I0098208

MUSINGS: LITURGICAL & CHARISMATIC

Giles Dimock, O.P.

Copyright © 2020 Giles Dimock
All rights reserved.
ISBN: 978-0-9886270-5-5

Cover art: *View of the Church of the Holy Sepulcher*
masar1920 / Adobe Stock Photo

Discerning Hearts®
www.DiscerningHearts.com

CONTENTS

FORWARD

At the beginning of an academic year while a student at Franciscan University, a new Dominican professor, Father Giles Dimock, started his lecture with a prayer in the most reassuring and melodic Northeastern accent, ending with a reverberating "Mary, Seat of Wisdom, pray for us." Whereas we were blessed with many outstanding professors who were devoted to the truth and were zealous for the mission of the Church, this Dominican exuded a love for the Church that many of us had never encountered before.

His command of the wisdom of St. Thomas, the treasury of sacred art and architecture, as well as the beauty of liturgical prayer, while affirming the very best in our charismatic piety, also challenged us. While at the time we would not have had the language for it, he helped us make connections to the broader tradition of the Church, and to understand what the Holy Spirit was doing in our hearts through a certain hermeneutic of continuity – to use a phrase from Pope Benedict. Whereas some charismatic circles saw spirit-filled praise as an activity reserved for a prayer meeting and the Rosary as an entirely unrelated devotion, he trailblazed a path of spirituality that was at once charismatic, Marian, and liturgical. He could do this because he had learned obedience in a very disobedient time, discovered beauty during a very ugly period, and humbly embraced the truth when many others walked away.

His teaching was forged in the furnace of Vatican II and its implementation. A love for the liturgy and for promoting beauty in the Church inclined him to religious life as a young man. Baptized "Richard" and raised in Connecticut, Father Dimock felt the call to priesthood as a young man, thinking first of the Franciscans, then the Benedictines, finally settling on the Dominicans. He was accepted by them and was given the name "Giles" in the novitiate. In the priestly ordination class of 1966, his was the first ordained at a Mass facing the people. As a young priest assigned to the Order's college in Providence, he became chaplain to a group of artists gathered around Marie Adélaïde de Bethune (known as Ade Bethune) of Newport who saw the need for renewal in Christian art and the restoration of beauty in the Church.

Renewal and restoration were needed. This was a time of crisis for society and for the Church. Priests and bishops attempted to respond. Some poor pastoral decisions resulted. The traditional piety of his youth was set aside but nothing meaningful put in its place.

Some saw Vatican II as an opportunity to advance different social and political agendas. Some truly great causes emerged such as the Civil Rights Movement. So did ignoble ones. In the wake of the sexual revolution and the emerging drug culture, he and his brother priests did not yet fully comprehend the catastrophic pastoral implications of the developing the contraceptive mentality among the faithful. As Father Giles points out in these pages, there was a domino effect in sexual ethics. Once the truth is betrayed in one area, it is impossible to uphold in other areas. Many began to question the value of any form of chastity and their own life-time commitments to celibacy. Half of his classmates would leave the priesthood in the following years.

If he, too, was caught up in the spirit of the time as a young priest, the Holy Spirit was also at work. He learned about the Charismatic Renewal at Notre Dame and got involved. He was prayed over, received a new outpouring of the Holy Spirit, and something changed in his heart. Sent to study in Rome, his passions were the liturgy and spiritual theology. Some Dominican Friars who were also introduced to the Renewal prayed together at the Angelicum and out of that, the Roman Prayer Group emerged. The holy friendships and renewed devotion of that prayer group would open him to deeper contemplation.

Along the way, he changed his mind about some of the teachings he had previously rejected and realized how important it is to rouse young people to aspire to noble values. He profoundly supported the ministry of John Paul II in this regard. His love for the discipline of religious life deepened. His gifts as a preacher and teacher were forged. In this experience of the Church in Rome, he glimpsed the beauty of the Church, not only of its art and architecture, but also of its very life. On this score, he was touched by the spiritual renewal that the Holy Spirit enkindled through the Second Vatican Council.

Before coming to Franciscan University, Father Dimock taught at the Josephinum, Providence College, and afterward at Holy Apostles College and Seminary. During his time at Franciscan University, he was the spiritual father for many men and women in their efforts to discern their vocations, choose careers and live holy lives. He was also a great support for Fr. Michael Scanlan TOR and the other Franciscans as they attempted to advance holiness of life, not only for the students, but within their own community. Deep friendships were formed and among these, his friendship with Fr. John Osterhout is particularly noteworthy.

He worked with Fr. John Osterhout TOR in the founding of the pre-theology program and Koinonia, the household for future seminarians, an effort from which I benefitted. After I graduated, he worked with Fr. John Osterhout at Steubenville's new campus in Gaming, Austria. They were also involved the pro-life efforts. He writes about a March for Life that he joined as an act of reparation for some of his political activities earlier in his priesthood. He also writes about visiting Fr. Osterhout when he was in prison for his pro-life civil disobedience. He accompanied Fr. Osterhout in his discernment to leave the Third Order Regular Franciscans and enter the Franciscan Friars of the Renewal, started by Fr. Benedict Groeschel. John became Conrad. I remember inviting Fr. Giles and Fr. Conrad to give a Parish Mission to Good Shepherd Catholic Church in Denver, Colorado. Many parishioners still remember their real-life stories of suffering for the faith, the power of the Eucharist, and the need for personal conversion.

Besides teaching at Franciscan University, this son of Saint Dominic also taught at the Angelicum where I again had him as a professor. He encouraged a small group of lay faithful to form a prayer group – not unlike the one he had been part of so many years before. Our prayer group was not as explicitly charismatic as what he experienced so many years before, but influenced by this same movement, centered on Eucharistic Adoration, Marian Consecration and pilgrimages. With his coaching, it became a blessing for many others, including future bishops. In particular, he helped us see the importance of making the Eucharist central to our prayer.

After Franciscan University, he went on to teach at the Dominican House of Studies where he also served as Academic Dean. There he also started a Dominican Third Order group for the lay faithful in Washington, D.C. He is now a senior priest at St. Patrick's parish in Philadelphia where he continues to work with Dominican Third Order groups and men's ministry.

It is important to mention the role and influence of Father Louis Bouyer on Fr. Dimock and his thought. The Oratorian gave him insight into Vatican II and provided a model for how to be a priest scholar. Sophisticated scholarship does not have to preclude simple piety. Instead it should safeguard it. Fr. Dimock fondly remembers when he chanced into a room to discover the great Fr. Bouyer deep in prayer humbly fingering the beads of his Rosary.

Now a word about the nature of this particular book. It is a series of articles written through the years on a variety of topics: The Holy Spirit, Devotion to Our Lady, Religious Life and the Priesthood, Liturgy and Devotion, Beauty and Goodness, and finally the Mission of the church. The National Catholic Register was very kind in granting the permission to reprint these works, many of which were published as columns in this paper.

These articles and other works have been carefully arranged into chapters so that each chapter treats a distinct topical theme. Together as a whole, these chapters tell a story, and that story unveils an outline of what the renewal of the Church actually means. I hope that you glimpse this beautiful horizon – for it looks out on a certain hope. As I read through these pages, the same sense of balance and love the Church comes through that first helped me discern how to respond to what the Lord was doing in my life. In times such as these, we need this same kind of wisdom more than ever if we are to find the most appropriate response to the beautiful things that the Lord is accomplishing in the face of today's difficult ambiguities and anxieties.

Dr. Anthony Lilles

INTRODUCTION

While I was a young friar teaching at Providence College I began writing regularly for the *National Catholic Register*. Early on, graduate students suggested that I publish my columns as a book. More recently, one of my students from Franciscan University of Steubenville, Dr. Anthony Lilles, Academic Dean of St. Patrick's Seminary in Menlo Park, renewed the same suggestion. Though written about many topics on life in the Church, the vast majority are on issues liturgical and charismatic. Where there was heavy duplication, some sections were removed, but overlapping and repetition is still found herein. May the reader enjoy them as much as I did writing them.

Feast of St. Dominic
2019

RENEWAL IN THE HOLY SPIRIT

1. Baptism in the Spirit

One hears a great deal about the Spirit these days. People refer knowingly to a "baptism in the Spirit" and to the gifts of tongues, prophecy and healing. What lies behind this unfamiliar terminology? What does "baptism in the Spirit" really mean? And is it Catholic? I would like to address some of the concerns orthodox Catholics have about the charismatic renewal and its role in tradition.

I first became acquainted with the charismatic renewal in 1967. As a newly ordained priest, I was sent to the Summer School of Liturgical Studies at Notre Dame. One evening I heard some Catholic "Pentecostals," as they were called then, explaining what had happened to them in their "baptism in the Spirit."

They said that prayer had become easier, that they were less conscious of their effort and more aware of God working in them. This rang a bell with me, because it seemed to confirm what our Dominican study of St. Thomas held – as one grew in prayer God took over more and more. Despite my initial openness, however, I was cautious about my involvement with this new phenomenon, for it seemed to smack of "holy-rollerism." While I prayed with these good people and allowed them to pray over me, I would not let myself be called a "Pentecostal." When I returned to Providence, Rhode Island I avoided prayer meetings that had sprung up there.

It wasn't until 1970, in Rome, that a little group of Dominicans including myself began praying in a tower of the Angelicum where I lived. Here I emerged as a full-blown charismatic.

By this time the Church had given the movement a certain guarded approval. Our Roman prayer group, which began in such a tiny way in the Angelicum, soon outgrew several subsequent sites as word of it spread. Finally, through the good offices of Father Frank Sullivan, we were able to meet at the Gregorian University. Those meetings grew to about 200 attending each Sunday afternoon.

People who came to our Roman prayer group began asking questions. Has this the blessing of the Church? Isn't there a danger of enthusiasm? What is "baptism in the Spirit"? How does it relate to the sacraments of Baptism and Confirmation? How can we trust something that had its origins in an anti-sacramental Protestant Pentecostal tradition? Since many of these questions still concern Catholics, let us examine the modern charismatic movement and the Catholic understanding of and participation in it.

The charismatic renewal takes its name from the *charismata* or charismatic gifts of the Holy Spirit that are listed by St. Paul[1] – wisdom, knowledge, faith, healing, miracles, prophecy, discernment of spirits and tongues. The gifts of the Spirit listed in Isaiah[2] – wisdom, understanding, counsel, strength, knowledge, piety and fear of the Lord – in the Catholic tradition are the gifts received in the Sacrament of Confirmation. Obviously, there is some overlap and surely all are the work of the Spirit.

The widespread experience of the *charismata* or charisms today can be traced back to Charles Parham, an American Protestant minister of the early 1900s. He felt that his Kansas congregation was spiritually complacent and dead. Parham and his congregation studied the Acts of the Apostles and saw that when the Spirit was given by the laying on of hands, there were usually signs and manifestations: tongues and prophecies. They prayed for the Holy Spirit and they received His gifts. Pentecostalism was born.

The first Protestants involved wanted to remain in their churches, but the seemingly extraordinary charisms and the accompanying exuberance were too much for the brethren. So, the Pentecostal churches were formed. In the 1950s, Neo-Pentecostalism finally was welcomed by the mainline Protestant Churches.

---

[1] 1 Cor. 12:8-10
[2] Isaiah 11:1-2

In 1967, as if in answer to John XXIII's prayer for a new Pentecost in the Church, Catholics began reporting that they had received these gifts as well. Now the question was: how could this be explained in terms of Catholic theology? After all, if this experience was genuine, its fruits were dramatic: powerful conversions, deep awareness of God within, renewed sacramental lives for members of the Church.

In the Pentecostal tradition "baptism in the Spirit" is the high point of Christian experience; it manifests itself charismatically, especially in the gift of tongues. Pentecostal churches consider baptism in water as a sign of repentance and regeneration, but not as an imparting of the Spirit. This comes later, in the "baptism in the Spirit."

Obviously, this cannot be squared with Catholic doctrine, which has always maintained that the Spirit is given by "water and spirit" in the sacraments of Baptism and Confirmation. Then what was this "baptism in the Spirit" that some Catholics received, and what should one make of the charismatic gifts?

Some Catholic theologians have tended to see the charisms as something given only to the early Church to help get it going. They say God now works primarily in the sacraments. If there are extraordinary charisms, they are found only in the lives of the saints. In such a view, ordinary charismatics are simply deluding themselves.

On the other hand, some charismatics mistakenly claim that at long last God has awakened the Catholic Church from its centuries-long "deep-freeze" by returning the Spirit to us today. Of course, such a view is myopic and not Catholic.

The truth is, the Spirit has never left the Church but has worked charismatically within it throughout history.

2. A Renewal of Grace

At a meeting of Catholic charismatic theologians at Notre Dame University, I heard a lecture by Father Louis Bouyer that shed new light on the relationship between the Holy Spirit and the Church. The great liturgical and spiritual theologian demonstrated that the Holy Spirit has always been at work in the Church, not only in ordinary sacramental ways but also through the various charisms. And the Spirit has been more evident in certain periods of history than others.

Bouyer discussed the manifestations of the Spirit in the Acts of the Apostles and the First Letter to the Corinthians and showed how martyrdom as seen by St. Polycarp and St. Ignatius of Antioch was a Pentecostal event in which "another will suffer for me." He suggested that the greater emphasis on structure in the post-apostolic Church attested to by the same St. Ignatius and the reaction of Montanist heretics with their super-spiritual rejection of the hierarchy might have dampened the enthusiasm of the Church of this time for the *charismata*.

But Bouyer went on to show how early monasticism was an essentially charismatic movement in which we find the Fathers of the Desert experiencing gifts of prophecy, knowledge, and discernment. Their teaching on compunction, or the gift of tears, as a sign of true conversion eventually resulted in the concept of monastic profession as a "second baptism."

In the Eastern tradition, St. Simeon the New Theologian (d. 1020) insisted that Pentecostal experiences did not belong only to the past but were something personally experienced now.

In the West St. Bernard and the Cistercian, Richard Rolle (d. 1349), and the Nine Ways of Prayer of St. Dominic suggested a charismatic approach. St. Thomas Aquinas treated all the gifts of the Spirit, personal and charismatic, in his *Summa Theologiae*.

It is also true, however, that in the Counter Reformation, St. John of the Cross distrusted extraordinary manifestations of the Spirit. His attitude is still found today, with many Catholics reacting against the excessive subjectivism that typified some of the Reformers. But St. John's approach was complemented by the more positive teaching of St. Teresa of Avila.

What this brief survey suggests is something of the richness of traditional Catholicism on the question of the special spiritual gifts or *charismata*.

In contemporary prayer groups when Catholics are prayed with for the "baptism in the Spirit" through the "laying on of hands" (which is not a sacrament but a gesture of support), they often experience a kind of breakthrough in their spiritual lives. This may be accompanied by charismatic gifts, the most common being that of tongues.

Some ask how they can receive the Spirit now. Did they not

receive It in Baptism and Confirmation? Simon Tugwell, OP, in his excellent little study *Did You Receive the Spirit?* answers that though the Spirit is given fully in the sacraments of initiation, there may be obstacles that keep the fullness of new life within the individual Christian from flourishing or from being manifested in all its splendor.

Some would see the "baptism in the Spirit" as a second conversion when what was accepted for one in the Sacrament of Baptism is made one's own in a fuller, more mature stage. Catholic charismatics, who see this experience as a birthright of all Christians, prefer to use the terminology of the "release of the Spirit." The gifts of Baptism and Confirmation are now made present in a deeper and richer way.

Another way of looking at the phenomenon of baptism in the Spirit is found in St. Thomas and proposed by Fr. Frank Sullivan of the Gregorian University in Rome. Sullivan refers us to the question of the missions of the Son and the Spirit in the *Summa*. The question is asked how a divine person can be said to come when He's already there. The Angelic Doctor answers that he can come in a new way for an *inhabitatio* (an indwelling of grace) or an *innovatio* (a renewal of grace).

This new coming, says St. Thomas, prepares one for a new state like monastic life or martyrdom, for the gifts of prophecy or miracles. This Thomistic approach allows us to see the work of the Spirit in Baptism and in Confirmation while also recognizing that the Spirit might still be given in a deeper way for special tasks and works in the Church and the world.

In my experience not only has the charismatic renewal rejuvenated my Christian life, Dominican life and priesthood, but it has done the same for most other charismatic Catholics I know. Occasionally one meets people who proclaim the renewal as the only way, but they are usually immature and do not realize "the Spirit blows where He will."

Others may act as if the gifts they've received make them holy or are the signs of their special status in the Church. But this is contrary to the teaching of St. Paul that the gifts are for the good of the Body of Christ – the Church. I have also met a few anti-sacramental charismatic Catholics with strong Protestant tendencies, but usually this deviation takes place when priests are not involved in prayer groups.

My charismatic brothers and sisters are deeply involved in the life of the Church, are most open to the teaching and authority of the Church and are very loyal supporters of John Paul II. From the welcome he has given various charismatic groups in Rome, I suspect he knows this.

3.   St. Thomas and the Spirit

At the Gregorian University in Rome in 1970 at the Sunday prayer meeting of our charismatic prayer group, a brother Dominican heard me explain the gifts of the Holy Spirit as charismatics experience them.

He challenged me to relate this phenomenon to St. Thomas' treatment of the charismatic gifts (or, as the Angelic Doctor called them, the graces freely given). I looked up the appropriate passage in the *Summa* and was surprised and delighted by what I found. Presenting his view of the gifts may help Catholics schooled in the more scholastic approach of traditional theology to relate to the gifts.

Thomas did not hold the opinion that the *charismata* were gifts only for the early Church, nor does the Church of today.[3]

The genius of St. Thomas is to situate these gifts in the broad context of the Christian life. For Thomas the Holy Spirit is the first gift. When He is given in Baptism and especially in Confirmation, those gifts listed in Isaiah[4] – wisdom, understanding, counsel, strength, knowledge, piety and fear of the Lord – are received by the Christian, along with faith, hope and charity and the moral virtues.

Thomas' treatment of the work of the Spirit, however, does not stop here. He goes on to consider the charismatic gifts (graces freely given) in relation to the whole Church – those charisms listed variously by St. Paul include wisdom, knowledge, faith, healing, miracles, prophecy, discernment of spirits and tongues.[5]

These charisms are not all given to everyone. Different members of the community receive different ones, all building up the Body of Christ. These charisms are manifestations of God's presence and power, and as such help people to experience God not only intellectually but in the totality of their being.

[3] see Vatican II's *Decree on the Lay Apostolate*, no.3.
[4] Isaiah 11:1-2
[5] 1 Cor. 12:8-10

These charismatic gifts, as considered by St. Thomas, are not sanctifying in themselves, but they help a Christian in leading others to God. Thomas sees those having gifts of wisdom and knowledge as having the grace of the work by which the intellect is instructed in the Word of God, moving man's affections willingly to hear that Word, drawing him to God and swaying him to do God's will.

For St. Thomas, the charism of faith (not the theological virtue of faith) is the super-eminent certitude of faith even to believing the impossible, which we often find in the lives of both saints and contemporary Christians.

He sees discernment as reading the secrets of heart which many saints had. As a more mundane gift, it is helping Christians with the proper advice to live their lives well.

St. Thomas sees gifts of healing and miracles as confirmations of sacred teaching, and we know that in the ordinary or extraordinary sense, healing and miracles have always been part and parcel of the Church's supernatural mission.

The gift of prophecy St. Thomas tends to see primarily as a foretelling of the future, which, indeed does happen, e.g., Our Lady foretelling World War II at Fatima. However, since the Hebrew word, *nabi,* means someone who directly speaks God's Word, this sense seems borne out in the experience of many today.

Finally, we come to the most controversial of all the charismatic gifts – that of tongues. In his first letter to the Corinthians, St. Paul speaks of this gift as used in a gathering to utter God's Word (when interpretation must be prayed for) but usually he speaks of it as a way of praising God. In contemporary experience this gift of ecstatic utterance (which is not manufactured or manipulated) is a gift of non-rational (not irrational) preconceptual praise of God in free sound. Usually it is a freeing experience and serves as a background to deep awareness of the Lord as one freely praises Him, even bringing one to a state that some would compare to infused contemplation.

St. Thomas' treatment of this gift is not along these lines. He sees it as a gift of speaking diverse tongues, as did St. Dominic, who once spoke to some German pilgrims who understood him, though he didn't speak German and they didn't speak anything else.

Even though Thomas restricts this gift to other tongues, it seems that we can find examples of ecstatic utterance in the Catholic tradition. Indeed, Eddie Ensley's little book, *Sounds of Wonder: Speaking in Tongues in the Catholic Tradition* does just that in tracing singing in tongues to jubilation in the early Church. Other examples include the prayer of St. Ephrem and the Desert Fathers, as well as St. Dominic.

Perhaps this gift, deeper than rational approaches to God in prayer, may be more frequently given than St. Thomas thought.

My purpose has not been to show an exact correlation between the gifts as described by St. Paul, experienced by people of today, and the thought of St. Thomas. Rather, it was simply to share the thought of a great and saintly theologian on these gifts as something he saw existing and working in the Church of his time. His analysis confirms that the experiences of many today are not something alien to the Catholic tradition, but something firmly entwined in it and enriching the Church of our time as well.

4. The Charismatic Movement and the Liturgy

Fr. Damasus Winzen, a Benedictine friend, once told me that if the Holy Spirit had been manifested in a powerful way before Vatican II, the old Tridentine Church could not have absorbed it – it would have cracked under the strain. However, Vatican II brought changes. The Church is becoming more pliable and flexible; all is in readiness for the work of the Holy Spirit. One evidence of God's timing is that the renewal and revitalization of the Roman Catholic liturgy is happening at the same time as the charismatic renewal.

Because liturgists now see more clearly the relationship among the various parts of the liturgy, they can prune away those elements which obscure the basic structure. They can even restructure the liturgy where a major overhaul is necessary. The liturgists have done this so that the Christian people might participate in the mysteries more fully. We might have expected these changes to foster a greater flowering of prayer and spirituality. Unfortunately, this has not happened. We must ask why.

There are many sociological explanations for the apparent collapse of the Roman Catholic Church in many areas of her life. We can easily perceive the confusion without reading any of the witty and sometimes unkind books exposing it. The basic ingredient missing in the life of the Church now – even in her liturgical prayer – is the deep and personal faith of believers. Nothing the Church does makes sense without faith. If we do not approach the liturgy in a spirit of faith and prayer, it can be a tawdry spectacle.

In their 1968 *Document of Music and the Liturgy* the American bishops recognized this close connection between faith and liturgy: "Good celebrations foster and nourish faith. Poor celebrations weaken and destroy faith." Similarly, even the most renewed liturgy becomes an exercise in aesthetics if celebrated by people without faith. Or, as the *Constitution on the Liturgy* warned, it becomes "the mere observance of the laws governing valid and licit celebration."

It is precisely on this level that the charismatic renewal contributes so richly to the life of the Church today and to the revitalization of her worship life. Charismatics have not so much contributed new forms of prayer to the liturgy (although the greater spirit of freedom and spontaneity in prayer must not be discounted); their contribution lies more in the deep and joyful faith in the presence of the Lord in the worshiping community as an experienced reality.

This was illustrated very graphically for me recently when a cousin of mine from California was visiting in the East. She had had wide experience of various experimental liturgies, both authorized and unauthorized, but she was overwhelmed by the very straight Mass celebrated by the Word of God Community in Providence. The setting was somewhat baroque: the vestments were old-styled fiddlebacks; only four hymns were sung, rather than the more important acclamations, such as the *Kyrie*, the *Sanctus*, and the Eucharistic Acclamation. Yet my cousin could see the faith and joy of people who wanted to be there to pray and sing the praises of the Lord who was truly present in their midst. This is the heart of the real renewal of the liturgy.

The charismatic renewal has brought other contributions to the liturgical renewal as well. Its great emphasis on the prayer of praise brings joy to any liturgist, especially since so much of the Office and the Mass consists of prayers of praise. Moreover, the charismatic renewal has developed a new form of prayer – prayer meetings – which could be called the modern lay celebration of the Liturgy of the Hours. All the elements are there: psalms, hymns, readings, and prayers. This form of prayer, which originated in the apostolic Church, has been revived by the Holy Spirit at just the right time in the Roman Catholic Church.

Since the Office was historically restricted to clerics and religious, the laity prayed many other devotions, some of dubious liturgical and theological worth. Some of these devotions, such as the Stations of the Cross and Benediction, grew up outside of the liturgy, or became in time somewhat alien to liturgical spirituality. Thus, the *Constitution on the Liturgy* of Vatican II recommended "these devotions should be so drawn up that they harmonize with the liturgical seasons, accord with the sacred liturgy, are in some fashion derived from it, and lead the people to it, since the liturgy by its very nature far surpasses any of them."[6]

By and large, this has never been done. Rather, most of these devotions have only been suppressed, despite the fact that they can be rethought.

Since these devotions have been suppressed or ridiculed, many Catholic Christians have stopped praying or have tried to find the whole answer to prayer in the Mass. However, Mass is not the answer, even though the Mass can be offered at any time of the day or night and in any place. The Eucharist is not meant to be the only form of Christian prayer. Christians need other forms to prepare to celebrate the Eucharist. We need other forms to carry the spirit of the Eucharist into the rest of the day. At one time, the Office served this function – and may yet again. Later, devotions served this purpose, though imperfectly. Now the prayer meeting, along with its many other aspects, fulfills this need.

It is obvious, then, that the "prayer meeting-Mass" is a mixed blessing, at least in my opinion. What Catholics do not need now in their spirituality is one more form of prayer turned into Mass. Rather, they need more non-eucharistic forms of worship. It seems to me also that the attempt to turn a Mass into a prayer meeting is fundamentally misconceived. We will always need prayer meetings, regardless of how we celebrate the Eucharist.

Of course, the eucharistic practice among charismatic Catholics varies greatly. For some a charismatic Mass is simply a dialogue homily, an extended prayer of the faithful, and singing in tongues as thanksgiving after communion. For other, it consists of a free form of prayer meeting with a preparation of the gifts and a eucharistic prayer tacked onto the end. Obviously, a charismatic community will

---

[6] Abbott's *Documents of Vatican II,* p.13

want to pray freely when celebrating the Eucharist together. But the basic structure of the Mass itself should be respected. After all, it is the same Spirit who breathes where he wills, who has led the Church to give us the new liturgy, a rich and flexible vehicle despite its imperfections. Since the spiritual gifts are under our control, this should mean in practice that we exercise the gifts the Spirit gives us at an appropriate part of the liturgy. Let me be specific.

In the penitential rite at the beginning of the Eucharist, people in a close-knit community might want to confess their faults, with everyone praying the *Kyrie* for them. Obviously, this is not sacramental confession.

The Liturgy of the Word is a part of the Mass especially dear to people who are enthusiastic about the Word of the Lord. If the readings are done meditatively with pauses between them, the Spirit might well inspire people to read other passages to buttress the main teaching. However, the constant nourishment of God's Word in the readings read in sequence is too rich a source of mature Christian spirituality to be lightly abandoned. Here also it seems that prophecies, the word of knowledge, and teaching might come forth, especially at the time of the homily. However, it would not seem wise for the celebrant to completely abandon his task as a homilist.

As we move into the Liturgy of the Eucharist, the most important point is that the whole Eucharistic prayer of praise begins with the preface and is meant to be *one* prayer and not interrupted. The *Sanctus*, one of the most important things to sing at the Liturgy, and the Eucharistic Acclamation, also to be sung, may provide brief pauses for singing in tongues and extending the praise, provided this is not so prolonged as to break the flow of the Eucharistic prayer. A long prophecy or teaching is clearly out of place here. Singing in tongues after communion is a beautiful and growing custom among charismatics. There are probably other ways to incorporate the gifts into the liturgy not mentioned here, but the principle remains that the basic structure of the liturgy should be respected.

The great contribution of spontaneity and free prayer should not blind us to the value of structure in prayer. We must pray in the mind as well as in the Spirit.[7] At times when the words will not come, it is good to be able to use certain formal prayers, as well as to pray in

---

[7] 1 Cor. 14:15.

tongues. It is also important to allow our prayer to be molded by the liturgy, to be stretched out to the full measure of Christ in the mystery celebrated, to be a part of something larger that unfolds gradually.

Fr. Simon Tugwell, OP, in his *New Blackfriars* article "Group Prayer and Contemplation"[8] says, "Our prayer does not originate with us, it is a cosmic process, it is a divine process, initiated by God himself; we are invited to take part in it, but it is not 'our prayer' primordially. We relax, we settle down into an ongoing process of prayer, we let it subtly and gently mold and sustain us. We do not – or should not – expect it always to be a great 'experience' any more than we expect our morning corn flakes to be a great 'experience.' But if we are deprived of it, we notice it."

Such is the value of structured, formal prayer. Even routine prayer has a good monotony to it, often covering the same ground more profoundly, ever plumbing the same mysteries in greater depth, so that we grow more deeply into the mystery of Christ.

We should be able to see how the charismatic renewal leads to true renewal of the liturgy. Charismatic prayer and liturgical prayer are complementary, each enriching the other, building up the Body of Christ, a people of praise. Indeed, this is now happening among us, not just in charismatic circles, but throughout the Church. We can already perceive renewal in the greater climate of faith and joy.

5. Wisdom from on High

At that time Jesus declared, "I thank you Father, Lord of Heaven and earth, that you have hidden these things from the wise and understanding and revealed them to babes."[9]

The wisdom that Our Lord is extolling here is the gift of one Holy Spirit that all of us received in Confirmation. Wisdom is the ability to see everything in the light of its highest cause, or if you will, in the depths of its most profound reality. A philosophical approach which is deeply analytical might turn us off as too "metaphysical," but the highest human philosophical wisdom, which is open to realities beyond physical, tangible reality is metaphysics. This branch of

---

[8] "Group Prayer and Contemplation," January 1971; now published in the book *Did You Receive the Spirit?*
[9] Matt.11:25

philosophy is further concerned with the causality of things, which leads ultimately to the first cause uncaused, but such wisdom garnered from thoughtful and correct analysis is not what the gift conferred by the Holy Spirit offers. It is rather, the interior enlightenment of the intellect of a Mexican pilgrim, crawling on his knees to Our Lady's Shrine at Guadalupe who sees the depth of reality through God's eyes. It gives him (or us) a naturalness (called "connaturality" by theologians) in making judgments about the things of God, but not because one has even studied theology or philosophy.

On the contrary, the gift of wisdom is found in all who are in the state of grace and its connaturality in judging the things of God even gives us a taste of God…"O taste and see that the Lord is good."[10] This experiential "taste" of God, this experience open to the humblest and simplest Christian, makes clear that the mystical life that many try to conjure up by New Age incantations or mantras is not a state we can work ourselves into, but rather a flowering of the gifts of the Holy Spirit – a life of holiness that Vatican II in its document *Lumen Gentium* makes clear all Christians are called to.

St. Thomas sees wisdom as perfecting the theological virtue of charity or gift-love, not the emotion of love. Faith, hope and charity are called theological virtues because they directly join us to God and charity, called *"agapē"* in the New Testament, is God's power to love shared with us, giving an ability to love that goes beyond the human both in loving God and one another. The gift of wisdom aids this virtue with God's judgment and vision of reality and deep experiential awareness of Him. However, when this experience fades, as it will from time to time, it's comforting to know that it is love that is important – our "experience" that may come and go. Not infrequently Charismatics who no longer find God so "tangible" as they did in their period of new conversion or first fervor tend to think they've done something wrong because God doesn't seem so close. It is important to realize that faith in His presence, hope in His promises, and love of Him even in the darkness are far more to God than the experiences He grants us, rich though they be.

Wisdom, as with all the gifts of the Spirit, is only found in those who are joined to God by love and not separated by mortal sin.

---

[10] Psalm 34:8

There is no mystical flowering of the gifts of the Spirit and contemplative union with God without a virtuous life, without a deeply moral life. Indeed, we can say with St. Paul "without love, I am a noisy gong or a clanging cymbal."[11]

According to Fr. Jordan Aumann's classical spiritual theology, this gift of wisdom which is lavished on us causes us to see all from God's perspective, even daily episodes of life. It opens the mysteries of faith so that they become the most real to us. It gives us the deepest contemplative awareness of the divine company of the Holy Trinity within us while causing us to love God in Himself and our neighbors for His sake in a heroic manner, doing in our milieu what Mother Teresa does in hers. Lastly, it is the perfection of the work of divinization that grace and the virtues work in our soul. Our Lenten penances clear the ground so that this may happen to us!

St. Thomas, as did St. Augustine before him, further connects each of the gifts of the Spirit with a beatitude from the Sermon on the Mount. We tend to be a little squeamish with this overly synthetic approach relating each gift to a virtue, a beatitude, and even a fruit of the Holy Spirit, but it certainly has to be admitted by us that those virtuous people who live in the Spirit will show the fruits of the Spirit in their lives and will be examples of the beatitudes, which are more perfect than the fruits of the Spirit.

And so, the medieval saw the beatitudes as works and rewards…works produced by the Holy Spirit in those who respond to the gifts of the Spirit and rewards that follow. St. Thomas thinks that the seventh beatitude, "Blessed are the peacemakers, for they shall be called the children of God,"[12] pertains to wisdom because its task is to set all in order, and peace, as St. Augustine says, is the tranquility of order. So, one possessed of wisdom is at peace within himself and such will be called children of God because they are "conformed to the image of His Son"[13] by grace, and the more so as they grow in the Spirit.

Let us pray then for grace… for the grace to see all from God's perspective rather than from a purely natural point of view or what is only politically correct, so that we can focus on true wisdom and the peace that comes in her train.

---

[11] 1 Cor. 13:1
[12] Matt. 5:9
[13] Rom. 8:29

6. Courage to Live

When confronted with the challenges of our increasingly secular culture, one finds that to be a believing and practicing Catholic in most circles is looked down on if not deliberately scorned. To refuse to accept the clichés that pass for wisdom, to refuse to live together before marriage, to refrain from homosexual activity if one feels inclined that way, to not accept abortion when one is caught off guard by a surprise pregnancy, to faithfully attend Sunday Mass, to really believe and actually pray, leads many of the "glitterati" to consider us beyond the pale. One who so believes and so acts must be a medieval peasant held in chains of superstition by religion, a cretin who cannot think for himself. To confront such an all-pervasive atmosphere, one needs the virtue of courage or fortitude, and the gift of the Holy Spirit by the same name.

The moral virtue of fortitude strengthens the will so that it will pursue the difficult good even when the path is arduous and fraught with danger even to bodily health and life, not to mention spiritual. Fortitude also helps the sensitive appetite as well as the will to seek the good presented by the mind enlightened by the Spirit and to not give in to our lower nature. Here we do not mean only sensuality, which is regulated by temperance, but also fear and recklessness as well. Fortitude prevents unreasonable fear from taking over and crippling our resolve in the face of criticism or persecution and yet restrains us from over-reacting with a bravado that accomplishes nothing. This virtue especially gives us the courage to endure what we cannot change, as the famous serenity prayer echoes.

Often, we cannot attack evils, but to suffer illness, persecution or death with a tranquil spirit requires the fortitude of a hero. Thus, Greek drama portrayed the hero of the tragedy as a man who knew how to accept death courageously, and the Church has always considered our heroes to be the martyrs who so courageously accepted death (the greatest of all fears, says Aquinas) for the sake of the Kingdom of Heaven. This Holy Week we follow the royal way of the King of Martyrs and His Cross.

Our spiritual journey obviously needs this virtue and its accompanying virtues: magnanimity whose large-heartedness is open to the truly heroic and often unconventional; patience which enables one to suffer with joy and even lightness of spirit; perseverance and constancy which allow one to go on in spite of the numerous difficulties which may be involved in reaching our goal this Holy Week and beyond.

The gift of the Holy Spirit which perfects fortitude is called fortitude as well, but it goes further than the virtues. It is rather an impulse of the Spirit that gives confidence in overcoming evils or enduring them until they are ultimately overcome. For any virtue to continue to operate in the challenge of the Christian life, the gift of fortitude is clearly needed, especially when sudden and strong temptations to commit a serious sin almost overwhelm one. One could fall without this divine instinct from within to fight or flee. This gift further gives us vigor in following Christ – "I can do all things in Him who strengthens me."[14] It overcomes lukewarmness in the Christian life. It won't settle for a dull respectability – or worse, a boredom with the things of God – but gives one high courage. Finally, it allows one to valiantly endure suffering with great heroism, joy and the peace that passes understanding.

St. Thomas links the fourth beatitude, "Blessed are those who hunger and thirst for justice, for they will be satisfied"[15] with the gift of fortitude. His reasoning is that this gift is about difficulty, and to hunger after justice or righteousness is difficult. Yet to hunger after justice or righteousness with an insatiable hunger requires a special gift of God to do more than the virtue empowers.

For me, the example of the virtue and gift of fortitude can be seen in seven of my friends who are being held in an Allentown, Pennsylvania prison for a pro-life rescue they performed last spring. In spite of their being kept long beyond their minimum sentences, in spite of some initial religious harassment, in spite of the men being held in 22-hour a day lockdown, they endure with fortitude and all the fruits of the Spirit: peace, love joy, etc. which they show especially to their warders. Not only did it show fortitude to stand against the establishment and not acquiesce in the routine contemporary slaughter of the innocents, but now to suffer patiently and joyfully with their Cross month after month, shows them as having an insatiable hunger for righteousness.

I visited them in December and said Mass for the men first, while

---

[14] Phil. 4:13
[15] Matt. 5:5

my friend Father John Osterhout, TOR, concelebrated with me. I celebrated Mass for the women later and the shining faces and loving words of all these pro-life prisoners so contrasted with those of their jailers that I wondered who was in bondage. This, even though two of the prisoners were man and wife recently off their honeymoon. Another, a young woman was recently engaged. Another, a female co-ed at the University of Steubenville. How will their example move us?

Let it at least move us to pray for the courage to live the Christian life fully, to fulfill our duties well, to carry our Cross daily and offer God the sacrifice of our daily lives as a penance as we walk towards Heaven.

7. Real Piety

This gift of the Holy Spirit, piety, brings us a special love for God precisely as He is the Father of our Lord Jesus Christ. Piety enables us to see the Father as the source of all supernatural life, who engenders this life by allowing us to participate in his inner life by grace.[16] St. Thomas links this gift with the moral virtue of justice that gives everyone his due. There can be no true religion without social justice: "Religion that is pure and undefiled before God and the Father is this: to visit the orphans and widows in their affliction and to keep oneself unstained from the world."[17] Religion itself, St. Thomas sees as an incomplete species of the virtue of justice because while the latter renders everyone his or her due, religion cannot hope to pay God back for all he has given us: life, being, grace, etc. Sacrifice is an attempt by primitive man and our patriarchs of the Old Testament to give God back an animal life in thanksgiving for the life he has given us. In the Mass, Jesus is made truly present so that his one sacrifice on the Cross for us may be perpetuated in the Mass for us to enter into the eternal sacrifice and offer in perfect thanksgiving the Son's Sacrifice to the Father, and in so doing, the Mass takes us beyond what the virtue of religion could accomplish alone. Religion reminds us that we worship God, depending not on whether we feel like it, but because it is our duty to honor and worship our Creator. The gift of piety adds to that a filial love and veneration to God as

---

[16] cf. 2 Pet. 1:4

[17] Jas. 1:27

Father through our Risen Lord and in the power of the Holy Spirit.

The recognition of the Fatherhood of God is much questioned today. It is said that God is beyond gender and this is true, but consequently some will not pray to the Father, Son and Holy Spirit, but in an age of personalism reduce these *Persons* to their *functions* of Creator, Redeemer and Sanctifier. The fact that Christ was a man and prayed to God as *Abba* or Father sets a direction in prayer that is normative for the Christian. C. S. Lewis sees us all as feminine or receptive in relation to God, as indeed God considered Israel His Bride and Christ is wed to us, the new Israel, as St. Paul says clearly in his letter to the Ephesians.[18] The feminine complementarity to the masculine appellation of *Father* is to be found in *Mother Church*, whose spotless model is the *Virgin-Mother Mary*. It is the gift of the Spirit, piety, that allows us to recognize this and not to be taken in by the politically correct slogans of extreme feminists.

The gift of piety enables us further to relate to all our brothers and sisters as children of the Father, as well as arousing this deep filial confidence and affection for and worship of God as Father through the high priesthood of His Son, our Risen Lord and in the Holy Spirit. Piety enables one to cherish the sacred liturgy and to savor the rites of this holy season. Aquinas further links the gift of piety with the third beatitude, "Blessed are the meek, for they shall inherit the earth."[19] He reasons that meekness or gentleness removes the obstacles to acts of piety and it is hard to imagine a proud and crusty type truly devoted to some practice of genuine piety like saying the rosary, the prayer of the humble.

Let us pray to experience the spirit of adopted children of God, our loving Father, through the first fruits of the Resurrection, Christ our Lord and Risen Brother. We pray as well to see all our brothers and sisters in this universal context of the children of God, His holy people, ransomed by his Death and Resurrection. We ask for total abandonment to the loving providential plan of our Father, to his loving arms, knowing he will continue to lavish the Spirit upon us as we went our way to Heaven.

---

[18] Eph. 5
[19] Matt. 5:4

RENEWAL OF DEVOTION TO OUR LADY

1. Mary, the Model for the Church Today

It has been my good fortune in recent years to be able to stop at Lourdes on several occasions. The first time, I went out of curiosity as a young liturgist who had little room for Mary in his life but whose views were to change dramatically. I had previously thought of Marian devotion as a later development in Christian piety, something that often detracted from the central liturgical worship of Christ and expressed a piety and devotionalism offensive to my aesthetic sense. In short, I was theologically, liturgically, devotionally, and aesthetically a snob.

The first thing that attracted my attention at Lourdes was that, although it was Our Lady's shrine, the focal point seemed to be not so much Mary as the Eucharist. This was true of the many Masses offered in many tongues for numerous pilgrims, the semi-weekly international Masses celebrated in the underground basilica for the ill from many countries, and the daily procession of the Blessed Sacrament with the blessing of the ill. I, a liturgist, came expecting to find only devotions and instead found at the center of Lourdes, the Eucharist, richly and liturgically celebrated by throngs of devout faithful, young and old. I found that I had to revise my thinking on Lourdes, on Our Lady and on Marian devotion, among other things.

I began to realize that Our Lady is more like us than unlike us; many of her prerogatives are signs of what is true of all Christians.

Her Immaculate Conception (her freedom from all sin from the moment of her conception, by the grace of her Son, so that she could be his worthy mother) is a sign of the grace that all Christians receive in baptism. Our Lady's Assumption (her body as well as her soul taken up into the heavenly reality so that her womb which conceived Christ would not see corruption) is a sign of our future participation – body and soul – in the resurrection of Jesus. I began to see that Our Lady was the pattern of the Church and of the individual Christian in responding to Christ.

The heart of the Protestant difficulty with Mary, says the Dominican Father Yves Congar, is that, for our Protestant brethren, nothing can be viewed as any sort of intermediary between God and man – neither Church, nor sacraments, nor the Mother of Jesus. It is also true that how one sees Our Lady colors one's view of the Church, the faith, theology, and even the most contemporary of questions – the role of women in today's Church. In so many issues, it seems to me, we need a woman's touch. We need a view that is more intuitive, less rationalistic, more contemplative – a revolutionary view which I think will come to us as we study seriously the woman, Mary, the Mother of God.

Mary, The Woman of Faith and Silence

Mary is the first Christian who hears the Word of God and keeps it[20] by her response in faith at the Annunciation.[21] She is the symbol of the believers of the Gospel and of the believing Church, for "Mary, by believing, conceived him (Jesus) whom, believing, she brought forth."[22] Our Lady's faith, which surely grew as she responded more and more to the paschal mystery, always had its contemplative dimension as she "pondered these things in her heart."[23] She is the Seat of Wisdom not only because the fruit of her womb is the eternal Wisdom of God, but also because that Wisdom found a fitting dwelling place in her, one of silence, presence, attentiveness and openness to God. John Lynch with reason called her "The Woman Wrapped in Silence" – a silence which is, in the words of

---

[20] Lk. 11:28
[21] Lk. 1:26-56
[22] St. Augustine, *Sermon* 215, 4: Migne P.L. 38, col. 1074.
[23] Lk.2:19-51

Romano Guardini: "much more than the absence of speech and sound, a mere gap, as it were, between words and sound; stillness itself is something quite positive...Stillness is the tranquility of the inner life; the quiet at the depths of its hidden stream. It is a collected, total presence, a being 'all there', receptive, alert, ready...attentiveness – that is the clue to the stillness in question, the stillness before God."[24] Such silence enables one to hear, for faith comes through hearing[25] but that demands "being inwardly present, listening from the vital core of our being; unfolding ourselves to that which comes from beyond, to the sacred word."[26] Such a listener to the Word and living receptacle of Wisdom was Our Lady, since her womb received the Word, but her mind first conceived Christ before he was physically conceived.

It is precisely on this level that in the post-conciliar Church Our Lady can teach us many valuable lessons. The renewal of Vatican II had us return to the sources of the faith – the Bible and tradition. In biblical exegesis we attempted to get at the most primitive level of the biblical data. In theology we became interested in distinguishing *the Tradition* from lesser traditions, which left us free to develop exciting new theories for the future. In recovering our more ancient liturgical traditions, we came up with a more streamlined contemporary rite of the Mass.

At this point we can ask questions and re-evaluate some of these emphases. Have we to some degree fallen victim to rationalism – accepting only those aspects of mystery which reason can accept? In our quest for the more primitive are we perhaps courting the classical Protestant error of leaving little room for development under the inspiration of the Spirit? In our view of the Church do we not frequently leave out the element of mystery, of the faith that goes beyond us, as we emphasize our community with one another in Christ while paying scant attention to the community of saints? Do our contemporary Scripture study and theology have that deeply contemplative vision which nourishes faith?

In many ways our more recent approaches have exhibited the most masculine rationalism of the Jungian *animus* and have not

---

[24] Romano Guardini, *Meditations Before Mass* (Westminster, Md., Newman), pp. 4-5.
[25] Rom. 10:14
[26] Rom. 10:14

allowed sufficient maturing in the deep recesses of the more feminine *anima* of the Church, where the central mysteries of the faith are cherished with reverence.

In her role of Seat of Wisdom, Our Lady can teach us this reverent attentive listening to the Word, while pondering it deeply and prayerfully with feminine intuition. She can help us to see the Church as more than an organization or even a community, but the great mystery of God dwelling among his people – Emmanuel, of which she herself is the sign – the ark of God, the tabernacle of the Most High, the womb of God, the *Theotokos*. We must allow the mysteries to grow in the womb of prayer, our ideas to be mulled over in faith.

This need for interiorization of the mysteries of faith, for deep, loving and prayerful consideration before theologizing was underscored at the opening of the academic year 1980-1981 of the Roman Universities in the homily of the Mass celebrated by Pope John Paul II. After all, theology is faith seeking understanding and this faith must be nourished by deep silent prayer as it undergoes the analysis of the intellect. Even then, the human mind of the believer seeks for the further inner revelation of the deep ramifications of truth, not forcing dogma to undergo the laboratory dissection of purely rational analysis. The Holy Spirit, by his gifts of knowledge, wisdom and understanding, enlightens those who are docile and reverent and who cherish the truths of the gospel. Our Lady as the eternal woman is the model of cooperation with the Holy Spirit in the silent depths of her womb-being.

Mary the Woman of Prayer

Mary is not only the sign of the Church, the Mother of the Church, but also the model of the Church at prayer. The *Magnificat*,[27] Mary's prayer *par excellence*, expresses her joy and thanksgiving for salvation history and her role in it, a foretaste of the praise and adoration to be offered in the Eucharist of her Son.

Mary is seen in the Gospel of John as a great intercessor, especially as she hastens the Lord's hour and causes him to perform the first of the signs which manifest the kingdom.[28] The changing

---

[27] Lk. 1:46-55
[28] Jn. 2:1-11

water into wine in turn foretells the institution of the Eucharist when the wine is mysteriously transformed into the Lord's blood to be poured out on the Cross along with water;[29] these are seen to be the sacramental signs of Baptism and Eucharist, according to the Fathers of the Church.

In John's Gospel, we see Mary as the new woman (Eve) standing under the Cross (tree) of Jesus (the new Adam) while, according to the Fathers, creation, which had gone awry, is reclaimed in the new creation of the Church born from the side of this sleeping Christ.[30] As Mary stands at the sacrifice, she takes part in the offering that her Son makes to the eternal Father, just as she once offered him in the Temple.[31]

Finally, Mary joined in the prayer of the apostolic community before and after the day of Pentecost.[32] Did she not teach them how to pray as she prayed in their midst?

Again, we have an example of great importance for the Church today. Many are seeking an experience of God in prayer. Many also turn away from our liturgies because they do not find them prayerful. It does not matter whether this is so because an old pastor rushes through valid confection of the sacrament on the grounds that it will work *ex opere operato*, or a young celebrant, using every gimmick imaginable, tries to manipulate the congregation to create a certain "experience." In either case the quality of prayer and reverence is felt to be missing. Here, Mary, the woman of prayer, the participant in the perfect act of worship of her Son on the Cross, the one who prayed continuously with the apostles, can teach us to celebrate the holy mysteries prayerfully, reverently and with love. Our relationship to this woman of prayer can help us to find the contemplative depths of the liturgy of the Church, to allow it gently to mold our prayer life, rather than to seize control of it to manipulate it for our own purposes.

A postscript might be added to this point. Prayer to Our Lady in her intercessory role ought to be worthy of her. It ought not to compete with the liturgy of the Church, especially the Eucharist to

---

[29] Jn. 19-34

[30] *Lumen Gentium*, no. 3 *Sacrosanctum Concilium*, n. 5, in Austin Flannery, O.P., Vatican II, Northport, N.Y., Costello Publishing Co., 1975.

[31] Lk. 2:22-39

[32] Acts 1:14

which Our Lady leads us. The liturgy itself often celebrates Mary's role in salvation history, as Pope Paul pointed out in *Marialis Cultus*,[33] but all prayer is not liturgical. Even here, however warm and devotional prayers to Our Lady might be, they ought never to be overly sentimental, for, as Vatican II reminds us in *Lumen Gentium*: "True devotion consists neither in fruitless and passing emotion, nor in certain vain credulity. Rather it proceeds from true faith, by which we are led to know the excellence of the Mother of God and are moved to filial love toward our Mother and to the imitation of her virtues."[34]

Our prayers ought to be simple, biblically and liturgically based. Pope Paul in *Marialis Cultus*[35] commended the *Angelus* and the rosary as such prayers. The latter, with its simple *mantra* of the *Paters* and *Aves* as a backdrop for contemplation on the central events of the paschal mystery, can lead one precisely to a deeper appreciation of the profound mystery celebrated in the Eucharist.

Mary, the Church and Womankind

Mary is the Mother of the Church since she was given to us in the person of St. John at the foot of the Cross.[36] Lumen Gentium quotes St. Augustine to the effect that Mary "is clearly the Mother of the members of Christ...since she by her charity joined in bringing about the birth of believers in the Church, who are members of its head." [37]

This motherhood of Our Lady is a type and exemplar of the motherhood of the Church, "for by her preaching and by baptism she brings faith to a new and immortal life, children who are conceived by the power of the Holy Spirit and born of God."[38]

Just as Mary's virginal womb was fruitful in bearing the Lord, so, as the Fathers of the Church loved to point out, is the Church's womb, the baptismal font, virginal and yet ever fruitful, giving new life through the pouring of water and the outpouring of the Holy

---

[33] Pope Paul VI, *Marialis Cultus*, *L'Osservatore Romano*, April 4, 1974, nn. 3-11
[34] *Lumen Gentium*, n. 67.
[35] *Marialis Cultus*, nn. 41-55.
[36] Jn. 19:26, 27
[37] *Lumen Gentium*, n. 54.
[38] *Lumen Gentium*, n. 64.

Spirit.[39] Thus, we can see how the Woman of the Book of Revelation is both Our Lady and the Church, who gives birth to many (spiritual) children through the power of the Cross under which Mary stood while the Church came into being. It seems to me that the role of spiritual motherhood is especially relevant when discussing the important question of the expanding role of women today, a role that complements the fatherhood exercised by the priest but does not take away from it.

The Church images Our Lady, and women are an image of the Church as we see in St. Paul's teaching on marriage that a man "must love his wife as Christ loved the Church,"[40] and she must be subject to him as to Christ.[41] The parallels here are man compared to Christ and woman to the Church, and the Christian pattern we see emerging out of this is not superiority of man over cringing subservient woman, but rather complementarity.

The man images Christ, the head of his body, the Church, by being head of the domestic Church, the family. The woman actively receives love and is cherished by her husband as the Church is cherished by Christ, her Bridegroom; the woman imaging the Church becomes the heart of the family, mothering the family in Christ. We have here differentiation of roles and complementarity springing from the very biological complementarity of man and woman.

Since grace builds on nature, it does not surprise us that this same complementarity overflows into Christian marriage and into the Church as well as into the respective roles of men and women. Many point out with chagrin that only a man can be an ordained priest, unaware of the fact that only a woman can be a consecrated virgin. The tradition of the Church is profoundly archetypal and iconographic, recognizing that a man, as the icon of Christ, is complemented by the woman as the icon of the Church.

Our Lady is the symbol of receptive love as well as the virginal yet fruitful motherhood of the Church, and the symbol according to their unique role, of all Christian women. So, we can pray with Archbishop Jadot that the Spirit will enlighten us to find woman's role in the Church — find those roles that *only* woman can

---

[39] St. Leo the Great, Tract XXV in *Nativitate Domini*, 5: C.C.L. 138, p. 123, cf. *Marialis Cultus*, n. 19.
[40] Eph. 5:25
[41] Eph. 5:22

fulfill – recognizing her unique mystery, not seeing her as a copy of man.

Yet Pope Paul pointed out in *Marialis Cultus* that many women today have a difficult time looking to Mary as a model because of her limited domestic role at Nazareth, and perhaps also because of sentimental portrayals of her as an utterly passive instrument in God's hands with no human initiative.[42] Her sociocultural background need not concern us, since she accepted God's will,[43] accepted the Word of God and acted on it, and was characterized by a spirit of charity and service,[44] which virtues all Christians can imitate regardless of their environment.

Also, while it is true that Our Lady is the model of response to God, this does not mean that she responded passively. At the Annunciation she gave her active and responsible, "yes," and so changed the course of the gloomy history of the world. Our Lady's piety shows forth in her *Magnificat,* and we find there a proclamation that God vindicates the humble and removes the powerful people of this world from their privileged positions[45] – hardly a resigned acceptance of the *status quo*! Mary as one of the *anawim* understood the plight of the poor since she herself experienced poverty and suffering, flight and exile.

At Cana, Mary, ever concerned with hospitality, was unafraid to take command of the situation and tell the steward to "do whatever he tells you."[46]

Finally, under the cross, Our Lady stood offering with her Son his suffering, love and obedience to the Father.[47] The Dominican, Fr. Gerald Vann, once pointed out that we should call Mary Our Lady of Compassion since she *suffered with (cum passio)* Christ, and as she did so she stood, the strong and valiant woman,[48] not swooning as some late medieval artists liked to portray. (To vindicate Our Lady's active courage, the Holy See had to condemn this sentimental devotion to Our Lady of the Swoon!)

---

[42] *Marialis Cultus*, n. 34.
[43] Lk. 1:38
[44] cf. Lk. 1:39-56
[45] Lk. 1:51-53
[46] Jn. 2:5
[47] Jn. 19-25
[48] Prv. 31:10-31

It is clear then that Our Lady offers Christian women a real model of faithful response, one that is responsible, self-possessed, serene in her role of wife, mother or consecrated woman. As Mary fulfills her complementary role, we can see how the beautiful complementarity of man and woman, Christ and the Church, enriches the human race and the new people of God.

Conclusion

In this article, we have tried to develop some of the major Marian themes which would be most helpful for the Church today. Many other rich biblical and patristic approaches to Our Lady's role could be mined; others that some might think of could be explored with great profit; but here we have one opinion.

It is clear, however, that this exploration will go on, for we have a Marian Pope, whose motto *Totus Tuus* proclaims him Our Lady's son. Before he was shot, John Paul II went from country to country consecrating the Church in each land to Our Mother, knowing that Our Lady never leads people to herself but to her Son, Jesus. One theologian said recently that Mary is like air, preparing the atmosphere for one's encounter with Jesus. Our saintly Pope seems to know this instinctively. May we follow his example.

2.   Mary and the Church

When I was a boy growing up in the fishing village of Stonington, Connecticut, we were often admonished to go swimming the 15th of August because "there's a cure in the water." This advice gave us on that day a spiritual (and I suspect Irish) reason for our usual summer occupation.

It's not surprising that folk customs for Marian feast days should abound, for simple, humble Catholics have always been close to the Mother of God. They know by the instinct of faith what Vatican II in its *Constitution on the Church* teaches more solemnly: Our Lady leads people to her Son and to his Eucharist.

Mary, Immaculate Ark of her Son, preserved from all sin by the prevenient grace of the Cross is the first human to share in the bodily redemption of her Son. As such she is the Bride, without spot or wrinkle, the glorious sign in the heavens of what we will become as

Church at the end of time.

As her Immaculate Conception by which she was preserved from any taint of sin (our tainted nature's solitary boast, as Wadsworth called her) is the triumph of grace into which we are plunged at baptism, so also is her Assumption the sign of the perfection of that same grace of her Son completed in us in our bodily resurrection.

Mary's privileges, then, are signs of hope for us the Church, and she is our model in corresponding to God's grace in always saying "yes." In the Gospel for this feast day she can rejoice in the "God who is mighty and has done great things in me."[49] And because of those great things we are among those generations who call her blessed.[50]

It is important to note that the human being chosen by the Father to be the model of the proper Christian response to his Son is a woman. Only a woman, who in her psyche and body is receptive, could be the model for the Christian who receives all from Christ.

Some reject this understanding, because they think such an approach casts woman as too passive a being. But to be receptive is a beautiful act of cooperation with man. In their deepest mystery, healthy men and women don't compete with one another, rather they complete one another.

So, in the Church, Mary shows us all how to be utterly open and receptive to the loving providential plan of our Heavenly Father, and how to complement one another, men and women, in the Church.

Many women in the Church today – even when quite orthodox in their beliefs – feel unappreciated and misunderstood. They are told they cannot be priests; therefore, some conclude they are nothing in the eyes of the Church.

Not only is this untrue, but it reveals a deeply clericalist view of the Church. The priesthood is seen as the only ministry in the Church; the many ministries in the Body of Christ enunciated by St. Paul and emphasized by Vatican II are ignored.

Secondly, such a view ignores the beautiful and noble role of wife and mother, the very foundation of human society, so constantly articulated by John Paul II.

---

[49] Lk. 1:49
[50] cf. Lk. 1:48

Finally, such a view does not come to grips with the divine plan of the complementarity of the sexes. "For, man and woman He made them,"[51] not unisex or self-sufficient.

Since grace builds on nature, it should come as no surprise that this complementarity is echoed in Christian marriage as well as in the Church in terms of the respective roles of man and woman. Only a man can be ordained a priest because he needs to be identified with Christ even in his sexuality to be His icon at the Eucharist. So also, a husband and father represent Christ to his wife and family.

But it is also true that only a woman can be consecrated a virgin, because only she can be the icon of the fruitful yet Virginal Church in her body in a way a man can never be. And only she can be the icon of the Church to her husband and to her family.

Men and women in the Church and in Christian marriage are a sign of the love between Jesus and His Bride, the Church. Man reminds us iconographically of Christ, though all Christian women are in Christ and women reveal the Church though all Christian men are in the Church.

Today we do not yet see many roles for Christian women that reveal this ecclesial sign. Yet when traditional roles are refurbished and new roles come to light, women will have their own strong identity. The Holy Spirit does not want women to be "mini-men" in the Church; so, the Spirit will open new doors, revealing new ways to find those roles that only women can fulfill.

Our Lady, as the symbol of receptive love and virginal yet fruitful Motherhood of the Church, will teach Christian women how to use their gifts in the service of the Lord and his Church. With Our Lady as a model, women will come to find themselves at the heart of the Christian family, and at the heart of the Church.

3. Women, the Woman, and the Church

John Paul II begins his great apostolic letter on the dignity of women, *Mulieris Dignitatem*, by placing all women in the light of *the* woman, Mary, the *Theotokos*, or Mother of God, for he says that "the central event, the key event in the history of salvation… is realized in and

---

[51] Gen. 1:27

29

through her."[52]   Thus, the beginning of his meditation on women shows a Marian emphasis, as does the whole document, in focusing on Mary as model of both mothers and virgins who reflect dimensions of Virgin-Mother Church in their lives. It is this mystical dimension of women and their role that I would like to reflect on, even though in so doing, I will not follow the inner logic of the pontiff's letter itself.

Towards the end of his letter,[53] the Pope discusses the Church, the great mystery, as bride in the light of the text from Ephesians in which Christ is the bridegroom.[54] This is a beautiful analogy, drawing on the biblical account of the creation of man and woman according to the image and likeness of God.[55] They were made in a "unity of the two," or a *communio personarum,* and this spousal relationship reflects Israel's relationship to God as bride to bridegroom.[56] The Pope refers us to Hosea, Jeremiah, Ezekiel and Isaiah, and is echoed in that of the bridegroom, Christ, to the Church, the new Israel, His bride. Thus, the love of God for his people, and Christ for his Church is spousal: "Husbands love your wives as much as Christ loved the Church."[57] The Holy Father points out that this love of husbands is affirmation in which the wife blossoms, and so it is also that we are all loved and affirmed by Christ as his Church. In turn, the Church can respond and blossom and be "without spot or wrinkle," at least in her teaching, sacraments and saints in the lives of all her members.

Yet in this lyrical celebration of marital love, John Paul II does not shy away from the difficult Pauline verse: "Wives, be subject to your husbands, for the husband is head of the wife."[58] What are we to make of this statement in the light of the earlier papal statement in this letter that the domination of woman by man is an unfortunate deformity of original sin?[59] We have to see how Christ is described as head of the Church in this same text. He is seen as head

---

[52] John Paul II, *Mulieris Dignitatem,* 3.

[53] *Ibid.,* 23.

[54] Eph. 5:25-32

[55] cf. Gen. 2:24

[56] *Mulieris Dignitatem,* 23.

[57] Eph. 5:31

[58] Eph. 5:22-23

[59] *Mulieris Dignitatem,* 10.

to give Himself up for her.[60] Here we find the same kenosis hymned by Paul in Philippians, that pattern of the Christian life for us all.[61] Husbands and wives are to exercise "mutual subjection out of reverence for Christ,"[62] and in that mutual kenosis or self-giving, each for the other, the man exercises a special headship following Christ who gave Himself up completely. It would seem that John Paul II is not abrogating the teaching of Pius XI on family roles in *Casti Connubii*, contrasting the headship of the man in the family with the special role of woman as the "heart" of the family,[63] but giving it a new context so that men who tyrannize over their wives can never claim the support of sacred scripture or tradition for their outrageous behavior. The Pope says that *mutual* subjection is something "new" from Christ and His Gospel[64] and, I would add, gives the kenotic background for the complementary roles of husband and wife, who further spend themselves completely in giving to their children as well.

It is this background of complementarity which sees that, since in his body man is a giver, and woman in hers is a receiver, we can see Christ as bridegroom giving to us – "He first loved us"[65] – and ourselves as Church responding by being receptive. The receptivity is not passivity, as some would have it, but an active welcoming, and women who know how to receive can help teach the whole Church to do so – even men. For, as the Pope rightly underlines, "both women and men are called through the Church to be the 'bride' of Christ..." thus the "feminine" element becomes the symbol of all that is "human," and men must learn how to love with a bridal or ecclesial love.[66]

It is the relationship of the masculine Christ to the feminine Church that sets the context of the papal discussion as to whether women can be ordained to the priesthood or not. John Paul, of course, answers according to the constant tradition of the Church,

---

[60] Eph. 5:25
[61] Phil. 2:5-11
[62] Eph. 5:21
[63] Pius XI, *Casti Connubii*: AAS 22 (1930); Washington, D.C., NCWC (1931) pt.I, p.II.
[64] *Mulieris Dignitatem*, 25.
[65] 1 Jn. 4:19
[66] *Mulieris Dignitatem*, 25.

but his reasoning is lucid and his handling of the questions this topic raises is firm. To those who say that the Lord, a man of his own times, could not have gone against contemporary social constraints, the Pope says, to the contrary, that Christ did not conform to any prevailing customs in regard to women and was even revolutionary in speaking openly to women and in dealing with them directly in a way that was unheard of.[67] And yet the Pope affirms that "in calling only men as his Apostles, Christ acted in a completely free and sovereign manner."[68]   Since the Lord chose only the Twelve to "do this in memory of me," and represent him and his Cross in the wedding banquet of the Eucharist, the priest acts *in persona Christi* as the bridegroom, through whom Christ gives the gift of Himself in his body and blood to the bridal Church.[69]

As an icon of Christ, a masculine sign of Christ and the ministerial priesthood, the priest is received by the laity, possessing the universal or royal priesthood of all Christians, insofar as they are Church or bride.[70] This masculine-feminine complementarity gives us insight into the very structure of the Church, not as a cold institution, but as the living and organic mystery with both its "Marian" and "Petrine" emphasis, to steal from Hans Urs Von Balthasar.[71]

Though the Church has a hierarchical or Petrine structure, this is not an end in itself, but is "totally ordered to the holiness of Christ's members."[72]   Holiness is the great mark of the Church. Newman, convinced that he had found all the other marks of the Church in Rome, had to wait for his encounter with Blessed Dominic Barberi, CP to see the mark of holiness incarnated in that humble Italian Passionist before he could enter the Church. One might ask then, who really has more power: Mother Teresa or the local bishop? While she has no juridical ecclesial power, her influence, flowing

---

[67] *Mulieris Dignitatem*, 12-14.

[68] *Ibid.*, 26.

[69] cf. *Inter Insignores*, 1976, AAS 69 (1977) 98-116.

[70] *Mulieris Dignitatem*, 27; cf. also Sara Butler's "Forum: Second Thoughts on Ordaining Women" in *Worship*, Vol. 63, No. 2, March 1989, and the follow-up discussion in *Worship*, Vol. 63, No. 5, Sept. 1989. Sara Butler points to the priest as an image of Christ, not only of God; so, the masculine sign is more telling.

[71] *Mulieris Dignitatem*, 27; cf. footnote 55.

[72] *Ibid.*, 22.

from the charismatic attraction of her simplicity and holiness, is worldwide…now even reaching to Moscow!

Our Lady, the figure and model of the Church, is "Queen of Apostles without any pretensions to apostolic powers."[73] We can say that she has greater influence in another order of being. The Pope affirms this in the example of holy women in the Church, down through the ages, who have excelled in the order of love; those virgins, widows, martyrs of the Apostolic Church, those holy women from the East, as well as Monica, Joan of Arc, Catherine of Siena, Teresa of Avila, Elizabeth Ann Bailey Seton, to name a few.[74] Holy women are an incarnation of the feminine dimension of the church. They can teach the whole church how to receive God, how to be holy, if only they would. Much discussion today focuses on how to obtain the power (juridical) associated with the hierarchical or ministerial priesthood. If one cannot become a priest with power one is nothing! Such a view is contrary to the Pauline sense of the body of Christ with its many ministries and functions. Questing for power delivers us once more into clericalism.

It is because "in God's eternal plan, woman is the one in whom the order of love in the created world of persons takes root," that she can teach us how to love,[75] for she is a helper to man, not his subordinate, who is loved to love in return, her spouse, her family, and even universally.[76] Woman has a special gift of self to give in the mutual self-giving of marriage, and so she is especially physically, psychically, and spiritually ready for the vocation of motherhood. The Pope sees women as mirroring Eve, the mother of the living, as they bring new life into the world and exclaiming in wonder as she did: "I have brought a man into being with the help of the Lord."[77]

Though both mothers and fathers mirror the Trinity in the generation of the Son by the Father, nonetheless, it is the mother in whom parenthood is realized more fully; for this generation absorbs the energies of her body and soul.[78] One might point out that the embryo comes materially mostly from the woman's body and that

---

[73] *Mulieris Dignitatem,* 22.

[74] *Ibid.*

[75] *Ibid.,* 29

[76] cf. Gen. 2:18

[77] Gen. 4:1; *Mulieris Dignitatem,* 18.

[78] *Mulieris Dignitatem,* 18.

mater, the Latin word for "mother" is the basis of the word "material." But it is not just the materiality of the womb that forms, but even the psychology of the infant, and later the child, is dependent on woman because women are better at paying attention to another person than men. Men are "outside" this event (forming and giving birth to the child) and must learn how to be a parent from the mother – or how to be a father from the mother. (In a lecture on *Mulieris Dignitatem*, given at the University of Steubenville in November 1988, Dr. Joyce Little of the University of St. Thomas, Houston, Texas, opined that because the mother is more closely involved with procreation of a child within than the man, John Paul can easily be interpreted as saying that woman is greater than man.)

Yet motherhood does not stop with having children, but in raising them, entrusted as children are to parents by God, to be a moral force for good. John Paul underlines this in his interpretation of Jesus' response to the spontaneous praise of his mother in the Gospel of Luke: "Blessed is the womb that bore you and the breasts you sucked."[79] The Lord says: "Blessed, rather, are those who hear the Word and keep it,"[80] showing that motherhood goes beyond the physical dimension, rich as that may be, to the spiritual order of teaching how to listen to the Word of God and keep it, as Mary taught her Savior-Son.[81] Further, mothers suffer for their children as part of the Paschal Mystery of the Cross and Resurrection, not only in the pangs of childbirth, but also in the trials of their offspring. The Pope goes on to list all the ways women suffer, including those exploited by the wounding of woman's human or maternal dignity.[82] One thinks of all those women pressured by males into the crime of abortion.

Though Pope John Paul does not elaborate this teaching as such, I think we can draw from his treatment thus far that Christian mothers are a sign of Mother Church. Just as mothers bear new life in their womb, so the Church bears new life through the womb of the baptismal font, according to the teaching of the Fathers, and feeds us with the pure milk of sound doctrine. The very potential of the body of the woman for bearing and nourishing life is the

---

[79] Lk. 11:27-28
[80] *Ibid.*
[81] *Mulieris Dignitatem*, 19.
[82] *Ibid.*

incarnational sign of the mystery of the Church – a sign that women bear in their bodies as men do not. Therefore, women can be a sign of the Church in their very embodiment, as men are signs of Christ in their bodiliness – a wonderful complementariness in physicality and symbol as well.

The Pope recognizes that women's call is not limited to marriage and motherhood but sees the place of virginity (or celibacy) as a call "for the sake of the Kingdom."[83] Such a vocation is a grace of divine initiative, but also a human response and free choice for both men and women which consecrates the person to God.[84] Some women, in following this path of virginity, confirm themselves "as persons whom the Creator, from the beginning, has willed for their own sake."[85] They give a "sincere gift" of their femininity to Christ, the bridegroom, in spousal love and are the sign, then, of the Church as faithful Bride. Masculine or priestly celibacy, says the Pope, is only analogous to this prime analogate.[86] One might note it is easier for men to see themselves relating to Christ as friends or followers, rather than as spouses, yet as we have seen earlier, this is the relationship common to the whole membership of the Church in relation to Christ: whether male or female, the relationship is spousal. However, because men, in their bodies are not *the sign* of the Bridal Church, they cannot be consecrated virgins even if technically they are such. It is only women, with their bodily configuration of inner space, and the interiority of the womb which renders them more capable for contemplation and prayer, who are able to be the signs of the Virgin/Mother Church at prayer. As such, with a much greater disposition for prayer, they are able to enrich the Church and exercise a spiritual Motherhood according to the Spirit among the young, those seeking Christian perfection, and especially in the way theology can be done.

My thesis is that Vatican II which, in its rich theological formulation, was humanly the answer to the problems of Northern post-war Europe as proposed by the *periti* (masculine) is correct in its main proposals, but that its reception has been somewhat mixed. The Church has built a new outer structure or house after Vatican II,

---

[83] Matt. 19:22
[84] *Mulieris Dignitatem*, 20.
[85] *Ibid.*
[86] *Mulieris Dignitatem*, 20.

and it is up to women theologians, mystics and authors such as Adrienne Von Speyer and Edith Stein, to make it a home, as women have done in the past. This will not be done by doing theology exactly as men, but by bringing their specifically feminine qualities to bear.

To conclude my reflections on *Mulieris Dignitatem*, it seems that we can say in summation that woman, according to John Paul II, is "married" to Christ either directly or through the sacrament of matrimony. In either case, she is a sign of the Church. As wife and mother, she is a sign of Mother Church and, like her, exercises a real physical and spiritual motherhood or, as virgin, she is the sign of the fidelity of the Church to Christ. So, woman is the sign of the Church (Virgin and Mother) and Mary is the model of both dimensions for the Church, as spelled out in the *Constitution on the Church*.[87] Mary is the model of all Christians in the Church, but more especially for women – a beautiful model of interiority and prayer, "who pondered these things in her heart"[88] and action: "Do whatever he tells you."[89]

Further, one might categorically state that it is impossible to understand the Church without Mary, its Mother and most noble member. Those who strive to do so speak only of "institution" rather than "mystery" which the contemplative, Marian, mystical and feminine dimension would yield. So, in this reflection we are back to where we started, with Mary. As the Bible starts with "the woman" in Genesis and ends with her in the Book of Revelation, so does the Pope in *Mulieris Dignitatem*, addressing her in prayer in his conclusion – he whose motto, "*Totus tuus,*" proclaims him her son.

4.   Medjugorje: Fruits of the Spirit

Medjugorje (pronounced Med-ju-gor-ee-ay) in Croatian means "between the mountains." In the valley between the mountains for the past four years, six young visionaries claim that they see Our Lady as she appears to them nightly.

She first appeared on the side of a low mountain until the Communists enforced a Yugoslavian law forbidding public worship anywhere but in a church. Our Lady graciously obliged by visiting

[87] *Lumen Gentium,* (Boston: St. Paul Editions, 1964) 63, 64.
[88] Lk. 2:19 and 51
[89] Jn. 2:6

the children in a sacristy chapel, and when the local bishop forbade them to meet there, Our Lady appeared in the rectory where only the children are gathered.

The Marian message at Medjugorje seems to be a continuation of Lourdes and Fatima, only with greater specificity. The world is on the edge of chaos, but prayer and fasting can alter the course, says Our Lady, who revealed herself as the Queen of Peace.

I had heard of the apparitions and knew of the message, and I had tried to keep the Friday fast with varying degrees of success. But I really didn't know what to expect when a married couple and I made the pilgrimage to Medjugorje. We contacted a Sister Janja, who speaks English, and she brought us to the home of a family who took us in for the week.

The hospitality of the villagers to the great influx of pilgrims, not asking any money though they seem to be of modest means, was for me a real sign of the authenticity of the visions – a flowering of the Christian life in the people, whom their Franciscan confessors say have steadily grown in virtue.

Another sign surely is the intensity of the prayer life there. Our Lady has asked for three hours of prayer a day. There seems to be no great problem in complying with this request in Medjugorje, since the evening service lasts at least three hours. At six o'clock in the evening the people pray ten decades of the rosary, invoke the Holy Spirit and then attend Mass.

Most of the liturgy is sung with deeply moving Croatian hymns and acclamations. The readings are often done in French, Italian or English as well as Croatian for the pilgrims who are there. The Canon is recited mostly in Latin for the sake of the many foreign priests who come as pilgrims. They distribute Holy Communion to the crowds of people.

At the end of Mass, after the seven Our Fathers, Hail Marys and Glory Be to the Fathers requested by the Blessed Virgin, there often are additional prayers. It is usually toward the end of the recitation of the rosary that Our Lady appears to the children, and all the while the church is a center of intense and joyful prayer.

The final and most impressive sign of the authenticity of what seems to be happening in Medjugorje is the obedience of the priests and the people to the local bishop. There are long standing tensions between the Franciscans, who evangelized this valley in the

1400s and still minister to the people of St. James' parish of Medjugorje, and the diocesan clergy, represented by a local bishop who doubts the authenticity of the visions.

For the time being, the local bishop has asked the visionaries not to await the apparition of Our Lady in the church; they (and she) have complied. He ordered the Franciscans to remove a rather crude statue fashioned after the description of Our Lady as she has appeared at Medjugorje, replacing it with the statue of Our Lady of Lourdes; this has been done. The bishop also told the visionaries not to lead the prayers (the seven Paters, Aves and Glorias) after Mass, and they have obeyed.

The visionaries themselves seem healthy and cheery, quite normal – not at all like the pious types one would expect to be so favored. One night my friend spotted them standing undiscovered amid the congregation; they were laughing and exulting over their temporary anonymity. Their relief is understandable when one realizes that the more fervent pilgrims make life difficult for them. The children are often besieged, the crowds allowing them little peace or privacy.

In charismatic circles one is used to testing any spiritual message or happening by asking whether the phenomenon in question manifests the fruits of the Spirit enumerated by St. Paul in Galatians 6 – peace, love, joy, gentleness, self-control, etc. – and whether any aspect of the phenomenon is against the teaching or discipline of the Gospel or the Church.

Here I think one must say that this does not seem to be the case. I think the fruits of the Spirit are abundantly evident in the lives and attitudes of the visionaries, the Franciscans, and the villagers. I am most impressed by their peaceful, trusting obedience, the knowledge that God will triumph if this is indeed of God.

Of course, I, as any faithful Catholic, await the final judgment of the Church. I went on pilgrimage not seeking signs and wonders (though apparently some have seen them) but finding signs of generosity, hospitality, fervent prayer, inner and exterior peace, and docile obedience. All of this convinces me that something extraordinary is happening Medjugorje.

5.   Medjugorje and the Facts

On the eve of Epiphany, I celebrated Mass for a small group of Dominican tertiaries and their families. There was a great sense of community and human warmth as well as a deep sense of prayer and reverence at the celebration of the holy mysteries. Other times I had been with this group, had preached to them, taught them, celebrated Mass for them, but had not experienced such unity and peace. I reflected on recent happenings in their lives to see what had made the difference, and I discovered one common thread in the recent experience of many of them – their exposure to the messages of Medjugorje. In that small Yugoslavian village, Our Lady speaks daily of peace, prayer, conversion and penance. I was seeing the fruits of that message in this little Dominican group, which through those fruits had grown from a collection of individuals into a community. When one considers the main thrust of these apparitions, one is not surprised.

On June 24, 1981 the visions began that have since occurred nightly in this village of 300 people. In this valley, at first on a low mountain, later in other places, a beautiful woman appeared who, when first queried by the youngsters, said she was the Mother of God. The six visionaries, now young adults – Mirjana, Ivanka, Vicka, Marija, Ivan and Jakov – when Our Lady appeared would all fall to their knees at once and would be in animated though inaudible dialogue with some unseen personage. To fake such synchronization and dialogue night after night for almost six years would be extremely difficult and false visionaries would ultimately break down. Further, these young visionaries are remarkably healthy psychologically and well balanced – not the church mice that skeptics might expect them to be. It is true that the local bishop (of Mostar) has many reservations about these apparitions and that the commission he set up to investigate them was not impressed that they were of divine origin.

Cardinal Ratzinger of the Congregation for the Faith did not find their conclusions sufficiently definitive and invited the Conference of Yugoslavian Bishops to appoint a new commission to investigate again the phenomena of Medjugorje, which include the visions themselves, the miracles of the sun (like Fatima) and a concrete cross on the highest mountain in the area seen spinning about by many observers. Of course, faithful Catholics will abide by the Church's final decision in this matter, though it is difficult for me to see how any decision could be given except that what is happening is from God.

Before we examine the message of Medjugorje, we might note that two of the visionaries stopped seeing Our Lady; Mirjana in 1982, and Ivanka in 1985. Also, the site of the apparitions moved from the mountain when the Communist officials insisted that the law be followed which allows public worship only in a church. Mary obliged and appeared in a sacristy of the church, and when the bishop forbade this, the apparitions took place in the rectory. Now having been forbidden again by the local bishop, they occur on the balcony of the church and in this we see Our Lady and the four visionaries obeying the bishop.

What does the "*Gospa*" (Croatian for "the Mother of God") say? Mary says that the world is on the brink of catastrophe and I should think this is clear to any thinking person. Even though we rejoice at the recent Summit agreement between Reagan and Gorbachov, nonetheless we know that there is a significant balance of terror in nuclear weaponry that could easily trigger total destruction of the planet. One could further cite the breakdown of family life and morality, the lack of respect for life as seen in the abortion "holocaust" and the enthusiasm for euthanasia, not to mention the increasing materialism of many and the dire poverty of so many more (both individuals and countries.) Our Lady says the only way to true peace is conversion, individual and collective. This will come about as people repent of their sins and change their way of life. "The word I want to tell the world is: be converted," echoing her Son, "turn away from sin, the Kingdom of Heaven is at hand."[90] Is it just a coincidence that the appearances began on June 24th, the feast of the great preacher of repentance, John the Baptist? Mary says practically, "tell the people to go to Confession and make amends for their sins," and promises that much in the Church would be healed by monthly sacramental Confession of Catholics.

The consequence of conversion is the call to deeper prayer. Our Lady repeatedly calls for people to "Pray, pray, pray" but not "only an increase in the number of prayers…but an attitude of continuous

---

[90] Matt. 4:17

longing and desire for God" – in short "pray always." The "*Gospa*" has even recommended four hours of prayer for everyone but did not start there. Like the good spiritual director that Our Lady is, she started by asking people to pray seven repetitions of Our Father, Hail Mary and Glory Be, a traditional prayer in the valley to which she added the Creed. She requested the rosary and once they were saying one chaplet asked for the other two so that all fifteen mysteries were meditated on each day. Gently and slowly as the people had begun and learned the first lesson, then Our Lady led them more deeply into greater challenges, but gradually so as not to frighten them. Our Lady did the same with fasting, at first asking everyone to fast on bread and water (the best fast) on Fridays and when they were doing that adding Wednesdays as well. Mary reintroduces fasting which most of us feel we can no longer do (yet we diet constantly) to prepare us for prayer and give intensity to the prayer life.

The "*Gospa*" as our spiritual director, teaches us about prayer in the messages: "The fundamental point about prayer is to have a great desire for God and for the salvation of souls…if you possess these desires you will pray and find the time for prayer." But if we have no time for prayer, are we really Christians? Our Lady seems to think not: "Christians who do not pray are no longer believers." She would like families to pray a half hour in the morning and in the evening and even tells us how to do so: "Pray sufficiently in the morning, read a page of the Gospel and root the Divine Word in your hearts and remember it during the day, live by it, particularly in your trials and, by evening, you will have become stronger." Here is our Lady's approach to inner peace – she says explicitly, "lead a simple, humble life, pray a great deal and do not delve into your problems but leave God to solve them." From this inner peace flowing from conversion to God and prayer comes the courage to be at peace with one's brothers and sisters, and as it spreads, peace can be given to the world. Our Lady's first message, after all, was "peace." She called herself the Queen of Peace and stated, "I have come to bring peace to the world."

What have been the fruits of these apparitions? What have been the results? Thousands now come there, and many are converted, especially through the Sacrament of Penance, and one might well find thirty or forty priests in the summer hearing confessions in the fields. The Franciscans say that serious sin has almost disappeared from their flock in the parish. The villagers themselves receive many pilgrims into their homes and would take no recompense until the Yugoslavian government insisted that this be done (assuring the government of its share.) They prepare wonderful meals for others to eat while they themselves fast. Many go to daily Mass or at least one representative from the family attends the evening Mass in the parish church which has become the focal point of the apparitions. This does not surprise us as Mary always leads us to her Son and His Eucharist.

From my two trips there I can recreate the scene. Each evening a full church prays ten decades of the rosary in preparation for the apparitions which usually occur approximately an hour later, after which the Mass is celebrated. This is a celebration of the Eucharist such as Vatican II envisaged with choir and people singing in their own tongue in full participation, with the readings done in their Croatian, but also in English, German and Italian for the pilgrims. The core of the canon is done in Latin, so many are the priests from diverse parts present and all in great reverence. The distribution of Communion is done in an orderly fashion despite the great crowds present and after Mass a devotion often extends the spirit of the Liturgy, such as Eucharistic Adoration on Thursday, Adoration of the Cross on Friday, devotion to Our Lady on Saturday or prayers for healing which are always needed. This celebration of the Eucharist is the center of life at Medjugorje (as indeed I have also witnessed at Lourdes) and is clearly experienced as the "summit" of the life of the Church and the "fount from which all its power flows," as the *Constitution of the Liturgy* of Vatican II states.

A final fruit I will simply mention is that of obedience to the Church in the person of the local bishop, who seems distant from or even at times a bit hostile to the phenomena occurring in Medjugorje. Despite this the visionaries and the Franciscan friars who man the parish obey their ordinary. I see this as one of the healthiest signs of God at work, even more impressive than the many conversions. The Friars, it might be noted, evangelized this area in the fifteenth century and have served the local people since then. When early in this century some of their parishes were handed over to the diocese, the people reacted wanting their own beloved friars instead, provoking a controversy still simmering and which may explain in some part the local bishop's coolness toward the Medjugorje phenomena. The

Franciscans who have been assigned to the parish are all well-educated men (the pastor has a doctorate in New Testament Theology) who keep enthusiasts from focusing too much on the apocalyptic aspects on the message, and keep orientating everyone who comes there to a more pastoral approach emphasizing the scriptural basis of personal conversion, prayer, and fasting.

It is true, however, that there is a frightening side to the message that the "*Gospa*" brings. Our Lady has shown to all the visionaries Purgatory, and four of them Hell, and these visions were extremely frightening, but has also shown two of them Heaven, which was delightful. She warned of the power Satan has, and also confided ten secrets about the future and a coming chastisement by God (that our prayers have already lessened but not removed), and has said that she will warn Mirjana three days before the chastisement, who can tell the priest of her choice and he will decide when to reveal it. However, we should not be frightened but know that "by prayer and fasting you can even dispel wars," and she further reminded the visionaries that "if you think about evil, punishment, war, you are on the road towards them. Your task is to accept Divine Peace, to live it and to spread it – not with words but with your life." This is in line with the message of Our Lady at Fatima in terms of praying for peace, and perhaps with the secrets she told Lucy. Fr. Stephano Gobbi, who seems to have received locutions from Our Lady, thinks so, but sounds the optimistic note that in this Marian Year the triumph of Mary's Immaculate Heart has begun and a reign of the mercy of Jesus will be ushered in by the chastisement which will be an era of rebirth in the Holy Spirit – a great Pentecost for the Church.

In some ways this fits in with a reported vision that Pope Leo XIII had when he saw Satan waging war against the Church for a hundred years, which time is now drawing to a close. Let the skeptic consider that the late nineteenth and twentieth centuries have been the times of massive apostasy of the Church because of a popularization of the ideas of the Enlightenment which lead to atheism and agnosticism. All through these times Our Lady has come as God's prophetess, proclaiming his word at Rue de Bac, La Salette, Lourdes, and Fatima, requesting prayer of reparation and sacrifice, then becoming more explicit in requesting the Rosary, Consecration of Russia to her Immaculate Heart, and the First Saturdays devotion at Fatima, all as a way to combat the errors of this century and bring people back to the Gospel. Medjugorje is in line with this divine development, only becoming more explicit still, asking for fasting, more prayer and a whole new converted life as already outlined.

Perhaps now it is clear how living these messages of Mary: peace through conversion and prayer, union with God and one another, would bring that deep unity and peace that I noticed in the Dominican group for whom I celebrated Mass. They were all afire with Our Lady's messages, and are now spreading the Gospel. Would that Mary's call might touch us all so that we might be converted and usher in the reign of her Immaculate Heart, a time of mercy and peace, a time of rebirth in the Spirit.

6. Medjugorje: One Pilgrim's Reaction

In the spring of 1985 I went on pilgrimage with a married couple and their beautiful three-year-old daughter to a little Yugoslavian village called Medjugorje, where it was claimed that the Blessed Virgin was appearing daily to six teenage visionaries – Jakov, Ivan, Mirjana, Vicka, Ivanka, and Marija. I went as someone open to the phenomena that were occurring there and yet with a bit of skepticism as well. I had heard of the main thrust of the messages received in the apparitions: fast, pray, be converted, make peace with God and with one another, and peace will come to the world. I had also heard of the "ten secrets" being confided to the visionaries gradually: secrets concerning the future of the world and some impending chastisement that had already been much reduced because of the prayers of the faithful. The "*Gospa*" – the Croatian word for "Mother of God" – told the visionaries that people have forgotten that they can even change the course of nature by prayer. Many people were reporting that extraordinary occurrences were taking place at Medjugorje – the dancing of the sun as had happened at Fatima, and the spinning of a concrete cross on the highest mountain in the area, or a luminous woman seen by many, standing beneath that same cross.

I had heard all of this both back in the States and also in Rome, where I was teaching at the time of my pilgrimage, and yet I wasn't sure how I would react to these phenomena occurring in Medjugorje, whose name in Croatian means "between the mountains." I was a bit afraid I would find mass hysteria, exaggerated super spiritualism, and unhealthy piety, but what I found was quite the opposite. We were received into people's homes without charge (the government has since made the town's people charge so that it will get most of the money). We found a vibrant atmosphere of faith and prayer which reminded me of Lourdes, and was yet much simpler and homier. Many pilgrims were drawn to do penance and confess their sins and the confessional lines were practically unending. I had occasion on a subsequent trip to be present when one of the visionaries, Jakov, experienced the apparition. He suddenly dropped to his knees and was conversing with someone not seen by us and there yet was a "presence" in the room as well as great peace. Four of the visionaries still claim to see Our Lady daily wherever they happen to be, whereas two, having received all ten of the secrets, now only see her rarely.

The Eucharist was the highlight of daily life as is always the case in great Marian shrines. The church was jammed with people before Mass reciting ten decades of the rosary. Usually during this time, the apparitions took place elsewhere. Mass would follow with vibrant singing of all the parts of the Mass in Croatian. The readings were done in that language as well as in Italian, French or English for other pilgrims who spoke those languages. The homilies (many of which have since been published in English) were excellent. The preachers were the Franciscan friars who run the parish, many of whom are highly educated, holding doctorates in theology and scripture. They never emphasized the apocalyptic or extraordinary in their sermons but tried to connect all of the messages with Gospel themes, which was easy to do since they are simply the core of the Gospel proclaimed afresh by the "*Gospa*" for the world today. I was very impressed by the faith of the people, their peace, joy and penance. Confessors say that serious sin has disappeared from the village. Finally, I was most impressed by the joyous Christian hospitality shown by the villagers, who took strangers into their homes as Christ.

These are my impressions of Medjugorje after close inspection in two trips there. I do not anticipate the judgment of the Church on the authenticity of these apparitions and am completely ready to accept its decision though it is my *private* opinion that they are genuine. It is not a secret that the local bishop does not agree with me, although the neighboring Archbishop does. After the diocesan commission investigated and came up with a negative verdict as to the authenticity of the visions, Cardinal Ratzinger asked the Yugoslavian Bishops' Conference to set up its own commission to examine the case in greater depth, and that work is going on now.

Some feel that there should be no credence given to the apparitions or the connected messages until the Church pronounces its judgment, but both at Lourdes and Fatima, this happened long after the events, and in the meantime, the people believed and prayed. In a recent pastoral letter written on Medjugorje, Bishop Michael D. Pfeifer of San Angelo, Texas, defended the view that as long as the messages were not against faith or morals, they could be accepted by faithful Catholics even before official approbation is given. He recounts that in his *ad limina* visit to Rome, the Pope, when asked about Medjugorje spoke guardedly but favorably of the many conversions that had taken place there. The Bishop also recalls John Paul's words to the Italian bishops, when they asked if their people could visit Medjugorje and the Pope responded, "Let them go to Medjugorje, if they convert, pray, confess, do penance and fast." These are the main themes of the *"Gospa"* at Medjugorje, echoing Gospel imperatives, which I saw lived out in the love, faith and service of the people there. "By their fruits you shall know them."

7. Mary's Greatest Church in Rome

One August 5th, while on a Roman tour, I found myself behind schedule, hurrying up the Esquiline Hill to the Basilica of St. Mary Major for Solemn Mass. I was a bit late but arrived just in time to hear the choir singing a wondrous *Kyrie*.

As the singers broke into an equally magnificent *Gloria*, I was amazed to see no one was paying attention to the music. Instead, all were applauding while looking in the direction of a side chapel, where a famous painting of Our Lady attributed to St. Luke is enthroned.

Craning my neck to see what the crowd was applauding, I caught sight of rose petals falling like snow from the dome of the chapel. Only then I realized we were witnessing a recreation of the legend of Our Lady of the Snows during the *Gloria* in this most venerable and popular of Roman churches.

Pious tradition has it that Pope Liberius and the wealthy Roman patrician John had the same dream on the night of August 4, 356, in which Our Lady asked them to build a church in her honor on the Esquiline Hill. The next day, though it was a blistering August day, the spot Our Lady indicated was covered with snow. Pope Liberius traced the outline of the building he wanted with his crosier, and John undertook to pay for and supervise its construction.

Each year on August 5th this tradition is recreated with rose petals. Along with the artistic and devotional treasures of this Marian basilica, this tradition has made St. Mary Major not only a very popular church, but one much prayed in by the Romans themselves.

Though not the first church in Rome dedicated to Our Lady – Santa Maria in Trastevere claims that honor – St. Mary Major's second and present edifice was built by Pope Sixtus III to commemorate the Council of Ephesus, which in 431 proclaimed Our Lady as *Theotokos*, "God-bearer."

This wonderful early Christian structure, with its semi-circular apse, triumphal arch and thirty-six marble and four granite columns, was decorated in the years 432-440 with beautiful mosaics depicting Old Testament events as well as New Testament scenes of the life of the Blessed Virgin. In the ensuing epochs, it acquired relics of what was said to be the manger from Bethlehem, the relics of St. Matthew brought back from the Holy Land in the 13th century and now resting under the main altar, an icon of our Lady called *Salus Populi Romani* ("Health and Salvation of the Roman People") said to have been painted by St. Luke, but believed by most art experts to date from the middle of the fifth century, at the earliest.

Behind the Renaissance altar canopy is the huge and magnificent mosaic of the Coronation of the Virgin by the Risen Lord, done by Franciscan artist Fra Jacopo Torriti in 1225, when his order was newly approved by the Pope. The coffered Renaissance ceiling of the basilica is decorated with gold – gold brought back to Ferdinand and Isabella of Spain from the New World by Christopher Columbus and given by them to Pope Alexander VI.

The canons of St. Mary's chant Lauds and Vespers on Sundays and assist at Solemn Mass sung by the professional choir. The ordinary Masses are celebrated by Redemptorist Fathers, whose college is down the street. The confessors are Dominican friars, whose black-and-white habits can be seen gracing the more open European-style confessionals.

Pope St. Pius V, who was also a Dominican, lies in a wall

mausoleum behind a sliver panel (which is lowered on his feast so one can see his effigy) in the lovely Blessed Sacrament Chapel. Just across the way, people attend the Masses, rosary and Litany of Our Lady in her chapel where her icon is enthroned.

Just down the aisle is the capitular chapel, where the Blessed Sacrament is exposed each weekday from 9 to 5, and where people join in the rosaries offered by adoring nuns or sit in silent prayer. Many seem to be either preparing themselves for the Sacrament of Penance or doing the assigned penances.

This is Mary's church, and it is clearly a house of prayer. During the Marian year it was a major pilgrimage site for visitors from all nations.

Now a $7 million restoration is under way to clean the church's facade and exterior sculptures, which are being corroded by acid rain and pollution, as well as the roof and inner coffered ceiling. The fifth-and 13th-century mosaics, the beautiful 13th-century mosaic-like floor and the side chapels will also be cleaned. This venerable basilica, Our Lady's home in Rome, really needs the face-lift and repair and now it is being done so it will shine forth in its ancient splendor.

8. Surprised by Beauty

On the vigil of the Assumption I was in Washington, D. C., to attend the solemn profession of two of my younger brethren at the Dominican House of Studies. That hot afternoon, I wandered across the street to visit the National Shrine of the Immaculate Conception. What I found – hordes of pilgrims and a Latin Mass with song – was not at all what I had expected.

Twenty years ago, as a brash young seminarian full of ideas on proper contemporary liturgical art and architecture, I pontificated on the fact that the completion of the shrine (decided on by the bishops of this country in 1953 after a building halt during World War II) was a tragic mistake.

I was certain that they should have used the crypt (begun in 1924) as a substructure for a far more modern edifice in the Bauhaus style, not continue with the Byzantine-Romanesque plans of Maginnis, Walsh, and Kennedy. In the critical circles in which I traveled it was considered a breach of good taste to have anything good to say about the shrine.

Yet the people came to see it, and to pray. As Msgr. Cartwright remarked in his *Catholic Shrines of Europe* about the grand Bernini *baldachino,* the ordinary people liked it both when it was considered fashionable to admire it, and later when it was considered unfashionable to do so. The pilgrims have continued to come to look at this great church, to pray, to gawk, to light candles, for they obviously feel at home in this shrine of their Mother. Now that she is more a part of my life, so do I.

Artistically, I found myself this time most drawn to the Crypt Church with its beautiful onyx altar and the Blessed Sacrament Shrine where the jeweled tabernacle is set before Bancel La Farge's exquisite mosaic of Christ, the Good Shepherd. In the upper church, one is overwhelmed by John DeRosen's masterful "Christ in Majesty" in the central apse towering over the lovely altars dedicated to the glorious mysteries of the rosary.

Of all the side chapels and shrines, my favorites are the side altars in the Rosary Chapel with their excellent statues of Saints Dominic and Catherine, the Chapel of Our Lady of Czestochowa, the Byzantine Ruthenian Chapel, the new shrine to Our Lady Queen of Ireland, and the new confessional chapel dedicated to St. John Neumann of Philadelphia.

One would be mistaken if one saw Our Lady's shrine only in terms of marble and mosaic. It is a very busy church with many Masses, including one Sunday Mass chanted in Latin and the principal Sunday Mass with its excellent choir doing Tallis, Byrd, and Mozart.

Confessions are heard three times a day, the rosary is recited daily in the Lourdes Chapel for peace, lectures are given, and Vespers chanted with the people on the Sundays of Lent by the Dominican friars from across the street.

My recent visit opened my eyes to this rich feast of color, art, liturgy, music and piety that preconceived snobbism had kept shut tight. While all that I've described is important – and the shrine's staff are to be commended for their pastoral sense and liturgical sensitivity – the many pilgrims appreciate the primary meaning of the shrine as our country's tribute to Our Lady.

Much of the shrine is new and this very newness speaks to us of the American Church with both its vigor and its lack of experience.

The passage of time, the prayers of pilgrims and their lighted candles will mellow this edifice, entwining it more and more around the hearts of American Catholics whose ancestors, in the words of Pope John Paul II, "came here from various countries of the old world...came together around the heart of a mother they all had in common."

May we continue to cherish their legacy to us, a deep love of Mary, the Mother of God, especially as it is symbolized by our own American shrine.

9. The Rosary: A Spirit-filled Prayer

The rosary, a Spirit-filled prayer? Isn't that a contradiction in terms? Its monotonous and repetitive form seems a far cry from the rush of the Spirit, the spontaneous joy that wells up in the heart when one is touched by the presence of the Lord, or the new awareness of the word of God awakened when the Scriptures seem to leap off the page. How can we settle for prayer formulas like the rosary when the Holy Spirit seems to give us new words of prayer, both in heartfelt inspiration in our own words and in the joyful utterance of tongues? What does the Rosary have to offer us?

These are good questions. I asked them myself. The answers came to me gradually from my experience in the charismatic renewal as I saw the need for the "spirituality of the long haul."

When I came into the renewal in 1967, I had long since left the rosary behind. Like many Vatican II Catholics, I mistakenly thought that the council had banished such devotions. In the first flush of prayer meetings, renewed interest in reading Scripture, and spontaneous prayer with friends, I had no need of the rosary.

Only after I'd been in the charismatic renewal for quite some time did I see the need for a quieter, more rhythmic type of prayer. I came to appreciate this form of prayer especially in the "dry" times when the Spirit did not seem so active. I realized that the rosary is not a prayer foreign to Scripture, but one drawn directly from it. Most of the mysteries are events in the lives of Jesus and his mother that are depicted in the synoptic Gospels.

Thomas Howard, a convert to Catholicism who treasures the riches of his Evangelical heritage, explains the rosary as a way of *gazing* on the Gospel events – prolonging the experience by entering deeply into them in prayer and meditation. The regular rhythm of the Our Fathers and the Hail Marys calms our spirit and creates an inner space where we can encounter the Lord as we ponder particular aspects of the mysteries of his life, Death, and Resurrection.

Pope Paul VI recommended praying the rosary in his letter *Marialis Cultus* ("To Honor Mary"). He pointed out that while the Mass makes Christ sacramentally present in the Paschal mystery of his life, Death and Resurrection, the rosary makes these same mysteries present to the mind in meditation – thus the rosary can prepare us to celebrate the Eucharist.

As a Dominican, I am proud of the tradition that St. Dominic received the rosary from Our Lady when he was in a deep depression over his inability to convert the Albigensian heretics in southern France. These heretics taught that all matter was evil and that whatever increased the material, for example, sex, marriage, and children, was to be avoided as well as material food and drink. The celibate "perfect" fasted as much as possible, but ordinary people were permitted to enjoy sex, provided they did not marry or have children. The old were encouraged to commit suicide. This was a very dangerous heresy, upsetting the whole fabric of Christian society, and fostering the same contraceptive and anti-life mentality that promotes abortion and euthanasia in our own era.

The tradition attributes St. Dominic's eventual success against the Albigensians to his preaching the rosary to them. Paternoster beads, on which lay people who couldn't read the 150 psalms in Latin recited 150 Our Fathers as a substitute, were known before St. Dominic's time. As Marian devotion flowered in the Middle Ages, Hail Marys were substituted for some of the Our Fathers. The Dominican author, Fr. Bede Jarrett, suggests that as Dominic, inspired by Our Lady, preached on the great mysteries of the Incarnation and the Redemption, the people meditated on these mysteries while they recited Our Fathers and Hail Marys. Hearing that matter and flesh were good enough for the Son of God to assume and that he suffered and was also glorified in the same flesh would have been a good antidote to the Albigensian teaching.

How can we effectively be led by the Spirit as we pray the rosary today? What do we meditate on while we pray?

Some find it helpful to read the pertinent Gospel passage before each mystery; others use the scriptural rosary, which has a passage from scripture for each Hail Mary. Most like to picture the scene. When I was young, our family had a small easel with 15 prints of paintings by the Old Masters illustrating the mysteries. During the family rosary, one child would flip to the next scene at the end of the mystery so that we all had an image to gaze on. We can do the same thing in our imagination. We can also apply the events we are meditating on to our own lives.

The *joyful mysteries* – the Annunciation, the Visitation, the Nativity, the Presentation, and the Finding of the Child in the Temple – all are chronicled by St. Luke in the first two chapters of his Gospel. At the beginning of his Gospel, he describes Mary's wholehearted surrender to the Lord. Mary embarked on a journey of faith. Do we do the same?

Upon hearing of her cousin Elizabeth's pregnancy, Mary lovingly hastened to her aid. Mary has often been likened to the ark of the covenant, which bore the presence of the Lord in the Old Testament. At the Dominican House of Studies where I was trained, there is a lovely lectern from which the word of God is read and proclaimed. An image of the pregnant Virgin stands atop the lectern. We were told that we were being trained as preachers filled with the Word, as was Mary. Is this not true of all Christians?

It seems to me that the birth of the Lord is a mystery of silence and humility. Mary pondered the visits of the shepherds and the Magi in her heart. Likewise, she pondered the prophecy of Simeon that her child would be a sign of contradiction, and a sword would pierce her own heart. These last two mysteries are especially relevant to parents today who must learn that their children are not theirs but belong to their heavenly Father.

Our Lord's sufferings are depicted in each of the Gospels and are the subject of the *sorrowful mysteries*: The Agony in the Garden, the Scourging at the Pillar, the Crowning with Thorns, the Carrying of the Cross, and the Crucifixion.

In his agony in Gethsemane Jesus suffered so greatly that he sweat blood and asked that this cup be taken from him if possible, but he surrendered to the Father's will. Do we do the same? It's helpful for us to know that the Lord struggled, that in his humanity he feared suffering. He was stripped of his garments and humiliated. Do we practice modesty, or are we into the excessive cult of the body that characterizes our society? The Lord's head was crowned with thorns as described by Matthew, Mark, and John. His crown was suffering – do we seek glory for ourselves? The head symbolizes our thoughts – do we keep control over them, or do resentful or impure thoughts control us? John describes Jesus as carrying his cross while the synoptics show Simon as helping him. How do I carry my cross, or help others to do the same?

Finally, the Crucifixion is the climax of all the Gospels. Our Lord suffered for me; he "loved me and gave himself for me."[91] Have I responded by crucifying my fleshly desires?[92] Am I grateful for the great gift of salvation that flows from the cross of Jesus?

The *glorious mysteries* – the Resurrection, the Ascension, Pentecost, Mary's Assumption into Heaven, and her Crowning – bring us to the triumph of salvation. In the Lord's Resurrection I am transformed, for in baptism I died to the old man and rose to the new in Christ.[93] I live a new life in his Ascension; in his risen humanity shown to the Father, my humanity – despite its present weakness – is affirmed. Meditating on the Pentecost event (see Acts 2) enables me to ask for a daily empowering of the Spirit. While Our Lady's assumption and crowning are not found in the Scriptures, the woman in Revelations, Chapter 12, clothed in the sun with the moon under her feet and crowned with twelve stars, is a symbol of Mary and the Church. Mary's bodily assumption into heaven is a sign of our sharing in her Son's Resurrection as she did; her crowning reminds us of the crowns promised to followers of the Lord.

As I have mulled over the mysteries, pondering their depths and penetrating their meaning for my own life, I have found myself led to a more contemplative prayer. Rediscovering the rosary has brought me into a deeper communion with the Lord and has enriched my life in the Spirit. I believe that many others who have experienced the Lord and are hungering for growth would also receive the same blessing that I have in praying the rosary. If only we "could find again the charism of the rosary," as the modern Irish preacher of the rosary Fr. Gabriel Harty says, "and use it as an instrument of healing love as it was meant to be, (we) would sweep over the earth and renew it in fire."

---

[91] see Gal. 2:20
[92] see Gal. 5:24
[93] see Rom. 6:1-11

RENEWAL OF LITURGY, PRAYER AND DEVOTION

1. The Mystery of Mass Still Remains

One of the liturgical pleasures of Rome (where I'm now teaching at the Pope's alma mater, the Angelicum) is that one can participate in the celebration of the Mass in a great variety of rites and in many settings.

The past two Sundays, I've been sallying forth to the basilicas of St. Peter and St. Mary Major to see how the Mass is celebrated in these holy churches. At both Solemn Masses, the celebration was in Latin except for the readings, which were in the vernacular. The Mass was facing the people, (as it has *always* been in these basilicas), and the music was exquisite Gregorian and polyphony.

At both Masses there were even acolytes bearing torches during the Canon and a thurifer incensing during the elevation. American liturgists have eliminated these touches, taking the line that whatever is not explicitly spelled out in the Missal of Paul VI must be suppressed, a strictness not found in the Roman interpretation.

If one regularly could find in the States, Mass in the new rite beautifully celebrated in Latin, with music reflecting our great heritage, as Vatican II mandated, perhaps there never would have been the great outcry – largely from the United States – for the Mass of Pope Pius V.

I suspect many people attending a Tridentine celebration will miss hearing the readings in their own language, for the 1962 rite does not permit this. They may also miss the greater variety of scriptural readings at Sunday and daily Mass that the new lectionary with its ancient liturgical principle of continuous reading has restored.

But I know they will positively enjoy the quiet reverence and dignity of a sober rite, a reverence which is quite compatible with the *Novus Ordo* and indeed is closer to the Church's understanding than clown Masses and other ill-advised attempts at celebration!

On the other hand, the Holy Father, concerned for the spiritual and pastoral good of *all* Catholics, has, after listening to many petitions from the people in the pews, granted an indult to allow Mass to be celebrated in the Tridentine rite for those who would benefit from it. After all, former Anglicans can retain something of their beautiful liturgical heritage, so why can't Catholics celebrate the rite of the Dominican Pope Pius V, which nourished the faith of saints and untold Christians from his time to Vatican II?

The outcry from liturgists that greeted the Pope's gracious concession has mystified me. I've long thought the option should be allowed. Are my fellow liturgists so insecure that they think the new rite will be supplanted? Do they actually think that all the genuine liturgical reform of Vatican II will disappear?

Or is perhaps this a signal that the Church recognizes its right to regulate its own liturgical life, and that endless experimentation is drawing to a close? I devoutly hope so, for constantly tinkering with the rites, whether by "creative" celebrants or trendy liturgical committees, does not nourish God's holy people.

The conditions for a local bishop to allow the Tridentine Mass are sensible. The attitude here in Rome seems to be that they should be interpreted generously – the old Canon Law adage applies; favorable privileges are to be extended.

First, those requesting the Mass must accept the validity of the new Mass doctrinally (although not necessarily the fittingness of its various translations). Even though some think this indult might be a bridge to the followers of Archbishop Lefebvre, the problems between the Lefebvrites and Vatican II are more complex than the Mass alone.

Secondly, the Mass is not *usually* to be celebrated in a parish church, but in an oratory, convent chapel, etc. It is up to the bishop whether such a Mass will be a regular occurrence.

Third, the Mass must be entirely in Latin and according to the

1962 Roman Missal, with no admixture of rites. One might hope that such a celebration in time might be able to adopt the new and better Lectionary, especially since even the 1962 rite allowed vernacular readings by indult in some countries before Vatican II.

Finally, the bishop is to submit a report to Rome on the outcome of this indult, not so the indult might be terminated, but rather so the pastoral fruitfulness of the present conditions may be judged, and Rome may be adequately informed, especially if changes need to be made.

In the past, requests for information were answered with the response that there was no desire for the Tridentine rite. But the numbers now attending such Masses seem to belie this facile answer. If there is a need, let it be. While it will obviously not undo the new rite, perhaps it will help us recover the reverence, beauty and dignity of the timeless mystery of the Mass as the Fathers of Vatican II intended it to be reformed.

Then this great mystery will shine forth in all its splendor – whether new rite, old rite or Byzantine Rite; whether simple or solemn celebration, whether accompanied by charismatic music or Gregorian chant – the eternal sacrifice of Christ, the Lord, Jesus.

2. It's the Mass That Matters

This pithy statement by the late Msgr. Ronald Knox, convert from Anglicanism and noted author, that it is the Mass that is the center of Catholicism, the core of life in the Church for the Catholic Christian, is quite literally true here at the Franciscan University of Steubenville. Whether one participates in the quiet early morning Mass frequented by the early risers, the Franciscan Community Mass offered at noon or the evening liturgy celebrated in charismatic fashion with free praise and contemporary music, it is the Mass, like a bright jewel that illumines the day of ordinary life at the University.

There are always those special Masses like that celebrated in Latin by me recently at which the *schola* sang a magnificent polyphonic Mass and the congregation joined in with some simple Latin Gregorian chants, or the rich Byzantine Divine Liturgy that my classes will be attending soon, or the very early Mass said for the pro-Life students before their weekly sidewalk counseling and picketing at Pittsburg abortuaries. There are also the Sunday liturgies, well planned and sung with all the ministries actively involved, but whether simply said or richly celebrated, whether in Latin or in English, whether Roman rite or Byzantine, here it is for the Steubenville family "the Mass that matters" at the center of our day.

The Mass of the Roman rite has a simple, rather straight-forward structure no matter where it is celebrated, and I would like to review that perhaps to help our readers experience as much in the Liturgy of the Mass as we do here. In doing so I'll examine a little of the history and theology of the Mass.

The first part of the Mass to be celebrated is the last to have been developed historically. Our entrance rite of a formal entrance of priest and servers entering to a hymn comes from the first days of freedom for the Church after the Constantinian peace where long processions of clerics entered the newly built basilicas while a Psalm was sung by the *schola* and people. Vatican II teaches us there is a presence of Christ in the people who are gathered in the name of the Lord "wherever two or three are gathered in my Name...."[94] and a presence of Christ in the priest who acts in *persona Christi*, a presence in the Word which we will next examine, and the Real Presence in the consecrated Eucharist.

Once the priest greets us in Christ's name, he invites us to consider our sinfulness and we confess that in the *Confiteor*, which the priests used to say in silence processing to the altar, or in the *Kyrie* or Lord Have Mercy in which we acclaim the Lord's mercy in forgiving our sins so that we can worship Him. This is not the sacrament of penance or reconciliation which is necessary for serious sin, but a recognition of our own unworthiness. We thank God for his mercy in the praise of the Gloria, a 2nd century Syrian hymn extending the angels' song[95] which here at Steubenville is often extended in free praise at charismatic Masses. The priest says, "Let us pray" and pauses to allow the Spirit to pray in each of our hearts before he "collects" the prayer of all in the collect and offers them officially in the prayer of the Church to the Father through the Son and in the Holy Spirit, Amen.

Now we are ready to hear the Word. This part of the Mass goes back to synagogue worship before Christ. This may have developed during the Babylonian Exile when Jews missed the Temple with the

---

[94] Matt. 18:20
[95] cf. Luke 2:14

Lord's presence. The Prophets began teaching and the rabbis developed the understanding that wherever ten good Jews got together to read the TORAH or the Jewish Bible, there God would be in their midst. The Lord Jesus in the quote we've already seen "cuts down" the number and says, "Where two or three are gathered, I will be with them." So it was that when St. Paul preached to his new communities of Christians, or when the Gospels began to be written down and were read to the early Christians, and so it is with us, when we hear the Word proclaimed in our midst. We are not just hearing ancient history in the First Reading of how God dealt with his promised people of old, or in the Epistle of St. Paul chiding the Corinthians or encouraging the Colossians or in the Gospel Jesus speaking to the crowds that followed him. Rather through those readings, God is speaking to me, here and now! How do I respond? "If today you hear His voice, harden not your hearts."[96] The homily helps me to apply the word to my daily life and here at Steubenville, we are blessed with many dynamic homilists.

After the Creed, the renewal of the faith into which we were baptized, we have the Prayer of the Faithful in which we pray not just for our needs but for those of the Church universal and for the needs of all in the world. When the gifts are brought forth, symbols of our work and lives being offered with Christ, we enter into the deepest part of the mystery, and we find ourselves back at the Last Supper and on Mount Calvary, at the heart of Christ's sacrifice.

The Lord Jesus, a good Jew, used the Passover sacrificial meal as a basis for the new sacrament of the new Covenant, the Eucharist. Just as Jews to this day gather to commemorate the Exodus event – God using Moses to lead them out of the slavery of Egypt – so Jesus used the framework of this celebration to institute a new sacrificial meal in which His leading us out of the slavery of sin by the sacrifice of the Cross on the morrow is made present. Just as the Jews believe that in celebrating the past even in the Passover feast, it is somehow made present as a sign of hope for the future, so Jesus intended that His Eucharist would make present His death on the morrow (Good Friday) and the Father's acceptance of it in the Resurrection. That is why He said, "Do this as a memorial of Me,"[97] not just a psychological memory, but the past event of Calvary really made

---

[96] Ps. 95
[97] Luke 22:19

present so we can enter in.

God doesn't need this holy mystery made present, but we do so we can offer our lives, joys and sorrows, hopes and dreams in union with the Lord's timeless, eternal sacrifice. And so, St. Paul would write… "as often as you do this you proclaim the death of the Lord until He comes."[98] Here is where our hearts and minds should be as we join the angels in their song of praise – Holy, Holy, Holy[99] – hear the great Eucharistic Prayer, or the Canon. Pay close attention when by the words "This is my Body"; "This is my Blood" uttered by the priest acting in the name of Jesus, the bread and wine are "transubstantiated," that is become nothing other than Jesus Christ, body and blood, soul and divinity, although sacramentally present under the forms of bread and wine. Since Jesus is truly present, He is our offering to the Father in the Spirit. We who are not worthy to offer ourselves, join in agreement with this great act of worship and praise as we say "Amen," the Hebrew word meaning "so be it." St. Augustine says where he heard the Amen in the Milan cathedral at a Mass celebrated by St. Ambrose, the congregation was so responsive it sounded like a mighty thunder!

Now we get ready for communion. We say The Our Father asking for what we need – "our daily bread" and for this Eucharist, which is our "super-substantial" bread. We pray for reconciliation with all, "forgive us our trespasses as we forgive those who trespass against us" and in the kiss of peace which is a reminder to be reconciled, "if you have anything against your brother, first go and be reconciled,"[100] before you come to the altar. We receive the Lord in Holy Communion, not just as individuals, but "we the many though we are, are we not the one bread,"[101] and through our communion with Christ in His sacramental body, we are joined to one another in His mystical body. Now we are more the Church, the Body of Christ, and we are ready to go forth and live in Him, and out of that peace to proclaim the Gospel.

A postscript is in order here. Because we believe the bread and wine become Christ sacramentally, we reserve any hosts remaining in the tabernacle, beautifully designed, and here we pray before our

---

[98] I Cor. 11:26
[99] Isaiah 6
[100] Matt. 5:23
[101] 1 Cor. 10:17

sacramental Lord. The students here at the University are often found so doing in the Eucharistic chapel. Often the Blessed Sacrament is exposed in a monstrance, a vessel designed like a sunburst to "show" the Body of the Lord. Here daily adoration in which our students bask in the Lord's radiant energy and prostrate themselves in humble prayer is found in the beautiful little replica of St. Francis' Portiuncula. In Eucharistic holy hours in Christ the King Chapel, the sacramental Lord is worshipped as King of this campus.

In sum, whether in simple Mass or more elaborate traditional or charismatic celebrations of the Eucharist, whether in prayer before the tabernacle or in the Blessed Sacrament exposed, the Eucharist is the sun and the center of the universe of the University of Steubenville. Our explanation of this great sacrament shows us that it should be also for us.

3. Love of the Mass

Recently I had the pleasant experience of participating in the Sunday Mass of the Catholic Fellowship of the Charismatic Community at Ann Arbor, Michigan. I had spent time with the young people comprising this community, had stayed with a young married couple with their two children, and on Sunday had the occasion to join the Catholic members of the Community in Sunday Mass. As we were leaving for Mass, almost everyone else on the street, all young Catholic families, were getting into their cars going to the same Mass. We arrived at a large university auditorium where Mass was to be celebrated because no Catholic Church was free this time Sunday morning.

I do not like Mass outside a church edifice, but this was a pleasant, old, rather classical auditorium with a semi-circular stage, with a background of organ pipes. Against this, to ensure a sacred setting, a crucifix was centrally placed flanked by two beautiful tapestry hangings (not felt banners with clichés of "peace" and "joy" all over them). This was the backdrop to the well-designed altar, lectern and chair. The other concelebrating priests and I vested and soon were processing down the aisle to a very exuberant entrance hymn, full of joy, but also reverent praise. This really set the tone of the whole celebration, for it was a rather straight-forward Mass with no gimmicks or illicit Eucharistic prayers, simply the Mass as intended by the Church well celebrated by the whole community, whose song rang out as an expression of praise, reverence and faith.

All that should have been sung was: Entrance Hymn, Responsorial Psalm, Alleluia, *Sanctus*, Memorial Acclamation, Amen, *Agnus Dei*, Communion Hymn, and Recessional, all led by an excellent and varied music ministry. The sermon was on the Gospel, brief and to the point. At Communion, the priests were instructed not to expect the people receiving Communion to look at them; rather they wanted to look at the host in adoration a moment before receiving…a most laudable practice. I wrote later to the Pastor that my experience was that this was exactly what the Conciliar Fathers at the Second Vatican Council had in mind -- the Mass celebrated in such a way that the people could participate and express their faith, but always the sacred Liturgy of the Church, not eccentric experimentation or secular additions.

I don't know why exactly, but this Mass reminded me of another quite different celebration of the Eucharistic mysteries. This time I was in Munich and attended Mass in the Michaelskirche, a wonderful old German Baroque Church which had been renovated for the new Liturgy without destroying its artistic character. A new altar facing the people was placed in a circular sanctuary under the central dome, while the lovely baroque old high altar continued to be the altar for the reservation of the Blessed Sacrament as it had always been. The Church was jam packed and the congregation sang out lustily a German entrance hymn. The ministers advanced towards the altar and the celebrant greeted us in German and led us through the penitential rite. I was totally unprepared for what happened next, for suddenly the choir in the balcony behind me broke into a delightful Mozart *Kyrie* which was followed by a Mozart *Gloria*, all accompanied by an orchestra. The Mass continued with German hymns alternating with the wonderful Mozart *Sanctus* and *Agnus Dei*. During the Canon of the Mass, a dozen acolytes in red cassocks and white surplices circled the altar swinging smoking silver thuribles, welcoming the coming of the Eucharistic Lord – another Liturgy well celebrated in another style with the joy of Mozart and the baroque splendor of its setting, but nonetheless the Liturgy of the Church, the sacrifice of the Mass, participated in by all – the desire of the Second Vatican Council.

I wish that more of those who complain about the new Liturgy, about the lack of reverence and mystery, about the loss of Latin and the poor translations could have attended these Masses with me. Then, they would have seen that the new Liturgy well celebrated can be just as reverent as the old. I think many who follow Archbishop Lefebvre or seek out Tridentine chapels are fleeing from the manifold abuses committed by many celebrants who take matters into their own hands and give us their eccentric version of the Church's Liturgy. Yet we must not be blind to abuses of former years either, Masses rushed through in fifteen minutes, overly operatic Mass settings and often very sentimental hymns. The answer to different abuses lies in the love of the Mass itself, the mystery of Christ truly present, who offers Himself to the Father for us now as He once did in a bloody fashion on the Cross. This central mystery is there whether celebrated with bright new charismatic music, or with the sheer delight of Mozart, or with deeply moving Gregorian for that matter, or even when celebrated poorly. When my Irish great-grandmother asked the priest what the difference was between a low Mass and a high Mass, he answered the difference was between a calico dress and a silk one.

And so it is with the central mystery of our faith, the Mass – many different styles and settings, but ultimately in the words of Ronald Knox, "It's the Mass that matters."

4. Latin Mass?

When I was in Providence, I had the good fortune to have a bishop in the diocese who permits a public Latin Mass, and a deeply moving experience it is. On the Second Sunday of Easter I took some of my students to Holy Name Church, a lovely old basilica built at the turn of the century whose interior is vaguely reminiscent of St. Paul Outside the Walls. The Church was three quarters filled with regular parishioners, rich and poor, black and white, and with others who came from all over the city especially for the Mass. The congregation sang fairly simple Gregorian chants for the *Kyrie, Credo, Sanctus, Pater* and *Agnus Dei* as well as *O' Filii et Filiae* as a recessional. The choir, under the able direction of the organist, sang a splendid *Gloria* by Refice, more polyphonic music at the offertory and communion – a *Cantate Domino* by Croce, *Jesu, Rex Admirabilis* by Palestrina, and concluded with a bit of Handel. How refreshing to the ear, how uplifting to the Spirit – a change from dreary, listless singing by a few scattered in a non-participating congregation or folk music poorly done by amateurs. This rather elaborate and rich musical approach contrasts with another deeply moving Mass I recently attended completely sung in Latin Gregorian by the monks and nuns of Still River in central Massachusetts. Here one found less brilliance, but a deeply contemplative peace as the beauty of the Latin chant washed away all the cares of the day.

Is this at core not what many people feel to be lacking in our current liturgical approach? Could not more bishops allow this kind of celebration which adds a greater richness and beauty to the church of God in this age of "pluralism"? The *Notificatio* of Paul VI which made his *Missal* binding on Latin Rite Catholics while allowing the vernacular, also encouraged ordinaries "to preserve one or more Masses in Latin – especially sung Masses – in certain churches, above all in large cities, where many come together with the faithful of different languages."[102] This is often done in many European cities but is virtually unknown here. The same Pope later in 1974 issued his little booklet of Latin Gregorian chants *Jubilate Deo* in hopes that the *Constitution of the Liturgy's* directive that "provision should be made, however, to see that the faithful can also say or sing together in Latin those parts of the Ordinary of the Mass that concern them"[103] might be fulfilled. Unfortunately, this has largely gone unheeded.

Is it possible that there would be no illicit Tridentine Mass centers had this policy been adopted? I've often wondered why there wasn't permitted a Tridentine rite alongside the new rite, where many people felt the spiritual need. I suspect some of the accusations of extreme traditionalists that the Mass was made into a Protestant communion service at Vatican II have not helped the cause. The rationale for this accusation seems to stem chiefly from the fact that there were Protestant observers at the Council. Or we find the idea expressed that the Tridentine Mass was that celebrated continuously from antiquity to Paul VI, not recognizing the manifold liturgical changes in the rites of the Church that have always taken place. So, one in good faith could talk about the Tridentine Mass celebrated by St. Thomas Aquinas, though of course he celebrated in the former Dominican rite, or by St. Gregory the Great, whose Mass would have

---

[102] *Notificatio* of Paul VI (1971) n. 48.
[103] *Ibid.*, n. 54.

resembled that of St. Pius V (Tridentine rite) *only in its core*, and indeed the new order of Mass would be closer to that used by St. Gregory. Even if the Tridentine rite were allowed, as it often is in England for various groups, yet the problem for most ordinary people with our current liturgy is the lack of the sacred, transcendence, reverence and beauty which the Latin Mass evokes.

Perhaps this column is too nostalgic and unrealistic in expecting many Latin Masses in the new rite although I am convinced that there is a need for them in larger cities. Nonetheless I am delighted to see that more and more Latin Gregorian and polyphony is being performed at regular Masses in the vernacular. Choirs are refurbishing their repertoires and finding that some of the classic Latin chants and motets are just the thing to enhance the more solemn celebrations of the liturgical year. In the Neo Gothic Dominican Church in New Haven, which is physically located in the heart of Yale University, the organist and choir there have a grand tradition of using the finest Church music from the past at the more solemn Masses and utilizing good vernacular hymns and acclamations as well. Here there are well done folk Masses, sung English Masses, but also solemn celebrations with Latin Gregorian and polyphony. At the Easter Mass, jammed with Yale students as well as older parishioners, was Carl Maria Von Weber's *Mass in G Major* with the proper Gregorian chants as well as motets by Mozart. One of the Good Friday services featured selections from Bach. Many young students commented how good it was to be in a church that seemed like a church, to hear music that was uplifting.

Are these young people telling us something? I think so, and perhaps we will be sufficiently "Catholic" to respond by exploring the great riches of our liturgical and musical heritage so that we can share it with them. Perhaps this will be the task of the upcoming conference on Gregorian Chant at Catholic University in Washington this June. One hopes to see the beginning of a new era when we shall again worship the Lord in the beauty of holiness, no longer afraid to utilize our great musical heritage in manifold ways.

5. Liturgy for the New Millennium

Catholics had many different liturgical hopes on the eve of the Extraordinary Synod in Rome last November. Some hoped that the

Tridentine Mass would be restored, others that the Latin liturgy would be strongly encouraged and still others that liturgical innovation would be suppressed or curtailed.

Of course, the rather carefully balanced document that emerged from the synod dashed these hopes, since it didn't have a great deal to say about liturgical matters. Yet what the Synod Fathers did express on this subject will set the liturgical tone for the '80s and into the next millennium.

In a much-needed treatment of the *mystery* of the Church (a recognition that the Church is a divine reality that can never be completely reduced to merely sociological categories), note is taken of the "signs of a new hunger and thirst for the transcendent and divine." Further mention is made of the fact that perhaps the spread of sects and cults might be due to the fact that the Church has "sometimes failed to sufficiently manifest the sense of the sacred."

When the synod document addresses the Sacred Liturgy itself, it generalizes, I think accurately, that liturgical renewal has been fairly well received. It also states, however, that active participation consists not simply in external activity but in "interior and spiritual participation in the paschal mystery of Jesus Christ."

Some liturgists have questioned whether "active participation" is a faithful translation of the Latin *participatio actuosa* which the *Constitution on the Liturgy* encourages. The Latin term means *real* or *actual* participation – translations that seem more open to the totality which includes the external doing, but do not seem to limit participation only to that "active" level. "Real" participation embraces the deeper movements of the heart and mind which flow from the external rite and are the richest fruits of the death and resurrection of Christ realized in us.

Finally, the synodal document stresses that the liturgy "must favor the sense of the sacred and make it shine forth" and "must be permeated by the spirit of reverence, adoration and the glory of God."

Do our current Masses manifest these criteria? If not, what can we do?

First, we must not be afraid to utilize the great music of our liturgical heritage: Gregorian chant, sacred polyphony and more traditional Catholic hymns. I had the good fortune during last Holy Week to participate in the services celebrated by the Dominican

Community of Saint Mary's in New Haven, Connecticut. The graceful old Victorian Gothic edifice has been magnificently restored by the Knights of Columbus for their recent centennial, for it was here that they were founded. Throughout Holy Week, English liturgies used the proper Latin Gregorian chants which were appropriately somber. Latin polyphony by Victoria, Lasso and Palestrina done by the choir was complemented by popular vernacular hymns and acclamations for the people.

The Vigil's music was more joyful, and on Easter Sunday itself the choir sang a Mozart Mass (the *Orgelsolomesse*) and a Mozart *Regina Caeli* in an explosion of Easter glory. Participation, both external and internal, was total. It was a clear sign of the thirst for the sacred in this search for a more solemn liturgy.

We must also be open to traditional devotions, the experiential prayer of the people. The pastorally wise Dominicans at St. Mary's, besides having the people join them for the Liturgy of the Hours during this sacred time, also said the rosary with them, and on Good Friday had Stations of the Cross at which the devotion of the crowd was deeply moving. Clerical distaste for popular devotions is a snobbism that fails to understand how the people's piety has always been influential even in liturgical evolution.

My deepest conviction is that *the* one devotion that will aid authentic liturgical renewal the most is Exposition of the Blessed Sacrament. Silent prayer before the Blessed Sacrament will help to restore that contemplative gaze to worshiping Catholics. It will help us get beyond the "how to" of liturgy to the "what" of it all – Jesus Christ truly and substantially present in His Body and Blood, slain and yet risen and victorious – the same Christ at Mass offering Himself to the Father for us and our *real* participation in that sacrificial meal.

We'll get beyond mere activity to *actual* worship, and in doing so we will find the experience of God for whom we thirst. As we respond in beautiful melody that transcends the purely reasonable and expresses our adoration, the glory and splendor of God will shine forth in us, in the Mass, in the Church, as the Extraordinary Synod prophesied in its document.

6. An Evolution of the Liturgy

On June 29th of 1988, the Catholic Church witnessed a sad and significant happening. Archbishop Marcel Lefebvre consecrated four bishops, thereby causing automatic excommunication for himself and them. This penalty (which is inflicted by the new Code of Canon Law and not by Pope John Paul II) is so severe because, by that act of disobedience in defiance of the Pope, Archbishop Lefebvre created a schism in leading his followers away from the unity of the Church, away from the communion with Peter, the keeper of the Apostolic Faith and living Tradition. This act has a certain tragic irony to it for the Archbishop's intention in ordaining the new bishops was to preserve the Faith of the Apostles and Tradition; but in the Catholic view, one cannot have these without the successor of Peter – *ubi Petrus, ibi ecclesia* (where there is Peter, there is the Church) – and by this very act the Archbishop has put himself outside the Church.

It is not the purpose of this article to explore in depth all of the theological or ecclesiological issues of this case nor to review all the liturgical abuses and dubious theological understandings of Vatican II which upset all true Catholics as well as the Archbishop's followers, but to focus on the liturgical questions that the Archbishop has raised, especially when he accuses the present rite of Mass as being untraditional or as nothing but a Protestant communion service. It seems to me that Archbishop Lefebvre's problem is not that he is too traditional as the news media would have it, but that he is not traditional enough, especially in the area of liturgy.

Let me explain what I mean. Archbishop Lefebvre has said that he wishes to have on his tombstone St. Paul's classic text which is the very core of Tradition: "What I received, I handed on to you."[104] The very word *Traditio* means the "handing on" of the Faith – and here St. Paul is speaking of the doctrine and Liturgy of the Eucharist. The Archbishop and his followers tend to identify correct Eucharistic doctrine and proper liturgical form with the Mass of the Missal of Pope Pius V, or the Tridentine Mass which came out of the Council of Trent. He and his followers seem to freeze Tradition at that point in time, not realizing that just as doctrine evolves, not from one truth

---

[104] 1 Cor. 11:23f

to another (as some moderns would have it), but as a deeper perception of the ramifications of the same basic truth of the Faith; so also, the Liturgy itself has evolved in the Church. Not only was there a long history of liturgical change and evolution to arrive at the liturgical form of the Mass canonized by the Tridentine Missal, but even that book was changed by Pope Pius X, Pope Benedict XV and Pius XII, whose changes in the Liturgy of Holy Week were really quite radical.

Cardinal Newman once said that to live is to change and to live long is to change much, and this is true of the living tradition of the Liturgy, which changes its form for the different pastoral needs of different epochs in the life of the Church, but does not change the substantial Eucharistic Faith it embodies, as Archbishop Lefebvre seems to fear. So, we are not surprised at the fact that the Liturgy of the Church has changed and continues to change.

Archbishop Lefebvre has said that he is loyal to Rome – not "the Rome of the new-modernist and neo-Protestant tendency," but "Catholic Rome, guardian of the Catholic Faith and of Rome, mistress of wisdom and truth." Love for and loyalty to Rome and its tradition also motivated the members of the Tridentine Commissions, established by Paul IV and Pius V in their work of liturgical restoration and renewal in the aftermath of the Reformation. The liturgist Theodore Klauser shows how these commissions tried to return the ancient Roman liturgical tradition to the "pristine norm of the holy Fathers." They were not satisfied with many of the accretions of their day and felt the need to modify and purify the Liturgy they had inherited in the light of tradition and the sources that they had, thus producing the Tridentine Mass so revered by Archbishop Lefebvre.

The Commission established after Vatican Council II also clearly espoused in the *General Instruction to the Missal* of Paul VI the principle of returning to the "usage of the holy fathers," but in-depth liturgical patristic and historical research have unearthed for us today a clearer view of what that tradition was and helps us to reclaim it afresh. Today's rites are often far more" traditional" since we may follow the practice of celebrating Mass facing the people as was done in ancient Rome, though never in the Eastern Empire. Three readings (or more) of the Scriptures were the norm for the Liturgy in the Patristic era, and it was in the language the educated understood (Greek in

Rome until the end of the third or beginning of the fourth century when Latin became the more common tongue); so, the vernacular in our time can be seen in the Tradition. When one compares our present rites with the ancient, one frequently finds them both more traditional and more Roman than the Mass as legislated in the *Missal* of St. Pius V, due in large measure to historical data discovered since Trent.

Finally, because of the presence of Protestant observers at Vatican II, the Archbishop suggests that their influence can be detected in the liturgical changes following the Council. Even if they did have an influence (for worship in one's own tongue and hymn singing is common to Protestant as well as Catholic worship), that does not mean that the Eucharist has been "Protestantized" as Archbishop Lefebvre charges, nor that it has become just a Protestant communion service. Catholic belief is that the Mass is a continuation of the sacrifice of Christ on the Cross and that has not changed, though there may not be as many sacrificial references in the current rite as in the Tridentine Mass and some theologians are attempting to express the concept of sacrifice anew.

Very simply, then, I have tried to show that Tradition is a living, vital reality and that we can see this in liturgical development up to and including the Tridentine Mass and after, too. Further, I have tried to explore how much more traditional and Roman, the present rite is. I believe that many of the followers of Archbishop Lefebvre are good people, tired of liturgical abuses and trendy, sometimes heterodox preaching. And I am in sympathy with their impatience.

Pope John Paul II bent over backwards to meet as many of the Archbishop's demands as he could. Now he promises Lefebvre's sympathizers who do not follow him into schism the Tridentine Mass, the rites and ceremonies of the old Church, if they need them for the peace of their souls. This is a wise pastoral decision and we can only hope that many will avail themselves of the generosity. Yet, pray that as the Church celebrates her own Liturgy with greater reverence and beauty, with sound preaching and good music both in Latin and in the vernacular, that our newly separated brethren will be drawn away from schism into deeper Eucharistic communion and will return to the fullness of living Tradition, the Church of Rome and its Bishop, John Paul II.

7. Baroque Liturgy on Trial

Since the liturgy of the baroque era is the Tridentine Mass, it seems sadly relevant to be discussing it now, when Archbishop Lefebvre has just gone into schism to preserve this very form of the Mass, which most contemporary liturgists consider to be a very poor liturgical form. All standard liturgical authors consider the Mass of this period to be excessively dramatic in its music and ceremonial, propagandistic in its architectural and artistic setting, and far too tightly structured in its ritual. The dean of liturgists and the man at whose feet I studied at Notre Dame and Brown universities, Fr. Louis Bouyer, in his *Liturgical Piety*, expresses most clearly this opinion. I used to agree, but have since come to an alternate view, which is difficult for me to express, so great is my respect and admiration for this knowledgeable liturgical scholar and theologian. Fr. Bouyer, on this topic in his book *Liturgical Piety*, states:

From the 16th and 17th century idea of court life Catholics derived their false notions of public worship (i.e., Mass as a performance). An earthly king must be honored daily by the pageant of court ceremonial, so also the heavenly king. The courtly atmosphere around Him was to be provided by the liturgy…as many handbooks of the period actually say it was considered to be "the etiquette of the great King." The most obvious features of it were those embodying the external pomp, decorum, and grandeur befitting so majestic a Prince. The lack of intelligible meaning in so many rites and even in the sacred words themselves, was, therefore praised as enhancing the impression of awe to be given to the dazzled multitude. So also, it would have seemed almost indecent to offer the common people any opportunity to participate directly in so sublime a performance. They were rather, only to admire it, dimly from afar, as a scene of unapproachable magnificence.[105]

Our author sees this "distorted interpretation of the nature of the liturgy"[106] as arising from three main factors:

1. The neopagan aesthetic world of the renaissance which substituted Greco-Roman mythology for biblical imagery to the detriment of the latter.

[105] Louis Bouyer, *Liturgical Piety* (Notre Dame, Ind.: The University of Notre Dame Press, 1954), p.4.
[106] *Ibid.*, p.5.

2. A violent hunger for the "super-human instead of the supernatural, as witness the paintings of Michelangelo" and the "enormous rather than the great as witness the statues of St. John Lateran with their hysterical gesticulations."[107]

3. A baroque Catholicism that was more loyal "though not genuinely Christian" which gradually withdrew into "a soulless kind of conservatism."[108]

This last point he has an ambivalence about since on one hand he charges the baroque era held no deep or positive inspiration of its own and simply fossilized the Mass, embellishing it with elements almost completely external and on the other hand, its "rigid and unintelligent traditionalism…was the providential means, whereby the Church managed to keep her liturgical treasures safe throughout a long period when scarcely anyone was capable of understanding their true worth."[109]   Bouyer compares the baroque preserving of the liturgy to St. Peter's chair (actually a throne from a much later period) enshrined in Bernini's magnificent slipcover or the columns of the Lateran Basilica absorbed by Borromini's pilasters.[110]

Actually, what many of us regard as the highest aspect of this era, its artistic achievement, Bouyer criticizes, especially the musical art form of the time, opera. He charges it with exalting sensual passion and utilizing "imagery almost completely decorative, flowering in courtly music and ballet."[111]   He decries its influence on the liturgy:

So, the faithful of the same period sought to find a religious equivalent of the opera in the liturgy. Churches came to resemble theaters in plan and decoration. The liturgical pomps displayed in such churches tended to smother the traditional text of the liturgy under an increasingly profane kind of polyphony, the text itself having little importance either for the performers or the onlookers. The liturgy became the pretext for an "occasion" similar to a soiree at court complete with a divertissement by Lully. The chief focus of liturgical life,

---

[107] *Ibid.*, p. 5-6.

[108] *Ibid.*

[109] *Ibid.*, p. 8.

[110] *Ibid.*

[111] *Ibid.*, p. 7

therefore, was no more the Mass, which included too many elements out of harmony with the mentality of the times.[112]

Instead, solemn Exposition of the Blessed Sacrament, a ceremony created and developed just in time to satisfy the tastes of the age, managed to assimilate perfectly the courtly ceremony then fashionable. In the presence of the divine King, a kind of heavenly grand opera could be performed with all the display of lights, jewels (mostly false), exquisite polyphonic singing and pageantry which commonly accompany a royal reception. And all this was pervaded with that type of sentimental piety, those panting after divine love, capable of competing successfully with the ecstatic expression of human love.[113]

We have quoted Fr. Bouyer *in extenso* because of his influence and because he states the case against the baroque liturgy so forcibly. Fathers Jungmann and Klauser agree with him in general outline, and yet each of them points out how the Tridentine liturgical commissions appointed by Pius IV and Pius V intended to return to the ancient Roman rites or "the pristine norm of the holy fathers."[114] These commissions investigated ancient sources and made use of them, though they didn't have our critical historical liturgical knowledge, and thought the Gregorian missal a pure Roman source, not knowing how many Franco-Germanic additions there were.[115]

The commissions also used the Greek Fathers as well as the Latin, under the impetus of the humanists to return to the sources.[116] This does not seem like pure anti-intellectual clinging to the past to me but investigating the Tradition as well as they could and making prudent reforms in the light of this legacy. Jungmann further catalogs the reforms of the Tridentine Fathers who:

    1. Threw out all sequences except four as being not in

---

[112] Louis Bouyer, *Liturgical Piety* (Notre Dame, Ind.: The University of Notre Dame Press, 1954), p.7.

[113] *Ibid.*

[114] Joseph Jungmann, SJ, *Missarum Solemnia* (New York: Benzinger Brothers, 1950), Vol. I, p. 136.

[115] *Ibid.*, p. 137.

[116] *Ibid.*

accord with the Roman Tradition.

2. Purified the Marian trophes (or trimmings) from the *Gloria.*

3. Recommended that the faithful receive Holy Communion each time they attended Mass, which was not the practice of the time, but that of the early Church.

4. Encouraged the printing of prayer books to follow the Mass, provided the canon was not printed.[117]

Such an approach hardly seems like "fossilizing" the liturgy, rather reforming it in the light of sound tradition.

Theodore Klauser in his research discovered that the Tridentine liturgical commissions weren't afraid to prune back the number of feasts that had sprung up like Topsy in the medieval epoch.[118] He even gives statistics to prove his point. In the years from 800 A.D. to 1558 A.D., 290 new feasts were added to the calendar, but that calendar promulgated by the Tridentine missal not only didn't introduce new feasts; in fact, it cut the number back to 133.[119] The commission tried to keep March and April free of feasts so as not to interfere with the venerable season of Lent. So anxious were they to return to the ancient Roman calendar, that 85% of the feasts that they kept were from the first four centuries. The emphasis was on the most ancient and Roman feasts, especially apostles, popes and martyrs.[120] They were looking for the "golden liturgical age" of the Fathers, as indeed many contemporary liturgists do, and they sought to root out later excesses. They were also interested in centralizing to curb liturgical abuses and the Roman Tradition gave them the unity they sought, although Pius V was prepared to allow rites 200 years or older (his own Dominican order) to keep their rites. Louis Bouyer shows that many gladly gave up their rites in exchange for the Tridentine missals "just off the press" with all conveniently located in one volume.

Perhaps the Counter Reformation liturgical reform was not quite so stilted and unthinking as Louis Bouyer makes out. Certainly, the

---

[117] Joseph Jungmann, SJ, *Missarum Solemnia* (New York: Benzinger Brothers, 1950), Vol. I, pp. 137-145

[118] Theodore Klauser, *A Short History of the Western Liturgy* (London: Oxford University Press, 1969), p. 125.

[119] *Ibid.*

[120] *Ibid.*

conciliar fathers at Trent thought they had intelligently revived the liturgy as we can see from these words from a sermon preached by Bishop Jerome Racozonus of Venice at the ninth and last session of Trent on December 4, 1563:

> You have thereby removed from the celebration of the Mass all superstitions, all greed for lucre and all irreverence…removed its celebrations from private homes and profane places to holy and consecrated sanctuaries. You have banished from the temple of the Lord the more effeminate singing and musical compositions.[121]
>
> Moreover, divine worship will be discharged more purely and promptly and those who carry the vessels will be so chastened that they will move others to follow their example.[122]

It is true that the primary concern of the Fathers at Trent was less liturgical than doctrinal, and was especially, to defend the faith against Protestant views. Therefore, the doctrines of the Real Presence of Christ in the Eucharist by transubstantiation and the Sacrifice of the Mass claimed their attention. Yet they treat of the need for liturgical rite and ceremonial:

> Since such is the nature of man that he cannot easily without external means be raised to meditation on divine things, on that account Holy Mother Church has instituted certain rites, namely that certain things be pronounced in a subdued tone (canon and words of consecration) and others in a louder tone; she has likewise made use of ceremonies such as mystical blessings, lights, incense, vestments, and many other things of this kind in accordance with apostolic teaching and tradition, whereby both the majesty of so great a sacrifice might be commended, and the minds of the faithful excited by these visible signs of religion and piety to the contemplation of the most sublime matters which are hidden in this sacrifice.[123]

---

[121] Colman J. Barry, O.S.B., *Readings in Church History* (Westminster, Md.: Newman Press, 1967), Vol. II, p. 104.

[122] Colman J. Barry, O.S.B., *Readings in Church History* (Westminster, Md.: Newman Press, 1967), Vol. II, p. 105.

Although Trent is open to reform it is an approach at once conservative and pastoral. In Chapter 8, we read:

> Although the Mass contains much instruction for the faithful, it has nevertheless not seemed expedient to the Fathers that it be celebrated everywhere in the vernacular. The holy synod commands pastors and everyone who has the care of souls to explain frequently during the celebration of the Masses, either themselves or through others, some of the things that are read in the Mass, and among other things to expound some mystery of this most Holy Sacrifice, especially on Sundays and feast days.[124]

We can only wonder at what state the Church would have been on the eve of Vatican II if these wise counsels had been followed and the explanations of the Mass had been widespread. Of course, this requires knowledge on the part of the priest, and this is encouraged in the catechism issued by Trent:

> The Sacrifice is celebrated with many solemn rites, none of which should be deemed useless or superfluous. On the contrary, all of them tend to display the majesty of this august sacrifice, and to excite the faithful, when beholding these saving mysteries, to contemplate the divine things which lie concealed in the Eucharistic Sacrifice. On these rites and ceremonies, we shall not dwell, since they require a more lengthy exposition than is compatible with the nature of the present work; moreover, priests can easily consult on the subject some of the many booklets and works that have been written by pious and learned men...[125]

Thus far, we have tried to show that Trent's liturgical sense was

---

[123] Roy J. Deferrari, *The Sources of Catholic Dogma*, a translation of Denzinger's *Enchiridion Symbolarum* – 30th ed. (St. Louis, MO: Herder, 1957), p. 290.

[124] *Ibid.*, p. 291.

[125] *Catechism of The Council of Trent,* translated by Charles J. Callan, O.P. and John A. McCue, O.P. (New York: Wagner, 1923), p. 259.

more sensitive to tradition and intelligent in handling it than credited by Louis Bouyer. In respect to his charge of the artificially and sensuous aesthetic of the baroque in art and architecture, art history would take a different tack, now acclaiming the baroque contribution as serious and not simply theatrical. Monsignor Cartwright remarks in his *Catholic Shrines of Europe*:

> There was a time when it was universally fashionable to make little of this baroque style with its bold and startling departure from architectural repose. But today most writers on art seem to have come around to quite a different point of view. Meanwhile Bernini's colonnade and canopy have stood through the years, admirable when they were not admired and admirable now that they are admired. A great many people have always admired them both when it was not correct to admire them and now that it is proper again.[126]

The wondrous new style burst the classical norms of renaissance art and architecture and as employed by the Church sometimes took its inspiration from the early Church. The basilican plan with a nave became popular instead of round renaissance chapels. Bernini's colonnades at St. Peter's reminds one of the cortiles before early Roman basilicas and his twisted columns for the baldachino are inspired by ancient columns from the Constantinian basilica there. In baroque churches, people were much closer to the altar and so could participate in the liturgy more closely, albeit silently. The magnificence of the surroundings is described by Jungmann:

> The Church became a great hall, its walls shimmering with marble and gold. The paintings on the ceilings which grew right out of the plaster of the entablature made the room appear to fade away into heavenly glory...The interior of the church has become a great hall filled with sensuous life.[127]

The liturgist's objection to this style is voiced by Klauser:

> During this period, the interior of the church itself became a

---

[126] John K. Cartwright, *The Catholic Shrines of Europe* (New York: The McGraw Hill Book Co., 1954), p. 22.
[127] Jungmann, *op.cit.*, p. 150.

throne room, whose main wall was completely covered with massive architectonic and often magnificent structures over the altar. The altar itself played only a subordinate role in the total aspect of this end of the church and had become debased to a mere detail by the tabernacle and the throne for the Exposition with all their trappings. On the other hand, the throne-room character of the baroque church interior excluded all side aisles…From every seat in the church people had to see the…monstrance as the heavenly Lord had to be able to see every one of His visitors. Hence the baroque period gave rise to a church interior which once more had the effect of gathering people together.[128]

Even though Klauser criticizes the throne-room concept, he can see some good in it and appreciate its beauty. Of course, the musical flowering is magnificent and too enormous to detail. From Palestrina's trying to follow the norms of Trent to Vivaldi and the great concert Masses of Haydn, Mozart, and Beethoven, the riches of the baroque Catholic heritage are too rich to recount here, but surely the beauty of holiness has never been better portrayed.

Before concluding, let us mention the liturgical scholars at work during this period unearthing ancient liturgical texts. We must note Cardinal Bona, Cardinal Tomasi (declared a saint by Pope John Paul II in 1986), the seventeenth century Maurists Mabillon and Martene, and the Oratorian Librun in the same era who translated the *Missale Romanum* into French in 1660 for purpose of study.

Finally, are there lessons we can learn from the liturgy of the baroque era, since we have seen that some of its positive aspects departed significantly from Louis Bouyer's analysis? It seems to me that the delight of this era in beauty in all its forms, painting, sculpture, architecture, and music, and their enthusiastic service of the Church and its liturgy, is something we ought to emulate. We now seem to cultivate the cult of the crude and the ugly. As Cardinal Ratzinger says:

More and more clearly, we can discern the frightening impoverishment which takes place when people show beauty

---

[128] Klauser, *op.cit.*, p. 139.

the door and devote themselves exclusively to utility....
"simple" liturgy does not mean poor or cheap liturgy; there is
the simplicity of the banal and the simplicity that comes from
spiritual, cultural and historical wealth.[129]

The Cardinal also expresses himself forcibly on a false archaism
which would exalt the patristic period liturgically and throw out every
development after:

> In reality the medieval Church (or the Church of the
> baroque era in many respects) developed a liturgical depth
> which must be carefully examined before it is abandoned.
> Here too we must be aware of the Catholic law of an ever
> better and deeper insight into the inheritance entrusted to us.
> Pure archaism is fruitless, as is pure modernization (*Ibid.*, p.
> 132).

Finally, I would like to suggest we could learn something from the
baroque liturgical approach to the sacred. Although there might have
been little external participation by the laity in a great concert Mass
(liturgists consider this a grave fault) nonetheless there was a great
reverence and such sublimity of artistic and musical form that one
was led to bow before the transcendent Lord. This value is so clearly
lacking in most of our contemporary liturgy, that the report issued by
the extraordinary synod of bishops of 1985, while noting the "hunger
and thirst for the transcendent and divine,"[130] admitted the Church
"has sometimes failed sufficiently to manifest the sense of the
sacred."[131] Attempting to correct too external or *active* a notion of
participation in the liturgy, the synod notes that what is to be sought
is "the interior and spiritual participation in the paschal mystery of
Jesus Christ."[132] The baroque liturgy did that in its day (critics
notwithstanding), but it remains for us to do likewise in our day.

---

[129] Joseph Ratzinger, *The Ratzinger Report* (San Francisco: Ignatius Press,
1985), p. 128.
[130] *The Extraordinary Synod of Bishops: 1985* (Boston: St. Paul Editions, 1985),
p. 44.
[131] *Ibid.,* p. 45.
[132] *Ibid.,* p. 52.

8. The Current Liturgy: An Alternative View

In my experience ministering to the rather varied members of the people of God today I find among them a twofold response when discussing with them the liturgical changes wrought by Vatican II. Most of the older people seem to be happy that they now understand the liturgy, "get more out of the Mass," and can participate more easily, and yet with young and old there is a widespread complaint of the lack of a sense of mystery, a missing reverence, a dissatisfaction with poor quality of current church music, and often simply boredom at the whole undertaking.

This reaction is profoundly disappointing to many of us who teach liturgy, who labored to bring about many of the changes or at least to popularize them. The present state of affairs is so different from the high hopes we had before the Council that the renewal of the Liturgy would reinstate the Paschal Mystery at the center of Christian life and piety, in the reverent and joyful celebration of the Eucharist, and the rediscovery by the whole Church of the riches of the form of prayer the Church has made its own, the Liturgy of the Hours. The reading of such liturgical giants as Jungmann, Casel, Bouyer, and others, and of their research opened for many of us a broader and richer vision of Christian sacramental life than the usual low Mass and rather sentimental devotions of our childhood. Yet despite all the best intentions of *Sacrosanctum Concilium* and the ensuing legislation, these hopes have not been realized, or very feebly so if we consider the life of prayer of the whole people of God. One could argue that the situation is worse, with a resulting banality that borders on squalor as Ralph Keifer was not afraid to label it almost a decade ago.[133] Why is this so and what can be done?

Several years ago, Archbishop Rembert Weakland pointed out that Vatican II, despite its lofty aim to adapt the liturgical forms of the Church to speak more effectively to contemporary man, nevertheless tended towards the intellectual approach of the "enlightenment" in holding that rational explanation is necessary for participation.[134] *The Constitution* says:

---

[133] Ralph Keifer, "Squalor on Sunday," *Worship* 44 (May 1970), pp. 292-296.
[134] Rembert Weakland, "The 'Sacred' and Liturgical Renewal," *Worship* 49 (Nov. 1975), pp. 512-529.

...both texts and rites should be drawn up so as to express
more clearly the holy things which they signify. The Christian
people, as far as is possible, should be able to understand them
with ease and take part in them fully, actively, and as a
community.[135]

And again:

The rites should be distinguished by a noble simplicity.
They should be short, clear, and free from useless repetitions.
They should be within the people's power of comprehension,
and normally should not require much explanation.[136]

Certainly, this concern for intelligibility for the sake of
participation is praiseworthy. Surely the rediscovery of the theology
of Saint Thomas in which he characterized the sacraments as *signs*
which caused grace *in significando* paved the way for considering how
well or poorly the old rites signified the deeper reality. Yet we can
ask whether Aquinas' notion of a sign was only cognitive and
recognize in response that meaning in liturgy cannot be only
intellectual. What does a Gregorian *melisma* mean intellectually, or
singing in tongues for that matter? If we cannot express it, as indeed
we cannot express the ineffable mystery, must it be eliminated?
There has been too much of a tendency to see the liturgy only as
didactic, reducing all to the level of a catechism lesson.

Our cerebral liturgies don't appeal to the whole person since
we've been so afraid of religious emotion (as fear of the Charismatic
Renewal bears out), too quick to identify the non-rational with the
irrational, not sufficiently aware of the role of religious experience in
liturgy and vice versa, of the role of ritual in religious experience,
although some psychologists are becoming more aware of this
delicate interconnection. In the first edition (1964) of his *Religions,
Values, and Peak-Experiences*, Abraham Maslow called ritual an "enemy
of true religion" and an "arbitrary trigger," citing such examples as
organ music, incense, chanting, etc. and making short shrift of them

---

[135] Constitution *Sacrosanctum Concilium* on the Sacred Liturgy, no. 21, *Vatican
Council II, The Conciliar and Post Conciliar Documents*, ed. Austin Flannery, O.P.
(Collegeville, Minn., 1975), p. 9.
[136] *Ibid.*, no. 34, p. 12.

all.[137] However, in the 1970 edition, he modifies his judgment:

> The profoundly and authentically religious person integrates these trends easily and automatically. The forms, rituals, ceremonials, and verbal formulae in which he was reared remain for him experientially rooted, symbolically meaningful, archetypal, unitive.[138]

In the Church, we need to rediscover this truth. We often have good rational excessively *wordy* services, with little appeal either to the whole person or to the need for transcendence. We're often very good at celebrating the ordinary, but not of transcending it. We're often self-conscious about ritual, reducing it to a minimum – eliminating as many ritual gestures as possible (e.g., hands extended at the *Pater Noster,* despite the fact that charismatics are picking up this gesture). So much of the body language of worship we have let slide by, appealing only to the mind, if that. We must be more sensitive to gestures, old and new: kneeling, standing, bowing, genuflecting, sitting, the Kiss of Peace, hands raised, and so forth. We must be re-sensitized to prayer and the sense of mystery, to the signs and symbols given us by nature and the Church: darkness and light, water, bread and wine, incense, oil, vesture, images, and so on. We must say less and utilize these *non-verbal* symbols more. The larger numbers of Tridentine Catholics and young traditional seminarians are telling us something, and their hankering for nostalgia must be challenged by catechesis in the authentic tradition of the Church which reverently celebrates the Mysteries of the Lord in such wise as to appeal to the whole person.

Another problem aspect of the new liturgy is the very concept of change in relation to the Paschal Mystery. After Odo Casel helped the Church to rediscover the centrality of the Paschal Mystery, the first liturgical reformers wanted the liturgy celebrated in such a way that the Mystery shone forth in all its splendor, yet, or course, remaining a mystery that could only be reached through signs, through *visibilia*. The theory was that when the signs were changed, all would be able to participate in the unchanging mystery. Yet the

---

[137] Abraham Maslow, *Religions, Values and Peak-Experiences* (New York, 1964), p. 31.
[138] *Ibid.,* p. vii.

problem remains that when there is too much liturgical change, people begin to feel that the underlying reality or mystery has changed, or worse still, that there is nothing there. This is true especially if intelligent liturgical planning of the liturgy is confused with endless manipulation of the rites to achieve certain effects, gimmicks masquerading as holy signs. Rather than allowing one to be molded by the Mystery of the Altar which transcends the here and now, celebrants and ministers become entertainers or leaders of psychological "group grope." The *Ordo Missae* and its rubrics as well as those of the other sacraments at least can preserve a sense of the mystery when observed with reverence and love. The creative use of silence can foster real prayer and participation in the Holy Mysteries and is an appropriate response to the ineffable.

The truism that "beauty may not save the soul, but it makes the soul worth saving" may not be completely correct since beauty as the outward splendor of the saving mysteries may indeed help to save man in his existential situation. Since we go to the invisible through the visible it is imperative that the latter be well made and noble as become vehicles of the divine. Surely this incarnational principle was the one behind the building and ornamentation of the great Romanesque and Gothic cathedrals, the delightful churches of the baroque era down to the somewhat derivative though cheerful and colorful Irish Victorian churches of the last century. All of these buildings were alive with color, light, and texture in terms of sacred images, statues, lofty altars, and stained glass. Visiting these churches or worshiping in them was often and still is a feast for the eye as well as a nourishment to faith.

Many churches needed change for the proper celebration of the new *Ordo Missae*, but surely not the vandalism and iconoclasm that have been committed on many charming old churches even in this country. Much is removed to be replaced with nothing and whitewashed interiors devoid of life are given as liturgical environments lacking even the quiet grace of Quaker Meeting Houses. Even the clean lines of our modern churches are often bereft of color and seem rather antiseptic. Instead of Vatican II's insistence that sacred images be few in number and well made,[139] there are none since they are viewed as distractions, and often fine

---

[139] *Constitution on the Liturgy*, nos. 124, 125, p. 35.

old images and candlesticks are sold to antique dealers who are aware that the secular world has discovered the world of Victorian art that Catholics are trying to erase.

Can we not preserve the best of the old with the freshness of the new as well? The Blessed Sacrament is frequently not in that prominent place that *The General Instruction of the Roman Missal* recommends,[140] not in a place inviting prayer and quiet contemplation; instead it becomes one more competing item of rather dull sanctuary furniture. To remedy the situation, we must be much more open to our artistic heritage. The Bishops' booklet on the environment of worship is a beginning, but surely the photographs of various architectural approaches are not representative.[141] The whole question of Church music is obviously related, but to discuss it would take us too far afield. We can only point out that the loss of "mystical" Gregorian chant precisely when so many young people are open to the contemplative is an ironic twist of our times.

In terms of the para-extra liturgical or devotional scene, one finds the same tendencies at work. *Sacrosanctum Concilium* recognized that popular devotions needed to be harmonized with the liturgy[142] since they were often alien in spirit to the liturgy as they sprang up when liturgical life was at a low ebb in the Church and when the piety of the people was no longer formed by the liturgy. Also, especially after the Counter-Reformation, the liturgy was officially so tightly controlled and usually so static that religious emotion often sought other outlets. Devotions often were the really felt prayer of many people while Mass was central though often not understood. Indeed, devotions along the lines of the cathedral rather than monastic type of liturgy sprang up at first as appendages to Vespers in the form of salutations to the Blessed Sacrament and the Blessed Virgin, later stealing the show in time and becoming popular in themselves.[143] Here was where the real life of prayer went on in the Church for most Catholics except for those special people who had been

---

[140] *The Roman Missal, General Instruction* (New York, 1970), no. 276, p. 24.

[141] Bishops' *Document on Environment*, Washington, D.C.: NCCB, 1979.

[142] *Constitution on the Liturgy*, no. 13, p. 7.

[143] For documentation of this phenomenon and a sympathetic treatment of popular devotions, cf. Carl Dehne's "Roman Catholic Popular Devotions," *Worship* 49 (Oct. 1975), pp. 446-460.

initiated into the intricacies of the Breviary, and here is where strong faith was generated.

The Council asked that devotions be reformed and brought into closer harmony with the spirit of the liturgy, a delicate task. Instead, we have suppressed them, leaving stranded many whose only approach to prayer was incarnated in these forms and have substituted Mass at all hours of the day. Though the Eucharist is the greatest prayer, we need forms of prayer to dispose us for its prayerful celebration and others to carry its spirit into the rest of the day, which is properly the task of the *Liturgia Horarum*, but all may not be able to begin there.

The Charismatic Renewal has filled the prayer void as did spontaneous prayer, but even these approaches (and I am a charismatic) need at times more structured forms of prayer. It would seem that the tide is beginning to change, and we note now, not only the Liturgy of the Hours, but new Office books like *Praise Him, Bless the Lord* and *Lord Hear Our Prayer*, which are modeled along the lines of the *Liturgia Horarum* but more adapted to the laity, sisters or seminarians in the beginning of their formation.[144]

The rosary is being rediscovered by many as a Christian mantra, a non-verbal rhythmic prayer whose meaning is not simply the words or the aspects of the Paschal Mystery contemplated, but a rich interplay of both. Fr. Schillebeeckx in his earlier book, *Mary, Mother of the Redemption*[145] suggested that there be new mysteries to ponder prayerfully, and indeed a commission in the Dominican Order is mulling over the possibilities. Stations of the Cross have been done in different ways, with a fifteenth Resurrection station and more modern meditations replacing the standard ones of St. Alphonsus.

Devotions centered around the Blessed Sacrament pose a more delicate problem, but one that we ought not fear to rethink. The liturgical renewal was aimed not at furthering prayer before the reserved Eucharist, but participation in Christ's prayer in the actual celebration of the Eucharist, in which communion the Christian

---

[144] These are excellent prayer books as well as simple Offices and are the work of William Story of Notre Dame – *Praise Him*, (Notre Dame, Indiana, 1973), *Bless the Lord* (Notre Dame, Indiana, 1975) and *Lord Hear Our Prayer*, (Notre Dame, Indiana, 1978).

[145] E. Schillebeeckx, O.P., *Mary, Mother of the Redemption*, London, 1968, p. 168.

community is made one with the Lord and, therefore, with one another. While we rejoice in the present awareness of the manifold aspects of Christ's presence in the Liturgy, especially that he is present horizontally in the midst of the assembly, nonetheless, this ought not to obscure our awareness of the abiding presence of the Lord in the consecrated species. The reserved Blessed Sacrament offers the more abiding aspect of Christ's eucharistic action for our contemplation. We ought not to set it aside lightly. We are sensitive to environment, but what of prayer environment? The reserved Eucharist makes one aware of Christ's presence localized so as to be more aware of it elsewhere. While one can experience Christ everywhere, usually human psychology demands a place, hallowed by association, evoking the memory of past prayer, sacred with the presence of the Lord, and prayer before that symbol which is the very reality it symbolizes helps to provide such a conducive place.

Having discussed prayer before the Blessed Sacrament, it is clear we must treat of Exposition and Benediction. Many liturgists see Exposition as an ambiguous practice because it arose as a kind of medieval "visible participation" of the Eucharist when very few received communion. Surely, we would not want to be returned to this mentality, but now, after all the pastoral, theological and liturgical emphasis on reception of communion, is there any danger of that? Could we not see Exposition as the contemplative prolongation of the Eucharistic action, a focusing of our prayer? When the Blessed Sacrament is exposed, we have here a Holy Mandala to contemplate as we pray, not eschewing the senses, but aiding them. Of course, Benediction as a rite completely by itself is forbidden, but now is seen as the conclusion to Exposition which can be done in a simpler fashion and should include some scriptural reading, music and silence. There is much room for creativity here, and I was deeply moved by how effectively this can be done on a recent visit to Lourdes. The traditional procession blessing the ill with the Blessed Sacrament concluded a service of Exposition in which Gospel passages of Christ healing were meditatively read interspersed with silence. Much can be gained in this silent and meditative type of prayer which is spiritual yet gives something for the senses to hang onto – worship for the whole person.

In a recent article Fr. William Leonard, who has taught liturgy for over forty years, states his conviction that we have been so caught up in the mechanics of change during the past fifteen years that we have not really taught people the theology of worship itself.[146] Though there is a tremendous interest in prayer now, it has yet to be related to the prayer of the Church, and I suspect this is true because so many of our celebrations are not prayerful, do not bespeak faith, and are often not seen as worship.

We need to get beyond the popular clerical mentality of seeing the liturgy as a series of gimmicks "to turn people on." We need to teach our people how to pray so that they will come to the Eucharist with prayerful hearts, ready to praise the Lord, not coming as passive spectators waiting to be entertained as before a television screen. This participation is only possible in faith, and so we must lead our people to experience the liturgy as a celebration speaking to the whole person under sign and symbol, lifting him up through beauty, respecting the rhythms of prayer and silence, but above all we must enable them to participate in the timeless, everlasting sacrificial prayer of Christ to the Father and in the Spirit. This bespeaks conversion, faith response, love, and prayer, which is where perhaps this article should have begun.

9.   A First Look at a New Liturgy

On the feast of the Conversion of St. Paul, I had the rare opportunity of participating in a celebration of Mass according to the *Book of Divine Worship: Being Elements of the Book of Common Prayer Adapted According to the Roman Rite for Use by Roman Catholics Coming from the Anglican Tradition.*

This long title describes the liturgy officially approved by the National Conference of Catholic Bishops and the Holy See as a pastoral provision for those former Anglicans who have entered into full communion with the Catholic Church, allowing them to retain certain aspects of the rich Anglican liturgical heritage.

The occasion was another theological assessment that was being conducted at the Dominican House of Studies in Washington, D.C., whereby Catholic theologians were assessing what areas in theology, liturgy and cannon law some former Anglican clergymen might have to study to apply for the Catholic priesthood.   Those who have

---

[146] William J. Leonard, "A taste for Liturgy," *Worship* 53, May 1979, p. 217.

already gone this route and been ordained as Catholic priests may celebrate this newly approved liturgy for congregations of former Anglicans where they exist.

The setting of this Mass was the lovely Gothic chapel of the House of Studies. Its high altar reredos with the fifteen mysteries of the rosary carved in wood formed the background for the stately and dignified celebration of the liturgy that unfolded before our eyes.

After singing "Who Are These Like Stars Appearing" from the 1940 hymnal, we launched into Rite One which closely parallels the Book of Common Prayer. The stately cadence of Elizabethan English and the incomparable beauty of Cranmer's translation of ancient Roman prayers helped to create an atmosphere of reverence and beauty. The readings were from the Revised Standard Lectionary, in which a more elevated language is used than that prepared under the auspices of the Catholic Biblical Association in wide use here in the States.

In the sermon, Fr. James Parker, who assisted in administering the pastoral provision, spoke movingly of St. Paul's journey from Judaism to belief in Christ, while bringing to the service of his Lord the best of his Jewish training. So, too, did Father Parker see the faith journey of these former Anglicans, many leaving behind security and position for the security of faith guaranteed by the See of Peter. Yet they brought with them much that is beautiful and holy from the Anglican tradition.

The Mass proceeded with the Prayer of the Faithful or what the *Book of Common Prayer* describes as praying "for the whole state of Christ's Church."

The Penitential Rite followed with the Anglican version of the Confiteor, the concluding prayer of which reminded this friar of the absolution of the now defunct Dominican rite. The gifts were brought forth and prepared, and after the Preface we heard a translation of the Roman Canon. This was similar to that vernacular version which many of us grew up reading in our hand missals as we assisted at Latin Mass before Vatican II.

We sang the "Our Father" in English Gregorian Chant and said the magnificent Prayer of Humble Access in preparation for Holy Communion. After Communion there followed vespers in Anglican chant and a communal prayer of thanksgiving. The rite concluded as we recessed out of the chapel singing Vaughn Williams' "For All the

Saints."

My reaction to our Church's newest liturgy was mixed. I was deeply moved by the beauty of the rite, and yet I found I've become more used to the sparser contemporary Roman rite than I thought.

Afterwards I spoke with the clergymen who were present, men grateful to the Church for the pastoral provision that allows them to retain something of their heritage while embracing the broader Catholic faith, and which further allows them to remain married while exercising their ministry. I marveled at the wisdom of our present Pope, so unyielding in matters of faith; and yet so generous in trying to answer real pastoral needs such as this.

Could it be that this pastoral liturgical provision for former Anglicans, as well as the new permission he so graciously granted of using the Tridentine Rite of the Latin Mass where there is real pastoral need, may be the leaven to restore dignity and beauty of holiness to the contemporary rites of the Catholic Church? While perhaps not intended, this would be a welcome result, should it happen.

10. The Liturgy of the Hours: The Church's Monotonous Prayer

I once heard a most unusual lecture in which a young man, a recent convert to the Faith with a decided Pentecostal background, sketched out for a charismatic audience how we should pray the Bible. He spoke of the Psalms as excellent prayers, sanctifying the whole range of human emotions as God was praised in the words of the Psalmist; he spoke of listening to the Word of God as it was proclaimed in the midst of the Church, allowing the Word to settle deeply in our hearts; and finally of offering "supplication, intercessions and thanksgivings...for all men, for kings and all who are in high positions, that we all may lead a quiet and peaceable life, godly and respectable in every way."[147]

It wasn't until after he'd finished that I realized that he was describing in biblical terminology the Liturgy of the Hours or The Divine Office that he and his wife pray together daily. Of course, he was right; the Church's way of praying the Bible is not a random approach, but an ordered recitation or singing of the Psalter and the

---

[147] 1 Tim. 2:1

ordered reading of the Word of God as found in the Sacred Scriptures. This the Church does in the Divine Office, that prayer she makes her own and to which she obliges some of her children (priests and religious) and to which she invites all.

Personally, my life revolves around this form of prayer and if I'm without my Breviary, I feel as if my day has no structure or purpose. For many the very mention of the word Breviary conjures up a black bound volume edged in gold that is "something Father says." While it is that, it is also much more than that, which will become apparent in examining something of the history and theology surrounding this prayer of the Church.

The origin of the Liturgy of the Hours is found in the Jewish tradition of synagogal worship which probably developed during the Exile as a substitute for Temple worship. The prophets taught that God's presence was not confined to the Temple and the rabbis developed this teaching to emphasize that where ten Jews gathered to read and study the Word of God, then God would be with them. We recognize immediately the connection between this and the teaching of the Lord that He would be with us wherever two or three gathered in His Name,[148] and for us this is especially true when we gather for Mass, but true as other times as well.

The Jews gathered at the synagogue two or three times a day as the Orthodox Jews still do, and when impeded said their prayers where they were. The Early Christians took this tradition of a regular prayer rhythm and made it their own, though at first not as communal prayer, for in times of persecution, they were only able to gather for the Eucharist weekly. Nevertheless, the ancient documents such as the *Didache*, Hippolytus and Tertullian all speak of regular times of prayer, and these were considered so necessary for the Christian life that neophytes had to promise to keep them before they were baptized, according Jungmann.

In the fourth century when Christianity was no longer persecuted, public morning and evening prayers were attended daily by the laity and clergy alike, while the emerging monastic movement found many other times to sanctify by regular prayer as well. In the course of time the set psalms and prayer times of the laity and the monks merged together into the pattern of prayer – Matins or vigils, Lauds

---

[148] cf. Matt. 18:20

or morning prayer, Prime, Terce, Sext, None (originally prayer times corresponding to the Roman hours of the day, but now forming one prayer called midday prayer) Vespers or evening prayer and Compline or night prayer. That became the rhythm of monks and clergy of the Western Church. Lay participation dwindled at this more clerical and stylized prayer of the Church in the Middle Ages and so it continued until Vatican II's *Constitution of the Liturgy* mandated that The Liturgy of the Hours be restored to the people, at least Lauds and Vespers – the two hinge hours of the liturgical day – something that is happening in religious and diocesan churches, in prayer groups and among lay people anxious to learn this mode of prayer the Church has made its own.

The General Instruction to the revised Liturgy of the Hours makes it clear that in this prayer we are joined to the prayer of Christ who is constantly making intercession for us and we, the Church, are making His prayer our own. We pray the psalms that Jesus prayed, listen to the reading of His word, the same psalms and readings used by the Church universal, e.g. The canons of St. Peter's in Rome, the monks of Solesmes, the Franciscan friars of Steubenville, the Dominican Sisters of Nashville, countless parish priests, communities of religious and laity both individually and in small groups all over the world in a method of prayer that avoids narrowness and particularity but that imparts an ecclesial spirit which plunges us deeply into the heart of the Church.

While priests and religious are obliged to this form of prayer, all Christians are obliged to pray regularly and sanctify the day at least by morning and evening prayers and here we have the official way of the Church to make holy the day. Many people only want to pray when the Spirit strikes them so they can respond spontaneously in that special moment of God's intervention – *kairos* – forgetting that unless we pray regularly within the rhythm of daily time – *chronos* – that *kairos* might well not happen. If I regularly miss my *prayers*, *prayer* is not likely to "happen" in my life, and The Liturgy of the Hours is the Church's remedy against this, even if at times this prayer is monotonous as some have complained. It's supposed to be. The very rhythmical mantra-like quality of the psalmody disposes one for prayer and for deeper mystical experience.

Prayer which begins in the heart in the desire to pray usually requires words, and the psalter supplies them in abundance. St.

Augustine tells us that God not only commands us to pray but then gives us His own words in the psalms. These poems of prayer have served Christians as vehicles of prayer as they did Jews before them and the remarkable thing about the psalms is the great variety of them: cursing psalms, psalms of praise, historical psalms, and psalms of complaint. For the psalmist we go to God in prayer *as we are* with our joys, sorrows, pain and lament, and as we make known to God what we're really experiencing, He is free to help us. Of course, He knows all along, but we need to admit our real problems in His sight so that He can be free to act, and the psalter helps us to do that.

Of course, we do not pray the psalms as Jews of the Old Testament but as those who see the consolation of Israel in Jesus, not only in the directly messianic psalms but in the fuller sense of scripture as meditated on by the Church seeing the new as the fulfillment of the old. Antiphons and titles of the psalms help us to do that. After speaking to God in the psalmody, we listen to His Word, being fed by that Bread[149] preparing us to be fed by the Bread of His Body.[150]

When we hear God's Word He is speaking to us, inviting our response, and so in the Liturgy of the Hours we respond with canticles and prayers and as we do so we pray – not just for our needs, but for those of the Church universal and the world, putting our own needs in a broader and more catholic or universal context. Indeed, this is one of the benefits of this form of prayer. The Liturgy of the Hours gives one a more Catholic sense, stretches one's heart to embrace the whole Church, the whole world, as does the Heart of Jesus. Finally, one's spirituality is also stretched to the fullness of the Mystery of Christ, by being plunged into all aspects of that mystery in the feasts and seasons of the liturgical year. Here we commemorate the promise, Incarnation, Birth, Life, Suffering, Death, Resurrection, Ascension of Christ and the outpouring of the Holy Spirit and we are stretched into the fullness of the Paschal Mystery. This, the Church's own form of prayer, is a marvelously rich one, giving one the mind of Christ, and the love of His Church. Is it any wonder the Church so highly recommends it – its own monotonous prayer?

---

[149] cf. John 6:32-40
[150] cf. John 6:48-59

11. The Liturgical Legacy of Pope John Paul II

When one thinks of the late John Paul II, there are some aspects of this person, bigger than life, a player on the world stage, a saint, presider of global ceremonies, yet at heart a holy priest, caught in the great mysteries he was celebrating. In my liturgical and theological formation in the Order, at Notre Dame, at San Anselmo, the professors that I really admired were those who believed in the mysteries they were teaching us about celebrating as well. Pope John Paul not only taught us all well about the holy mysteries of the Mass and the sacraments but was seen "praying" them by millions of people all over the world. Even if one knew little about Catholic doctrine, watching him celebrate, one would know that something truly "awesome" and important was happening at the altar when he was the celebrant of the Mass.

Right at the beginning of his papal ministry, the Pope issued in 1979 his first encyclical, *Redemptor Hominis*, in which he put the mystery of the redemption at the center of his mission. As he explores how the mystery of the Death and Resurrection of Christ frees us and the world, he situates the Eucharist as the summit and center of this redemption realized as the Mass is celebrated. He teaches us that the Eucharist is a sacrifice sacrament, a communion sacrament, and a presence sacrament.[151]

In his 1980 encyclical on the Eucharist, *Dominicae Cenae*, the Holy Father treating of the Eucharist under the aspect of sacrifice, strongly stresses that the Mass is a sacrifice, because the bread and wine become:

> ...truly, really and substantially Christ's own body that is given up and His blood that is shed. Thus, by virtue of the consecration, the species of bread and wine re-present in a sacramental, unbloody manner the bloody, the propitiatory sacrifice offered by Him on the cross to His Father for the salvation of the world.[152]

Thus, the sacrifice sacrament. This reality offered "once and for all"[153] on Calvary is made present now so we can enter into this

---

[151] *Redemptor Hominis*, n. 20.

[152] *Dominicae Cenae*, n. 9.

[153] Heb 7:27

mystery. As we are joined with Christ, as we receive him into our very being, we are made one with him and one another. As John Paul II says:

> Therefore, in Eucharistic Communion we receive Christ, Christ Himself; and our union with Him, which is a gift and grace for each individual, brings it about that in Him we are also associated in the unity of His Body which is the Church.[154]

And so, we see his affirmation of the Eucharist as the communion sacrament, though of course he treats it much more richly.

Finally, in *Dominicae Cenae*, we find the Eucharist seen as a presence sacrament. Because Christ is present in the Eucharist "worship must be prominent in all our encounters with the Blessed Sacrament." Because the Lord is truly present in this sacrament, we must not stint our adoration for:

> The Church and the world have a great need of Eucharistic worship. Jesus waits for us in this sacrament of love. Let us be generous with our time in going to meet Him in adoration and in contemplation that is full of faith and really to make reparation for the great faults and crimes of the world. May our adoration never cease.[155]

In this document the Holy Father stresses the sacredness of the Liturgy as a quality that is inherent because the Mass is a holy action, the holy action of the High Priest of the New Covenant who is the "offerer, the offered, the consecrator and the consecrated."[156] Therefore, the Church has the duty to "safeguard and strengthen the sacredness of the Eucharist."[157]

Pope John Paul II did this not by changing the Liturgy, but by celebrating it well and devoutly and by teaching Catholic doctrine clearly on this great mystery. One action of the Pontiff was somewhat controversial. In hopes of luring the Lefevbrites back from potential schism, John Paul issued *Quattuor Abhinc Annos* in

---

[154] *Dominicae Cenae*, n. 4.
[155] *Ibid.*, n. 5.
[156] *Ibid.*, n. 8.
[157] *Ibid.*

1984 allowing the use of the 1962 *Missal* for groups of Catholics that found adjusting to the Mass of Paul VI difficult and felt drawn to the Old Rite. Unfortunately, Archbishop Lefevbre consecrated four bishops and was excommunicated, so in hopes of attracting some of his followers who did not want to follow suit, the Pope issued *Ecclesia Dei Adflicta* urging bishops to be generous in permission to celebrate the Tridentine Mass. The Pope was moved by pastoral concerns to bring all Catholics into the unity of the Church.

All along, Pope John Paul II was encouraging the priests of the church by issuing each year letters for them on Holy Thursday treating the priesthood, the Eucharist and the Mass. On Holy Thursday, 2003, in place of the usual letter, the Pope issued his fourteenth and last encyclical, *Ecclesia de Eucharistia*. He died two years later, so we might consider this his legacy to the church.

This document is not only official teaching that hands on the tradition of the Church, but also is a deeply personal reflection on what the Eucharist means to him. He sees this great gift of the Eucharist, the *mysterium eucharisticum* as flowing from the *mysterium paschale* as indeed does the Church. The Mass, in a way encapsulates the whole Triduum, since Holy Thursday and the institution of the Eucharist was celebrated in the light of the Death on the Cross on Good Friday which further climaxed in the glorious Resurrection on Easter. This mystery is the "foundation and well spring (of the Church) ... this is as it were gathered up, foreshadowed and 'concentrated' forever in the gift of the Eucharist."[158] And so, at Mass the Church becomes the Body of Christ fed on the Body of Christ. This is so because Christ speaks through the priest using the voice of the priest, turning the bread and wine into His own Body and Blood.

The Pope remembered celebrating Mass in the Cenacle, in his first parish church, for students in Cracow, as Pope at St. Peter's in Rome. He also reminisced about celebrating in chapels built on mountain paths, on lakeshores and seacoasts, in stadiums and city squares. These many venues reminded the Pope of the cosmic dimension of the Mass. Even if celebrated on a "humble altar of a country church" it is celebrated "on the altar of the world." It is cosmic because it is the sacramental representation of the sacrifice of the Cross... "it is

---

[158] *Ecclesia de Eucharistia*, n.5.

the sacrifice of the Cross perpetuated down the ages,"[159] and the Cross is the center of the cosmos.

The Pope found it necessary to stress the sacrificial dimension of the Mass because some strip the Eucharist of its sacrificial meaning "as if it were simply a fraternal banquet."[160] He insists that it is a "commemorative representation" (*memorialis representatio*) because "we who are many are one body, for we all partake of the one bread."[161] We, the mystical Body of Christ, become more so feasting on the sacramental Body of Christ and our communion is deepened.

Thus, the communion sacrament is also the sacrifice sacrament and when the Pope treats of the presence sacrament, he is not afraid to stress beauty as the setting for the reservation for the *panis angelorum*. He states the Church has never been afraid of extravagance in creating an atmosphere of beauty in "architecture, sculpture, painting and music."[162] How much do we need that emphasis now!

I'd like to conclude my reflection with a personal memory not of the World Day Masses at which I concelebrated with the Holy Father in various capitals of the world, but rather my experience at his early Mass in his private chapel at the Vatican. We were ushered in, the priests all vested, and we found the Pope kneeling in rapt prayer. At times we could hear him groan in prayer,[163] the Vicar of Christ with all the cares of the world upon him. Then he vested and began the Mass. It was in Latin, though the readings were in English. I read the Gospel, and later stood next to him during the Eucharistic Prayer during which I had a part to read. John Paul was so caught up in the holy mysteries that he was celebrating that so were we. This living example crystallized for me all he had written and engraved it on my heart.

12. The Liturgy in the Thought of Pope Benedict XVI

Much of the liturgical thought of the present Pope can be seen in his autobiography *Milestones* which chronicles his life until he was

---

[159] *Ibid.,* n. 11.
[160] *Ibid.*
[161] I Cor. 10:17
[162] *Ecclesia de Eucharistia,* n. 49.
[163] cf. Rom. 8:26

called to Rome. In *Milestones* he describes the Liturgy's effect on him in his youth as the church year was celebrated by his parish church,[164] especially the darkening of the church for the somber season of Lent. His parents' gift to him of a child's missal like their own hand missals drew him more deeply into the holy mysteries as a boy.[165]

When he entered the seminary, he encountered the new personalism of M. Buber alongside the teaching of St. Thomas whose "crystal clear logic" was "too closed in on itself, at least in the rigid neo-scholasticism" that was presented at the University.[166] He was influenced by M. Schmaus who left neo-scholasticism for the new liturgical movement which presented the faith more in the spirit of returning to the Sacred Scriptures and the Fathers of the Church.[167] A personal note could be added here: I find myself in sympathy with him, for I recoiled from an extremely rigid Thomistic formation to study Liturgy and later rediscovered the great wisdom of our elder brother, St. Thomas. The "new theology" was in the air. One of his professors was influenced by the "mystery theology" of Dom Odo Casel, OSB,[168] another saw the Mass as the center of each day, while the study of Sacred Scripture was seen as the soul of theology... many themes that would be taken up by the Constitution *Sacrosanctum Concilium* of Vatican II.

However early on, young Joseph Ratzinger had reservations: a certain "one-sided rationalism and historicism" of the liturgical movement in which some saw "only one form of the Liturgy as valid," i.e. that of the early Church.[169] This was not true of De Lubac whose teaching on the unity of the Church as sustained by the Eucharist was deeply influential in his thought.[170]

Ratzinger's account of the consideration of the Liturgy at Vatican II at which he was *peritus* is interesting. He states that the liturgical schema at the Council was not expected to be controversial since no

---

[164] Pope Benedict XVI, *Milestones: Memoirs, 1927-197,* (San Francisco, CA: Ignatius Press, 1998), p. 18.

[165] *Ibid.,* pp. 19-20.

[166] *Ibid.,* p. 44.

[167] *Ibid.,* p. 49.

[168] *Ibid.,* p. 55.

[169] *Ibid.,* p. 57.

[170] Pope Benedict XVI, *Milestones: Memoirs, 1927-197,* (San Francisco, CA: Ignatius Press, 1998), p. 58.

one expected major changes. However, from France and Germany pressure was brought to bear to reform the Mass according to the purest form of the Roman Rite in accord with those reforms of Pius X and Pius XII. A model Mass along such lines was rejected by a synod of conciliar fathers in 1967, but it still became the working model for the new Mass.[171] *Sacrosanctum Concilium* said Latin was to be preserved and that the faithful were to be able to sing the Ordinary of the Mass in Latin and clerics were to pray the Office in the same way. This soon became a moot point.[172]

Ratzinger's reaction to the introduction of the Missal of Paul VI was somewhat negative, but not completely so. He was dismayed by the prohibition of the Missal of Pius V (really, simply a reworking of that used by the Roman Rite since Gregory the Great).[173] He felt that this was a breach in practice and in this can we not see a hint of the Papal *Motu Proprio* to come? He felt that much that "should have been guarded (has) been neglected and that many treasures…have been squandered away"[174] in the new liturgy made by a committee.[175] This often is celebrated in a lackluster way that is boring and bereft of artistic standards.[176] So not all who criticize the current liturgy as banal, in the community celebrating itself are not necessarily integralists.[177] His criticism is "that the liturgy is not celebrated in such wise that the givenness of the great mystery of God among us through the action of the church shines forth."[178] The Church gives us the ritual, but cannot generate the power, the energy at work in these rites, rather it is the wholly Other [179] acting. We can participate actually and really and personally often in deep silence.[180] We participate in the Mystery which is still incomprehensible.

In the *Feast of Faith*, Joseph Ratzinger states that he is grateful for the new Missal of Paul VI for the newly added prayers and prefaces,

---

[171] *Ratzinger Report* p. 122.
[172] *Ibid.*
[173] *Ibid.*, p. 146.
[174] *Ibid.*, p. 127.
[175] *Ibid.*, p. 148.
[176] *Ibid.*, p. 127.
[177] *Ibid.*, p. 119.
[178] *Ibid.*, p. 120.
[179] *Ibid.*, p. 127.
[180] *Ibid.*

many of which came from other Western rites: the Gallican, Mozarabic, and Ambrosian. He feels the offertory prayers of the old Mass were misleading in that they tended to identify the offering of Christ's Sacrifice with this part of the Mass rather than with the consecration itself. Much of Ratzinger's criticism seems to be the interpretation of the new Liturgy in a nontraditional way, with a hermeneutic of discontinuity rather than continuity. Therefore, he was happy with the indult of Pope John Paul II, and perhaps why he followed it with his own *Motu Proprio*.

One of Ratzinger's great theological concerns is to show that the "Eucharist is more than a brotherly meal."[181] It is primarily the common sacrifice of the Church in which the Lord prays with us and gives himself to us."[182] In *Feast of Faith*, the future pope makes it clear that while the Eucharist has the "context of a meal," it is the "*Eucharistia*, the prayer of *anamnesis* or the verbal sacrifice in which Christ's sacrifice is made present."[183] Therefore, it is not worthless to attend even if one cannot receive, i.e. divorced and remarried Catholics.[184] This sacrifice is a feast in which we transcend ourselves into something greater...we enter into the cosmic joy of the Resurrection, the *Mysterium Paschale.*[185] In *God is Near Us* he sees the Eucharist as the wellspring of life from the side of Christ opened in sacrifice, fully present to us all scattered over the earth and to the saints in heaven.[186]

Since Christ is truly present to us in the Eucharist in his risen body,[187] we respond not only by receiving, but also by adoring him in gestures and postures, with kneeling and silence.[188] A rediscovery of the common meal aspect does not wipe out the need for adoration.[189] People, he says, have forgotten that adoration is an intensification of communion, so the *Corpus Christi* procession is an intensification of the communion procession,[190] a walking with the Lord.[191] In *Feast of*

---

[181] *Ratzinger Report*, p. 132.
[182] *Ibid.*
[183] *Feast of Faith*, p. 93.
[184] *Ratzinger Report*, p. 132
[185] *Ibid.*
[186] *In God is Near Us*, p. 42.
[187] *Ibid.*, p. 78.
[188] *Ibid.*, p. 91-92.
[189] *Ibid.*, p. 95.

Faith, he gives the history of this procession, the Lord, as head of state, visits the streets of each village,[192] a triumphal procession of Christ the Victor in his campaign against death.[193]   It is a good practice even if a medieval development and not of patristic origin,[194] because the Church is living and the medieval Church and that of the baroque era developed a liturgical depth which must be examined before it is abandoned.[195]

In the *Spirit of the Liturgy* our author points out that the medieval transubstantiation debate is the origin of tabernacles of various sorts, exposition, monstrances, processions: "all medieval errors" according to some, but Ratzinger profoundly disagrees.   He traces Eucharistic reservation to the early Church which kept it for the ill and attributes the Franciscan and Dominican evangelization and emphasis on the Eucharist for the Eucharistic doves, ambries, sacrament towers which were developed to reserve the Eucharist.[196]   He states that this medieval devotion was a "wonderful spiritual awakening" and further that "a church without the Eucharistic presence is dead," a statement with which I heartily agree.[197]   Let us conclude this section with his observation that since the Eucharist is the center of life of the Church, it presupposes the other sacraments and points to them.[198] It also presupposes personal prayer, family prayer, extra liturgical prayer such as Stations of the Cross, the Rosary and especially devotion to Our Lady.[199]

Our author has a definite perspective on church architecture.   In his *Spirit of the Liturgy*, he quotes Bouyer to the effect that just as the synagogue faced the presence of God in Jerusalem, so early churches faced East where the sun rose, seeing in this Christ, the Sun of righteousness, "coming forth like a bridegroom leaving his chamber."[200]

---

[190] *Ratzinger Report*, p. 133.
[191] *God is Near Us,* p. 110
[192] *Feast of Faith,* p. 127.
[193] *Feast of Faith*, p. 130.
[194] *Ibid.*, p. 132.
[195] *Ratzinger Report*, p. 132
[196] *Spirit of the Liturgy*, p. 80, 89.
[197] *Ibid.*, cf p. 90.
[198] *Ratzinger Report*, p. 134.
[199] *Ibid.*
[200] Ps. 19

We process towards the New Heavens and the New Earth and Christ the Light of the World.[201] The image of Christ seen in this way quickly merges with that of the Cross on the eastern apse of the church according to Ratzinger.[202] The altar under the cross in the apse is the "place where heaven is opened up" and there we are led to eternal glory.[203] Following Bouyer, he states how in the early Syrian churches, the faithful first gathered around the bema for the Liturgy of the Word, and then approached the altar and the East for the Eucharist, facing in the same direction as the celebrant. They were all directed to "*converti ad Dominum*," to look East with him.[204] In Rome, St. Peter's, because of the topography of the Vatican Hill, faced West in its apse rather than East, and its altar in the middle of the nave of the church faced the East through the main doors.

When St. Gregory the Great had the altar brought forward over the tomb of St. Peter, he set the stage for the later development of Mass *versus populum*.[205] Since other churches in Rome copied St. Peter's,[206] this custom of facing the people (though not found outside Rome) became the ideal of liturgical renewal even though it was not explicitly mentioned in *Sacrosanctum Concilium* of Vatican II. Ratzinger is strongly of the conviction that more important than priest and people facing one another is the mandate that they all face *ad Dominum*. Since re-orienting so many churches would be a daunting and expensive proposition, he suggests having the cross hang above the altar or on the altar, so all can be oriented *ad Dominum* rather than towards one another. Those who have participated in Papal Masses at St. Peter's or followed those celebrated by the Pope in his visit to our country note that the cross (crucifix) was always on the altar facing the Pope, as often were the candles.

Ratzinger is much drawn to beauty as the radiance of the truth, and states in *Feast of Faith* that Christians must make the church building a place where beauty is at home. He further states dramatically that without beauty, the world becomes the last circle of Hell.[207] Theologians who do not "love art, poetry, music and nature

---

[201] *Spirit of the Liturgy*, p. 68-69.

[202] *Ibid.*

[203] *Ibid.*, p. 70.

[204] *Spirit of the Liturgy*, p. 72

[205] *Ibid.*, p. 26.

[206] *Ibid.*, p. 27.

can be dangerous (because) blindness and deafness towards the beautiful are not incidental. They are necessarily reflected in his theology."[208] Holy images are necessary, and all historical forms of art from early Christian to Baroque lay down the principles for sacred art for the future.[209] One should not jettison all art which developed after St. Gregory the Great.[210] Solemnity and beauty are the wealth of all (including the poor) who long for it and even do without necessities to show honor to God.[211]

Our present pontiff, a musician himself, has a great interest in encouraging good church music, even devoting a book to the subject: *A New Song for the Lord*. His own brother was priest choirmaster of the great cathedral of Regensburg, whose name is synonymous with the great tradition of beautiful chant and exquisite polyphony. The Pope thinks that for the sake of popular participation, we've used "utility music" for the people to sing, i.e. that which is cheap and trite, the lowest common denominator. Simple liturgy need not be banal, because true simplicity can come from a spiritual, cultural and historical wealth.[212] The Church must rouse the voice of the Cosmos, elicit the glory of the Cosmos itself making it, too, glorious, beautiful, habitable and beloved.[213] He quotes St. Thomas Aquinas in the II-IIae of the Summa q 91, a I, resp. 1 to the effect that delight in the Lord, joy in a shared presence of Him, is the result of our praise through which we ascend to God and are brought to a sense of reverence since "vocal worship is necessary not for God's sake, but for the sake of the worshipper."[214] Man wants to sing, for according to St. Augustine "to love is to sing,"[215] but listening is also a form of participation. Listening to great music can be interior participation, so hearing the choir singing great works of choral music can rejoice the heart and raise up the soul and complement simple but good music the congregation can manage.

---

[207] *Feast of Faith*, p. 130.
[208] *Ibid.*
[209] *Spirit of the Liturgy*, p. 90.
[210] *op. cit.* 130.
[211] *Ibid.,* p. 131.
[212] *Feast of Faith,* p. 128.
[213] *Ibid.,* p. 129.
[214] *Ibid.,* p. 105
[215] *Spirit of the Liturgy*, p. 90.

In his Apostolic Exhortation on the Eucharist, *Sacramentum Caritatis,*[216] Benedict XVI, in his first papal teaching on the liturgy, articulates in his own original manner the classic Catholic beliefs on the Eucharist as a mystery and sacrifice. The relation of the Holy Trinity to this mystery and indeed especially the Holy Spirit in particular, the relationship of the Church to the Eucharist as well, the Eucharist and the other sacraments are all treated. Finally, the Eucharist is related to eschatology and Our Lady in the Pope's treatment.

It is his understanding of the *ars celebrandi* of the Eucharist that seems most to pertain to the subject matter of this paper. His emphasis on celebrating the rite itself is welcome and even his insistence that this is the best way to ensure *actuosa participation.*[217] Further, he draws our attention to respect for the liturgical books, proper liturgical vesture and colors, the liturgical furnishing and sacred space for art, words, gestures and silence which in the liturgy operate "on different levels of communication which enable [engagement with] the whole person."[218]

He highlights the architecture of the Church and its proper disposition for the celebrating of the sacred mysteries,[219] and singles out the location of the tabernacle. It must be marked by a lamp and readily visible to all in the church. Old high altars may be used or a central location in the sanctuary provided the celebrant's chair is not in front of it. Chapels of reservation may also be used according to the judgment of the ordinary.[220] Liturgical music must be good and respect the great heritage of the Church, a theme we have seen before. The structure of the Mass is discussed as well as the Liturgy of the Word with its homily. He speaks of the need of good preaching using the Lectionary texts, and not being afraid to use the four pillars of the Catechism: Creed, Sacraments, the Ten Commandments, and Prayer.[221] In the Liturgy of the Eucharist, he calls for restraint in the expression of the sign of peace.

Themes we have seen before, appear in this document: the

---

[216] Issued after the October 2005 Synod of Bishops on the Eucharist.

[217] *Sacramentum Caritatis,* n. 38.

[218] *Ibid.,* n. 40.

[219] *Ibid.,* n. 41.

[220] *Sacramentum Caritatis,* n. 69.

[221] *Ibid.,* n. 46.

interiority of active participation is underscored[222] as is Eucharistic Adoration.[223] He raises the question of very large concelebrations which might lose their focus, the unity of the priesthood,[224] and underlines, too, the need for the study of Latin for those studying for the priesthood to be able to celebrate in Latin and to sing in Latin as well.[225]

As Pope, Benedict XVI has given us a beautiful theology of the Eucharist in *Sacramentum Caritatis*, he has also set a new direction in the liturgical life of the Church through his *Motu Proprio* making the old Latin Mass of Pius V more available. Let us examine this document to see what effects it may have in the life of the Church.

Benedict XVI begins by emphasizing the role of the popes ensuring worthy ritual be offered the supreme majesty. He explains that particular churches concur with the universal Church not only in doctrine, but also in sacramental signs and in usages universally accepted by apostolic tradition. This tradition must be observed not only to avoid errors, but also to transmit the integrity of the Faith, because *lex orandi statuit lex credendi* (St. Prosper of Aquitaine). He then praises St. Gregory the Great who helped to codify the Roman Rite and had the great Order of St. Benedict disseminate it all over Europe. He praises the Dominican saint, Pope Pius V, for his renewal of that same rite at the time of Trent.

The far-reaching reform of the Roman Missal by Pope Paul VI and the translation of it into the vernacular he cites as well as the 3rd typical edition of Pope John Paul II. However, he notes that "no small numbers" had affection for the old rite and that same Pope allowed the old rite under certain conditions in 1984,[226] and further encouraged the bishops to be generous in providing for those attached to the old rite in 1988.[227] Because he sees that there is still a need, and after consulting with the consistory of Cardinals in 2000, Pope Benedict XVI issued his own *Motu Proprio Summorum Pontificium* of July 7, 2007. The provisions are as follows:

art. 1. The Missal of Paul VI is the ordinary expression of

---

[222] *Ibid.*, n. 52.
[223] *Ibid.*, n. 66-68.
[224] *Ibid.*, n. 61.
[225] *Ibid.*, n. 63.
[226] *Quattuor Adhinc Annos.*
[227] *Ecclesia Dei.*

the prayer of the Church in the Roman Rite and the Missal of Pius V, reissued by Bl. John XXIII in 1962 is the extraordinary form, never having been abrogated, a two-fold use of one and the same rite.

art. 2. Each priest of the Latin Rite may use the 1962 Missal or the current 1970 Missal at any time (except for the Triduum), *without* permission of the Holy See or the local bishop.

art. 3. Communities of religious wishing to use the 1962 rite may do so; if permanently, major superiors must see to the provisions of their own law.

art. 4. Such Masses may be attended by the faithful who freely ask to come.

art. 5. In a parish where there is a stable group of the faithful who desire the old rite, the pastor should, under the guidance of the bishop accede to their request:

    a.   Either on working days, or one such Mass on Sundays.

    b.   Pastors should allow the extraordinary form for marriages, funerals, pilgrimages, etc.

    c.   Priests who do this must be in good standing and qualified (able to pronounce Latin).

art. 6. In the extraordinary form, the readings may be in the vernacular.

art. 7. If laity asking for this are not satisfied with the pastor's approach, they may inform the bishop and if he cannot satisfy their request, the Ecclesia Dei office in Rome may be contacted by the laity.

art. 8. Bishops may also refer requests to that office.

art. 9. Pastors may use the older ritual for the other sacraments, bishops may confirm in the old rite, clerics may say the 1962 Roman Breviary.

art. 10. Parishes for the 1962 rite may be erected by the bishop.

art. 11 & 12 *Ecclesia Dei* will continue to exercise the Holy See's authority in this matter.

In an accompanying letter the Holy Father expresses the fear that some have that this permission would be turning back Vatican II. He states that the ordinary form for most Catholics will be the present rite. Some feel that this move will bring disunity in the Church. He thinks that the use of the old rite requires liturgical formation, the knowledge of the Missal and Latin and that will not be true of most. Therefore, the usage will be smaller. He does note that the two uses of the Roman Rite will be mutually enriching, with new saints and prefaces for the old Missal and greater reverence for the Mass in the new Missal. He hopes that this will bring greater unity in the Church, especially it would seem with the dissidents on the right, and this has already happened.

So, we have seen the liturgical thought of Joseph Ratzinger in its evolving from boyhood and seminary experiences to those at Vatican II, as university professor, Archbishop of Munich, as head of the C.D.F. and finally as Pope and yet we see an underlying consistency of principle. How his theology and pastoral direction will affect the Liturgy of the Church as well as his *Motu Proprio,* we shall watch with interest.

13. Restoring a Sacred Spirit

From the cliffs on which the University of Steubenville sits, as you look down on that little industrial city along the Ohio River, your eye is caught by the graceful Renaissance dome and twin towers of the parish church of St. Peter. It's one of those grand old churches that has been lovingly remodeled for the new liturgy while preserving its distinctive character. In all my travels, I've come upon few older Catholic churches as beautiful as this.

Building a new church according to the description given in Chapter 5 of the *General Instruction of the Roman Missal* and the document of the American bishops, *The Environment for Worship*, is a much easier task than remodeling an existing building. These documents envision a liturgy that reconstructs the golden age of worship (i.e. the patristic era): They presuppose an assembly hall focused on an altar which faces the people; the celebrant's chair and lectern face them as well, since participation is paramount.

How to design churches meeting these requirements and providing some sense of awe? Now there's a challenge. So many churches today – with wall-to-wall carpeting, purely functional furniture and no sacred art to speak of – seem not that different from dental offices. Sometimes the sterile whitewash is so pronounced and the stainless-steel fittings so severe that we're even reminded of an operating room.

The point is this need not be so, as can be seen in the new Dominican Chapel at Providence College in Providence, Rhode Island. It's an octagon with a warm, orange brick interior and a sloped modern ceiling of white plaster and light walnut. As you look forward through the rows of massively modern choir stalls, your focus is the white marble altar flanked by a pulpit and the Blessed Sacrament shrine with its magnificent tabernacle – a modern version of a Carolingian reliquary.

The area behind the altar bears the celebrant's chair over which is affixed to the brick wall a modern crucifix of the crucified and yet victorious Lord. Against this wall is also found a fine old rosary group with St. Dominic receiving the rosary from our Lady, all beautifully polychromed. Such an environment arouses reverence and rejoices in the Catholic incarnational tradition of elevating the senses through sacred art.

But the job of remodeling an older church with its great high altar which served as a throne for the Blessed Sacrament often replete with adoring angels and with side altars and shrines for statues of the saints, is a harder task. The concept of liturgy at work when these fine old structures were built was silent participation by sight. You watched as the sacred drama unfolded, led by the priest who faced "liturgical East" along with the whole assembly. To change such a structure for the renewed liturgy poses problems. But it can be done.

Sometimes the altar table can simply be removed and brought forward, thus having the advantage of Mass facing the people with the background as it always was. Sometimes a new altar that blends with the environment can be built much closer to the people, and the old high altar can simply become the altar of reservation, as is the case at St. Peter's in Steubenville. Sometimes precious marble work can be recycled, preserving good art and saving money at the same time.

Side altars, if they have artistic merit, can remain as shrines for appropriate statues. The custom of banishing all statues to a single room where they stand cheek by jowl on a shelf for those "who need that kind of thing" is especially reprehensible.

Directives issued by Rome are often broader and more flexible than local liturgical "experts" will allow. In a recent private chat with a highly placed Vatican official, we both agreed that American mania to remove all altar rails from churches, especially where they might be of artistic merit, was quite unnecessary. Further, the dismantlement of pews and the arrangement of new liturgical spaces that discourage kneeling is really *not* in the spirit of the Roman reform. If the Blessed Sacrament is to be reserved in a new place – a separate chapel, as the *General Instruction* encourages, or on a side altar – it ought to be a *special* place, prominent and dignified, inviting prayer and contemplation, and not some virtually forgotten corner.

Traveling in Europe and viewing beautiful new churches and old ones remodeled tastefully has convinced me that the iconoclasm which characterizes so much of the American approach to church edifices need not be the case.

Let's hasten the day when our venerable buildings are gently recycled and new ones intelligently planned to provide a better atmosphere for worship, one that encourages the participation of the people in the Holy Mysteries and at the same time provides a setting that helps to manifest true sacredness.

14. Eucharistic Exposition

I can never experience the fading of October into November without recalling the feast of Christ the King, which used to be celebrated on the last Sunday of October in the old calendar and is now celebrated on the last Sunday of the liturgical year in November. My boyhood memories include walking through the small Connecticut village I grew up in, past eighteenth and nineteenth-century homes on a golden New England fall afternoon, seeing red, gold and orange leaves brilliant against the blue sky as I made my way to our little frame church.

The parish custom was to expose the Blessed Sacrament all day on this day dedicated to the Kingship of Christ, so that all could spend some time before the Lord praying for peace. After coming in from the brightness of the day, my eyes had to adjust to the dim light of the vestibule, but once inside the church, my gaze was immediately swept up to the high altar all resplendent in golden lace where the Blessed Sacrament, in a golden sunburst, was enthroned in a blaze of candles and a forest of gold and white chrysanthemums. I can remember spending long periods of silent prayer in the hushed reverent atmosphere, aware of people going and coming, making visits, whispering prayers and lighting candles. I wonder if this type of prayer prepared me for the contemplative aspect of my Dominican vocation, as indeed the Dominican custom of Third Sunday adoration later nourished it.

It might seem at first that this nostalgic picture has nothing to say to us after Vatican II, but I think it does. The great desire among the young for contemplative prayer suggests that we ought to explore approaches to silent prayer, both old and new. In prayer before the Blessed Sacrament exposed, not only are we praying before the face of the sacramental Lord in His Real Presence but also we have a visual focus that can help us to guard against that distraction that comes from the senses, for here we have something (Someone) that engages the mind, heart, *and* the senses. So many forms of prayer seem to try to ignore the body, but we do so at the peril of ignoring the Incarnation. The Catholic liturgical tradition is to elevate all the senses through the beauty that delights the eye and ear, sanctifies touch and even is expressed in the fragrance of the sweet aroma of Christ.[228]

The new rite of Exposition promulgated in 1973, it seems to me, is especially well suited to help create the atmosphere where we can easily encounter our Lord in the silent prayer of the heart. The main concern of the new rite is to relate Exposition to the Mass so that this prayer in the Presence of Christ is seen as a contemplative extension of the Eucharist, where the Lord is present in His saving Sacrifice to offer our worship to the Father and bring God's grace to us in Communion. It would seem appropriate, then, to use the altar of Sacrifice so that this connection is more clearly seen. Also, in the case of Solemn Exposition, it is recommended that the host be consecrated in the Mass which precedes it, with the Blessed Sacrament being placed in the monstrance right after Communion, when the Exposition commences. The Mass then concludes simply with the post-Communion prayer, and there is no blessing because the Exposition itself is seen as a kind of prolongation of the Mass which will conclude later in the day with the blessing, i.e., Benediction of the Blessed Sacrament. Here we clearly see the thrust of the new rite.

---

[228] cf. Eph. 5:3

It is also recommended that there be prayers, songs, and readings to direct our attention to the worship of the Eucharistic Lord. Everything is done to focus on Christ in this great mystery. Music and readings may help to create the prayer environment, to dispose us to respond in periods of silent prayer which is also encouraged. Before, we often used to have Benediction by itself, but now it is seen as the conclusion to our adoration, whether of long or short duration. The hymn just before the actual Benediction may be the *Tantum Ergo*, *O Salutaris* or any Eucharistic hymn. The new rite may also be celebrated simply with only four candles if desired.

Recently Pope John Paul II ordered daily Exposition in the Blessed Sacrament Chapel of Saint Peter's Basilica, thus creating there an oasis of prayer away from the hordes of tourists. He is known to be a person of deep prayer who loves to pray before the Lord in the Blessed Sacrament. May we follow his example and create the atmosphere in which others may join us.

15. A Sign of the Church: The Sacrament of Marriage

Weddings these days are often a liturgical nightmare replete with gimmicky liturgy, freely written and possibly invalid vows, secular readings from such "profound" classics as Kahlil Gibran's *The Prophet, The Little Prince,* or *The Velveteen Rabbit* and pop love songs like "Follow Me," "We've Only Just Begun," and "You Light Up My Life," celebrating romantic love rather than *the sacrament* of matrimony. In one case of a valid second marriage recently, the bride requested, "Second Time 'Round," and was quite chagrined when the choirmaster refused her request! Of course, this is not just a post-conciliar problem, since many of us can remember strains of Mendelssohn, "O Promise Me" and "Because," as pre-conciliar wedding favorites.

On a splendid October day in the rolling Maryland countryside, I recently attended a wedding which was just the opposite of what has been described above – rather it was a real community celebration of the Christian sacrament of marriage. A young couple from the Lamb of God, a charismatic community from Baltimore, exchanged their vows amid members of their community, friends and relatives in a simple but deeply moving ceremony which lasted two-and-a-quarter hours.

Libertyville, Maryland, the groom's home, reminded me of the little town where I made my novitiate in Ohio – the same early nineteenth-century brick homes on tree-shaded streets. Here the Catholic church with its towering white steeple dominated the town, and from the adjoining cemetery (where the names on the tombstones bespoke the English Catholic heritage of that area) one could see cattle grazing in neighboring pastures. The white interior of the old brick church had recently been remodeled for the new liturgy with taste and reverence for its Neo-Classic lines and mellow nineteenth-century paintings.

Before the actual Mass, everyone in the crowded church prayed for the couple in songs and hymns, ranging from Bach's "Jesu, Joy of Man's Desiring" to recent guitar compositions in the folk idiom. We were led in prayer by one of the lay leaders, a friend of the groom, so that when the wedding party entered, all were in a prayerful, joyful attitude.

For the entrance hymn, we sang all the verses of "Crown Him with Many Crowns," and the Mass proceeded in the usual fashion. The groom led us in a meditative guitar responsorial psalm, friends did the readings, and the father of the groom, a married deacon, witnessed the actual ceremony of the exchange of vows straight from the Ritual. He seemed moved by being the Church's minister at his son's wedding, and watching them, so were we.

After the exchange of vows, many of the leaders of the community came forward to "pray over" the couple, i.e. pray for them and show love and support by the biblical gesture of laying on of hands. As one looked at the radiant bride and the handsome groom surrounded by their friends, one could only think of Jesus, loving His Bride, the Church, and the Church responding in kind.

The real nature of the Church as the Body of Christ was revealed in the community aspects of this ceremony, and those of the Bridal mystery of the Church in the vows, themselves. The Mass proceeded with the prayer of the faithful, Roman canon, sung acclamations, charismatic songs and traditional hymns at communion time. After communion, the bride and groom prayed in thanksgiving for the gifts of life and love from their parents. The thanksgiving was echoed in the praise of the community as it took up the recessional "Holy God We Praise Thy Name" with great gusto.

Community participation did not stop at the Liturgy but

overflowed into the reception at which we ate a meal prepared by the women and served by the men. We were entertained by community dancers doing various ethnic dances, and many joined in the Virginia Reel that followed. This was a many-leveled celebration: sacramental, ecclesial, communitarian and familial, the kind of celebration of marriage that mirrors the mystery of the Church in relation to the Lord and proclaims the Kingdom among us. May we see more marriages like this among God's people!

16. Christian Death

November is the month in which the Church prays for the dead, so that those who are no longer with us but who may not be ready for the vision of God in heaven may be helped by our prayers in the communion of saints, so that their purifying stay in purgatory might be shortened. This is the whole intent of funeral Masses, Masses and prayers for the dead at any time, but especially in the month of the Holy Souls, November.

Many funeral celebrations today seem to have lost this focus. It may be true that the Black Mass with its severe *Dies Irae* and starkness may not have been as comforting to the mourners as it might have been, and perhaps was not as reflective of our belief in the participation of the just in the Resurrection of Christ, yet its constant refrain of "resting in peace" – which is still found in the Masses of the Dead in the Missal of Paul VI – set the proper tone. In Masses of Christian Burial, we pray that the dead may rest in peace, that their purification, if necessary, may be brief and helped by our prayers. This is a quite different tone from so many funeral celebrations today that seem to instantly canonize the departed person. Also, the traditional sobriety and *"gravitas"* of the Roman Liturgy – underscored by the English liturgical scholar Edmund Bishop of the turn of the century – allows something of the grieving process to take place. We can't expect that those who have recently lost someone dear, especially if unexpectedly, will be happy – will be able to enter into a triumphant celebration of the Resurrection that vies with the celebration of Easter itself.

In a well-planned and well-preached funeral, the mourners may be led from the deep emotional sorrow that they are experiencing to a peaceful acceptance of the consolation of the faith that the just will rise again in Christ in the fullness of His Resurrection. In the meantime, they can be helped by our prayers as we, in turn, hope to be helped by the prayers of others in the communion of saints. Many funeral celebrations today seem to confuse the hope of the faith with a kind of simplistic happiness that Elizabeth Kubler-Ross has taught us is impossible in the emotions accompanying the mystery of death.

The last time I was in England, I attended the funeral of a good pastor, much loved by his people, who had died suddenly. His parish of Yardley Wood was a suburb of Birmingham, and due to the high unemployment in the area, many men who ordinarily might not have been able to attend a 10 A.M. funeral were free to do so. Be that as it may, the church, a somewhat Romanesque structure gently and tastefully remodeled for the new liturgy, was jam-packed with diocesan clergy, ecumenical visitors, religious, and families of the parish. Archbishop Maurice Couve de Murville, vested in purple rather than white, presided with great dignity.

As the funeral began, everyone sang the *Requiem* in Latin and the *Kyrie* in Greek. Our response to the first reading[229] was Gelineau's "The Lord is my Shepherd, there is nothing I shall want." We heard St. Paul to the Romans,[230] sang the Alleluia, listened to the proclamation of the Gospel,[231] and heard the homily which attempted to plumb for us the mystery of Christian Death. A rousing hymn in English – "Lord, Accept the Gifts We Offer" – was sung at the preparation of the gifts and the *Sanctus*, *Pater Noster* and *Agnus Dei* were all in Latin Gregorian. After the Communion Antiphon *Lux Eterna* was rendered, the congregation launched with great gusto into "O Bread of Heaven" and "Jesus, My Lord, My God, My All." The funeral concluded with the *Salve Regina* and the *In Paradisum* in Gregorian, and as the coffin was being carried out, all joined in "Sweet Savior, Bless Us E're We Go."

This funeral – dignified and sober, yet hopeful and peaceful, provided the proper orientation for this parish grieving over the sudden loss of its much-loved pastor. The Latin requiem was used and yet there were plenty of popular vernacular hymns as well. The tone of hope and prayer for the dead pastor was that he might rest in

---

[229] Isaiah 25
[230] Chapter 8
[231] Matt. 5:1-12

peace and that his family might be comforted. There was Christian confidence in the rising of the just in the Lord's Resurrection, but it was not celebrated as if it were at the Easter Vigil. The purple vestments – the proper Roman color rather than the experimental white used in the States – accorded more with the natural emotions of the grieving congregation.

This was a subdued yet hopeful celebration of the Mass as a sacrificial prayer for the dead, which was in complete accord with Catholic teaching. I only hope my funeral is such, that people avoid a hasty canonization attempt, and simply pray for the repose of my soul as the Church would have them do.

17. Louis Bouyer: Life and Work

In learning, it seems to me, that the greatest thing that can happen to one is to sit at the feet of a great teacher. I've had that good fortune a few times. While studying Liturgy at San Anselmo in Rome, I had the opportunity to have Fr. Burchard Neunheuser, OSB, as my teacher. He was a student of Odo Casel, OSB, who lectured in Italian, his text was a readable Latin, and once after class when he was answering questions in Italian, French, German, and English, he stopped and had to ask, "In what language am I speaking?" Once while I was teaching at the Angelicum in Rome, I decided to take some courses to fill out my background in certain areas. I learned much from the spiritual master, Fr. Jordan Aumann, OP, in his Course on Spiritual Theology. Earlier in our Dominican stadium I had Fr. Urban Voll, OP, teach me moral theology and he actually set St. Thomas in the context of his times and discussed the contemporary controversies, making it all very exciting and fresh, something not all of his Dominican confreres did.

Finally, when I began my teaching career at Providence College in 1967, I was given a course on the Church to teach. It just so happened that on the other side of the city, the Visiting Catholic Professor at Brown, the prestigious Ivy League university, was Fr. Louis Bouyer, of the Oratory. He offered a graduate seminar on *Lumen Gentium* of Vatican Council II. The text was still in Latin because it was so "hot off the press" that it hadn't yet been translated. A Dominican confrere and I sat in on it with Brown's Dean of Theology, grad students and ministers of all denominations… all very exciting.

I also audited a course of his, Ecclesiology: 1800 to the Present, but when he began the class, he said that one couldn't understand the ecclesiology after 1800, unless one had the New Testament, Patristic, Medieval, and Reformation ecclesiology as a background. So, in his black corduroy suit and Roman collar, sitting at a desk and reading in a monotone voice from a neat little notebook, he gave me the most exciting course of my academic career. The ideas of our heritage, the Sacred Scriptures, and the Fathers as understood by the Church, medieval doctors and modern theologians came alive as he unpacked their understanding of the Church. This was a life-changing course.

Bouyer was born in 1913 to a mother of Spanish/Italian descent and a father of French Protestant origin. His mother made her First Communion, but her anti-clerical father let her go no further. She became a nanny to wealthy Protestants who supplied her religious education. When she became a nanny to a family in England, she was introduced to the *Book of Common Prayer* which she used and later passed on to her son, so his Anglican sympathies began early. His father, a high school graduate, worked in the first electric company in Paris and he loved art, whereas his mother's side was musical, all playing instruments. Indeed, his maternal grandfather played in the orchestra for the Opera.

The family attended the Reformed Church in Paris, where he was baptized. Bouyer always felt that his family was *naturaliter Catholica* in terms of its core beliefs in which young Louis was raised. His mother's sudden death in 1923 was a great shock to him when he was eleven. It was recommended by a psychiatrist that time in the countryside would allow him to regain his equilibrium. He was already a precocious reader, polishing off all of Sherlock Holmes' adventures, as well as those of Alexander Dumas of *The Three Musketeers* fame. In the peace of the countryside, he read some Protestant spiritual authors which helped him to deal with his loss. Back in Paris, his school educated him in the Classics, Latin and Greek, physics, and chemistry.

He and his father began attending a Lutheran church in Paris where the pastor took a more "Catholic" approach to their liturgy. At this time, since his father had remarried, through his stepmother he met some Catholic cousins which broadened his religious horizons. At the time, he also read Newman's *Sermons*, Wadsworth's poetry and the French historian of spirituality, Bremond.

Louis Bouyer began thinking of becoming a Lutheran pastor as a young man. The circles in which he traveled were broadly ecumenical. He got to know the Dean of the Episcopal Cathedral who sent him to the St. Serge Institute founded by the Russian emigres fleeing the Bolshevik revolution. Here he met Bulgakov and started reading the Greek Fathers.

As a young man, Bouyer read Lutheran periodicals in which he encountered the ecumenical movement in the Life and Work project of Nathan Soderblom who was encouraging social work in common by all the churches. Even though Catholics were officially aloof, around that time, Cardinal Mercier had sponsored the Malines conversations with the Anglicans. Bouyer encountered Lutheran pastors of an ecumenical bent, seeking one Church of Christ.

He enrolled in a Protestant Theological Faculty in Paris, where both Lutherans and the Reformed (Calvinist) students studied side by side. Bouyer felt he got a good education there: some of the Calvinist professors interested him in the thought of St. Thomas Aquinas. He formed close friendships and started praying the Roman Breviary in Latin with one of those friends, rather than the *Book of Common Prayer*. He also attended lectures by the Catholic Etienne Gilson, and was drawn to St. Thomas, if not to scholasticism. He was now reading more of the Orthodox: Soleyev, Florensky, Bulgakov, and he met Lorsky. He also read the Benedictines Odo Casel, Vonier, Marmion, and made a retreat at the Abbey of St. Wandrille. These Catholic and Orthodox influences led Bouyer to discover a deep Catholic tradition which was aided and abetted by his reading Claudel and Peguy.

Now travelling in more "Catholic" Lutheran and ecumenical circles (he would call it the "Evangelical Catholic Lutheran" circle), he went to Strasbourg to study for the Baccalaureate (we would say Licentiate) because his Paris college was getting more liberal. He studied the Greek Fathers, more Pseudo-Dionysius, the Rhineland mystics, had a course with Oscar Cullman, and began to see the New Testament in a unity with the Fathers. He wrote his thesis on "Newman and Alexandrian Christianity."

Back in Paris in 1936 as Vicar to a small Lutheran Church, he wrote a novel (he wrote several under different *noms de plume*). Further contacts with Catholics such as Lambert Beauduin, OSB, and

Yves Congar, OP, had him questioning whether "Evangelical Catholicism," as he called his re-Catholicizing Protestantism, while yet being faithful to the true elements of the Reformation, might mean that he belonged in the Catholic Church. He spoke with an Oratorian, made a retreat at their boarding school, and shortly thereafter was received into the Church at St. Wandrille. He wondered if he had a monastic calling and poured out his soul to a monk who assured him that the Oratory was right for him, even though Bouyer saw its problems.

While discerning which vocation to follow, Bouyer was also meditating on the Triduum and produced a manuscript that was later published as *The Paschal Mystery*. He entered Oratory novitiate which, like mine, was dreadful. He felt that most of the prayer that should have been done in common, like the Divine Office, was done individually, and that which should have been done privately, like devotions, was done in common. This line of thought he developed in his book *Liturgical Piety*, the first book of his I ever read, and it made a great impression on me. However, he thought that some devotions like the rosary could easily be harmonized with the Liturgy since they both had as their object the Mystery of Christ. I remember when I took his course at Brown, I went to his office, knocked at the door, and opened too quickly and found the great Bouyer telling his beads.

Bouyer began his study of Catholic theology at the *Institute Catholique* where he said he had excellent courses. The professors presented the teaching without any anti-Protestant bias or polemic and made him feel that he didn't have to repudiate any basic Protestant insights. He said here was planted the germ for his book *The Spirit and Forms of Protestantism*, in which he singles out Christian truths fostered by the Reformation, which could find their place in the fullness of the Church, e.g. the beauty of holiness in Anglican worship, the emphasis on God's sovereignty in Calvinism, the role of faith in justification, a Lutheran concern, etc., and when I read it later this book also made a great impression on me. Perhaps because our separated brethren discarded some truths, they made more of the New Testament values they kept. Bouyer said elsewhere that they were permanent values of this Protestant tradition, such as a deep love of the Bible, the deeply personal nature of the life and consciousness of grace effectively gratuitous to the highest degree.

In 1944, Louis Bouyer was ordained a priest, prostrate over the grave of Fr. Condren (the second Superior of the French Oratory after Cardinal Berulle) and he was asked to teach at the *Institute Catholique*, while living at a different Oratory which was more to his liking. The priests there were serious, cultured, and fostered St. Philip's charism of friendship and charity. While teaching at the Institute, he helped to found the National Center for Pastoral Liturgy along with A.M. Roguet, OP, along the lines of Lambert Beauduin's idea of teaching the people about the Liturgy so they could participate in it. Later he would withdraw because it went in a different direction.

Upon the recommendation of the same Beauduin, Fr. Bouyer was offered summer courses at Notre Dame (USA) by Fr. Michael Matthis, CSC, in 1952. One of these courses was published as *Liturgical Piety*, to which I've already alluded, and which was later to be pivotal in my teaching. Other books flowed from courses he taught there: *Rite and Man* and *Liturgy and Architecture*. He taught with a stellar faculty such as Fr. John Quinn, Deacon Bouman from Nimegen. The fame of that grew so that when I attended it in 1967 and 1968, it was *the* place to study Liturgy. 1968 was the year he published his monumental work *The Eucharist*. While I was studying at Notre Dame, I got involved in the Charismatic Renewal. I remember that the leaders of the Renewal invited some theologians to put this experience into the context of the life of the Church. None did this more brilliantly than Fr. Bouyer, situating the charismatic experience in the heart of the Church, using the witness of the early church and the Fathers of the Church.

After a stay in England, he published *Newman, His Life and Spirituality*, and a life of St. Philip Neri: *The Roman Socrates*. While acting as spiritual director of the seminary in Strasbourg, he managed to put together the first volume of *The History of Spirituality: New Testament and the Fathers*. Volume II on medieval spirituality, written by Bouyer and two Benedictines, followed, and Volume III on the spirituality of the Orthodox, the Anglicans and Protestants was done by Bouyer.

A controversy at the *Institute Catholique* pitted the Jesuits, especially Danielou, against Bouyer and it reached such proportions that Bouyer resigned his post. At that time, he was invited to teach at Brown University in Providence, Rhode Island – for him a wonderful experience, as it was for me, his student. Later, he taught at Salamanca, Oxford, our own CUA, and Mt. St. Mary's Seminary in Emmitsburg, Maryland. While teaching there, he worked on his trilogy: *The Eternal Son, The Invisible Father,* and a work on the Holy Spirit that has not been translated into English. He also wrote a book on Our Lady, *Seat of Wisdom,* and his ecclesiology, *The Church of God,* which I had occasion to use in class.

In preparation for the Council, he was placed on the Commission for Seminaries, which he didn't think accomplished much. He worked on ecumenism with the Russian Orthodox at Bari, where he said he pursued the common discovery of ecclesial fullness, trying to distinguish the essentials from the non-essentials of the Faith. Because of his reputation in ecumenism, he was appointed by Pope John Paul II to work on Catholic-Orthodox reunion, having previously been named by Pope Paul VI to meet with the Anglicans in Malta.

His work on the Liturgy, especially his book *The Eucharist,* caused Paul VI to name him to the *Concilium* charged with carrying out the liturgical reforms of Vatican II. He worked under Cardinal Lecaro, but the one that got things done was Bugnini, "a mealy-mouthed scoundrel" as he styles him. Bouyer was not satisfied with the new Eucharistic prayers, but happy that the Roman Canon was left alone. Eucharistic Prayer III incorporated well an ancient Gallican anamnesis, and he felt that he and Dom Botte, OSB, did good work on Eucharistic Prayer II, and he approved of the many fine prefaces taken from ancient sacramentaries. He was upset at the loss of Septuagesima, the Octave of Pentecost, the changing of so many saint's days. He approved of the broader use of Scripture in the new Lectionary if not specific choices. Often in a controversial decision, he said Bugnini would end discussion by saying, "the Pope wants it." Afterward, when visiting Paul VI, Bouyer was asked by the Pope why such a decision was made and Bouyer said, "We were told you wanted it." De Lubac also complained that the French Missal of Paul VI had many mistranslations that Bugnini had approved as in conformity with the Latin. Later, Bugnini was relieved of his duties and sent as a papal diplomat to Iran!

After the new Liturgy was in place (in its beginning form) I ran into Fr. Bouyer at the Notre Dame Summer School. He invited me to have a drink with him before supper in his rooms. The room we were in was right next to a chapel for private Mass. Some priest was saying Mass for a group of students and the walls were thin. The folk music came pounding through the walls: "Sons of God, hear His holy word; gather 'round the table of the Lord. Eat His Body, drink His Blood, and we'll sing our song of love, Alleluia," etc. Bouyer grimaced and said, "We never intended that!"

Fr. Bouyer was invited to sit on the newly established International Theological Commission by the Pope. He recounts how the Jesuit Rahner would ramble on and once, when Bouyer was seated next to Cardinal Ratzinger, he heard him whisper, "another monologue on dialogue." The Commission answered to the CDF (Holy Office), which never passed their reports to the Pope. When Paul VI complained that he had never received a given report to Von Balthasar, he responded that he had sent it in months ago. When they researched a position paper on the limits of theological pluralism and handed it in, the same thing happened, so Bouyer resigned the Commission.

Feeling that many had misunderstood the conciliar documents and were pursuing the reforms of Vatican Council in an erroneous way, he wrote *The Decomposition of Catholicism*, which was much appreciated by Cardinal Heenan and more importantly by Paul VI, who gave him a pectoral cross as a sign of appreciation. The Pope invited him to join him on retreat at Castel Gandolfo, but Bouyer declined the kind invitation. Paul VI wanted to make him a Cardinal but gave up on the idea since the French bishops would have opposed it.

Though an Oratorian, Bouyer retired to the Benedictine abbey of St. Wandrille where he could study and pray. He felt that both he and Paul VI were failed Benedictines…they loved the monastic life, but it was not theirs to live. Here, Bouyer ended his memoirs.

A postscript: Fr. Bouyer ended his days with the Little Sisters of the Poor in Paris. His short-term memory failed, but not his long-term. He lived more in previous epochs of history than his own. He constantly prayed the Eastern Jesus prayer and the rosary with the Sisters, thus confirming one of my fondest memories of him.

THE RENEWAL OF THE LITURGICAL SEASONS

1. The "O" Antiphons

On December 17th, the attention of the Advent Season turns more to the Incarnation, Our Lady's part in this great mystery and the great advent or coming of the Lord by his birth of the Virgin Mother. The "O" Antiphons which are verses to be chanted before and after the Magnificat at the end of Vespers each night originated in Rome, where we find the classic seven antiphons, although in the Middle Ages, more antiphons were added in local churches. The seven "O" antiphons can also be found in the verses of the familiar Advent carol "O Come, O Come, Emmanuel."

First Antiphon - December 17th: *O Sapientia*
O, Wisdom, O holy Word of God,[232] you govern all creation with your strong yet tender care.[233] Come and show your people the way to salvation.[234]

In this ancient antiphon the Church cries out to Christ, as the Wisdom of the Father, the eternal Word proclaimed by John in his prologue,[235] who was with the Father in the beginning of the creation of the world which he continues to govern. We, the Church cry "Come," the most primordial of all prayers, because we know we've

---

[232] Sir. 24:3
[233] Wis. 8:1
[234] Is. 40:3-5
[235] John 1

"messed up" the wonderful order of creation with human sin and manipulation and need God's Wisdom, whose "thoughts are not our thoughts."[236]   Only he can show us his Son who is the way to Salvation; to saving us from ourselves and leading us to righteousness in thought and action, which the term salvation implies.

Second Antiphon – December 18th: *O Adonai*
O Sacred Lord of Ancient Israel[237] who showed yourself to Moses in the burning bush,[238] who gave him the holy law on Sinai. Come stretch out your mighty hand to set us free.[239]

This antiphon brings us back to the Exodus event. God revealed himself to Moses in the burning bush which the Fathers of the Church much later will see as a sign of the Blessed Virgin, whose virginity ever burns brightly without being consumed by the divine motherhood. God gave his name Yahweh to Moses, and with that power over him; for to the Hebrew to use one's name is to have intimacy with that person and thus to have power over him. Yet God cannot be like the gods of the pagans who are coerced by magical practices and so his name is not to be pronounced but instead "Adonai" or "Lord" is used.   In the fulness of time the Messiah will come and tell us to pray in his name of Jesus, with all the implications of that.   We pray now that he come again with outstretched arm, that is with power to set us free. In the words of St. Justin "He stretched out his arms on the cross," and was rendered powerless and received from his Father the power of the Spirit to set us free from our sinful selves.

Third Antiphon – December 19th: *O Virga Jesse*
O Flower of Jesse's stem, you have been raised as a sign for all peoples;[240] kings stand silent in your presence;[241] The nations bow down in worship before you. Come, let nothing keep you from coming to our aid.[242]

---

[236] Is. 55: 8-9
[237] Exod. 6:2
[238] Exod. 3:2
[239] Exod. 6:6
[240] Is. 11:10
[241] Is. 5:15
[242] Heb. 2:3

Here we call on the Lord as the seed, flower or descendant of the root or stock of Jesse, the father of King David. The Messiah comes from a royal line sprung from his human ancestor Jesse. He is the sign born of the Virgin, for all the nations to see. The East portrays the prophecy of Isaiah, "the Virgin shall conceive and bear a son," with the child enclosed in a circle on his mother's breast and calls that icon the Virgin of the Sign. We call on him now to come and help our sinful and weary world.

Fourth Antiphon – December 20th: *O Clavis David*

O Key of David, O royal Power of Israel, controlling at your will the gate of heaven,[243] Come, break down the prison walls of death for those who dwell in darkness and the shadow of death,[244] and lead your captive people into freedom.

The Lord Jesus is invoked here as the Key of David,[245] the one who can open the gate into the kingdom because he is the gate.[246] He knocks at the door of our hearts[247] leading us out of the darkness of sin into the true freedom of the children of God, which is freedom from sin and the resulting joy and delight.

Fifth Antiphon – December 21: *O Oriens*

O Radiant Dawn,[248] Splendor of Eternal Light,[249] Sun of Justice;[250] Come and shine on those who dwell in darkness and the shadow of death.[251]

The Lord here is invoked as the Light of the World[252] coming as the real *sol invictus* at the end of time calling us out of darkness into his own wonderful light. The gloom of mid-winter can be seen as the hopelessness of ancient paganism or our own contemporary angst from which we desperately need deliverance.

---

[243] Is. 22:22
[244] Luke 1:79
[245] Rev. 3:7
[246] cf. John 10:7
[247] Rev. 3:19
[248] Zech. 6:12
[249] Heb. 1:3
[250] Mal. 4:2
[251] Luke 1:78
[252] John 8:12

Sixth Antiphon – December 22nd: *O Rex Gentium*

O King of all the nations, the only joy of every human heart,[253] O Keystone[254] of the mighty arch of man;[255] come and save the creature you fashioned from the dust.[256]

This antiphon rejoices that the Lord is king not just of the Jews but us Gentiles as well, who makes them one people, one temple, in which he is the keystone, the crowning glory that holds all in place.[257] We beg the Lord to return again to save weak humanity made in Gods' image but disfigured by sin.

Seventh Antiphon – December 23rd: *O Emmanuel*

O Emmanuel,[258] king and lawgiver,[259] desire of the nations,[260] Savior of all people, come and set us free, Lord our God.

We have here a variation on the theme that Jesus, who is Emmanuel – God with us – is present in the Church and in the world as king and lawmaker; yet we need him to come again, we desire him to come and set us free from ourselves through Christ, through his saving birth, life and teaching, death and resurrection and his return in glory, all of which are implicit in our Advent prayer. Vespers on the 24th is no longer Advent, but the first Vespers of Christmas, whose special antiphons take up the theme of the Birth of our Savior.

2. Christmas: Rebirth of the Spirit

The born-again phenomenon is all about us. We see it in print, witness leading personalities on television speaking of how their lives have been changed by the Holy Spirit and perhaps have friends who have themselves had this experience.

Once upon a time "born-again" terminology would have automatically conjured up fundamentalist Protestantism to Catholic

---

[253] Haggai 2:8
[254] Is. 28:16
[255] Eph. 2:14
[256] Gen. 2:7
[257] Eph. 2:20
[258] Is. 7:14
[259] Is. 33:22
[260] Gen. 49:10

ears, but this is no longer the case, particularly because of the rise of Catholic charismatics.

Of course, no orthodox Catholic would hold that his sacramental baptism did not confer the Spirit which was only later conferred in "the baptism in the Spirit." Those of us who have had this experience usually became aware of a deepening of what was already there or, in the case of some, a dramatic rediscovery or release of the Holy Spirit so intense that it could be called a rebirth (what the classic spiritual writers used to call a second conversion).

All of us must be "born again"[261] and we are, when we are baptized through water and the Spirit. But perhaps after this initiation into the Christian Life there are stages of a deeper rebirth as we commit ourselves again and again to the mystery of the life of Christ within us.

The Fathers of the Church seemed to think so, as I discovered last Christmas while preparing my homily for midnight Mass. I was reading the Advent-Christmas volume of *The Liturgical Year* by my old liturgy professor at San Anselmo in Rome, Fr. Adrian Nocent, OSB.

In his treatment of our birth in the birth of Christ, he pointed out how the liturgy of the Church uses such terms as "renovation" and "regeneration" when speaking of our newness of life in the newborn Christ. St. Leo, using Pauline terminology, wrote that the Incarnation took place so that we might "be a new creation, a new work of His hands." The Christmas liturgy focuses on the Incarnation as the beginning of the Paschal Mystery, the Death and Resurrection of Christ, by which we are saved. The Missal of Pius V contrasted our "new birth" with the "old slavery" of sin in the prayers for Christmas Day.

Christmas was seen by the Church as a new beginning. St. Ambrose held that the Church came into being the moment of Christ's birth: "Christ is born, and the shepherds begin their watch, gathering into the Lord's house His flocks, that is the nations that hitherto had been living like beasts." The renewal brought by Christ's birth is not restricted to humanity, but is shared by the whole creation, the cosmos.

Since we celebrated the Lord's birth during the winter solstice, when the pagans celebrated the "birthday of the sun," St. Maximus of

---

[261] Cf. John 3:3

Turin wrote: "The people are quite right, in a way, when they call this the birthday of 'the new sun'… We gladly accept the name, because by the coming of the Savior not only is mankind saved but the very light of the sun is renewed."

Not only is man "enlightened" by the birth of Christ, the Sun of Justice, but His presence in the flesh bestows an added nobility on all material creation, animate or inanimate – for God's plan was "to unite all things in Him, things in heaven and things on earth."[262] Thus, in the great mystery of the Nativity of Christ we celebrate our restoration, renewal and rebirth through His Birth, Death and Resurrection, and the participation of the whole creation in this saving mystery.

As we prepare for the great feast – singing our carols (with their references to rebirth), gathering gifts, trimming trees and building our creches – let us prepare our hearts as well so that the solemn splendor of midnight Mass will be the beautiful sign of the light of Christ within us – inspiring our "rebirth" at the celebration of His birth.

3. My Twelve Days of Christmas

The world begins celebrating Christmas with Macy's Thanksgiving Parade or even right after Halloween in some shopping malls. The decorations are up long in advance; carols are played in commercial anticipation; parties are over long before the main event; and when some people take down their trees the day after Christmas, we can well understand, so tired could one become of the world's way of celebrating this feast. The Church, on the other hand, prepares by Advent, solemnly celebrates Christmas with its Octave, with a whole constellation of feasts for twelve days until Epiphany, and even after until the Baptism of the Lord officially closes the season two or three weeks after it began. This is how the Church wants Christians to celebrate with the liturgical cycle, and I try as best I can to comply. Last year, I had a wonderful time in doing so.

My Christmas began with a gathering of former students and members of a prayer group I used to direct, who assembled on Christmas Eve for a vigil service of the Office of Readings of the

---

[262] Eph. 1:10

Liturgy of the Hours. During the vigil service, we prepared ourselves by listening to St. Leo's wonderful homily on the dignity of the Christian because of the Incarnation and by singing carols as prelude to the simple, yet solemn Midnight Mass that followed in the cramped oratory. The next day I spent visiting my family, exchanging gifts, watching my nieces and nephews open theirs, and walking up to our parish church with my sister so I could say Vespers in front of the creche. After a few pleasant days with my family, I set off for New York City to visit an old college friend in the "Big Apple."

It might seem at first glance that this city is not the place to be for so holy a season, but actually it bedecks itself in such splendor that one can overlook the seedier sides of urban existence, and rejoice in the shining lights, the tree at Rockefeller Center before which skaters zip by, the tree in the Metropolitan Museum covered with baroque angels singing above the eighteenth century Neapolitan crèche, and the famous window of F. A. O. Schwarz where animated toys jump and cavort. It was the churches and museums that my friend and I hit as we used to in our youth – those lovely churches of the upper East Side all bedecked in their Christmas finery, starting with our own lovely Gothic St. Vincent Ferrer, the baroque St. Jean Baptist, the more staid and stately St. Ignatius on Park Avenue, and the charming St. Thomas More. We visited the Frick Museum, whose inner court cast a mellow light on pale pink poinsettias, and whose Holbein portrait of St. Thomas More was freshly restored. St. Patrick's was awash with visitors and its great pillars were hung with wreaths, its exquisite high altar banked with red and white poinsettias, its Lady's Chapel bathed in a golden light, while crowds jammed around the crèche. Downtown we stopped in old St. Paul's where Mother Seton prayed as an Episcopalian. It was all open and decorated. We then walked 'round to old St. Peter's, Barclay Street, Mother Seton's Catholic parish, only to find it locked tighter than a drum, as we also found *Old* St. Patrick's Cathedral.

On New Year's Day after saying Mass and preaching in our lovely Goodhue Gothic Church of St. Vincent, I headed for the country, silence, and rest, all of which I found at Still River, Massachusetts in the priories of Saints Benedict and Scholastica. The Brothers and Sisters know how to celebrate Christmas there, and every aspect of the beautiful colonial homes and chapel is magnificently decorated with colored lights on the trees outside, reflecting on the snow, making the whole scene look like one straight out of a postcard. The quiet countryside, the peaceful Gregorian chant, the joy of religious prayerfully celebrating the season set the tone, but so did the homemade Christmas goodies still around.

Finally, for Epiphany I went to Newport, Rhode Island to celebrate a Vigil Mass of that feast in a couple's home, whose twenty-second wedding anniversary it was. They and their five children (two of whom attend my college) hosted our little Dominican Third Order group while their mother and father and three others were received into the Order. We sang the Mass, blessed the house, had the children put the three kings in the crèche and picked cards which were gifts from the Christ Child. On the latter were virtues to be cultivated for the New Year. The people who bit into the three beans buried in the Epiphany cake were proclaimed kings, and nonetheless discovered they had the duty of praying for the rest of us that we be able to grow in the practice of the virtue received. The feast, itself, found me at Portsmouth Abbey, the mellow contemporary monastic architecture a delight to the eye, and the good taste of the English Benedictine Congregation evidenced in the staid and solemn Liturgy, at which a former student of mine made his monastic profession. The afternoon was spent at Ade Bethume's where the St. Leo League met to study slides of the recently beatified Fra Angelico's murals in San Marco (Florence) followed by Mass celebrated with Gregorian, the last carols of the season and a potluck supper. My celebration of the Twelve Days was completed, and I had time to meditate on and celebrate all the different aspects of the great mystery of the Incarnation for us.

Not everyone's celebration of Christmas could be the same as this errant friar, but that we allow ourselves to be lifted by the Liturgy of the Church and taken into its depths as the Church contemplates the great mystery of Christmas - Epiphany becomes all the more important as the world secularizes this feast more and more. How a family would do this is of course, different, but I can remember in my home on Christmas not beginning Christmas Eve until the statue of the infant was placed in the crib by the youngest child and all sang a carol. Advent wreaths on the table lit at meals help preface for the feast; the rosary said in front of the crèche, as we used to do, helps to focus on the mystery. Epiphany customs already described can help as well as other traditions described in the leaflets published by Liturgical Press: *Family Advent Customs in the Home* and *Family Christmas Customs in the Home*. However, it is done – by the individual, the family or the parish – we Christians must reclaim Christmas for the great spiritual feast and season that it is and not allow its tinsel to be ripped off by the world the day after.

4. Lent: A Method of Prayer

Now that Lent is upon us, we might ask ourselves what special practices will help us in our struggle against sin and in our desire to grow closer to the Lord. The traditional means hallowed by Jewish usage, recommended by the Lord in the Gospel of Matthew and emphasized by the Fathers of the Church, are prayer, fasting, and almsgiving. Prayer is God's action in us, but we can cooperate by disposing ourselves to pray.

First, one ought to find a quiet place where one can pray undisturbed – a corner of one's room or a church or chapel, perhaps kneeling before the Blessed Sacrament. In my room a favorite icon of Christ or a crucifix helps me to concentrate. My tools are the Bible (it's usually best to start with the New Testament) and perhaps another simple book of devotion or spirituality. I sit or kneel, get myself ready, and begin.

There are many different ways to pray. I use the letters which make up the word ACTS to help me focus on the goals of prayer, which are – adoration, contrition and consideration, thanksgiving, and supplication.

We begin with *adoration*, but it is first necessary to "put oneself in the presence of God" by reminding oneself that God is within the soul of each Christian by grace, wanting to communicate with us even more than we do with Him. This awareness leads to adoration or praise in which we think of the greatness of God the Creator, Redeemer and Sanctifier and thank Him and praise Him for all He's done for us in general – bringing us into existence, preserving us, protecting us, etc. – but also in particular – for giving us family, friends, etc.

Praise and adoration set up the proper stance before God who loves us, and yet we are sinners who've committed many sins that tried to crowd God out of our lives. We have flouted His law and need to repent or express our *contrition*. We can think of recent sins, past sins or even reflect on what we might do without His grace. Our aim is not necessarily to feel the emotion of sorrow but to resolve to change, to allow ourselves to be converted. Humility flows from such considerations.

Now we are ready to consider the truth of the teaching of Jesus in His word by reading or what the monks call *lectio*. We select a passage in the Gospels – perhaps that of the day – and read it slowly, allowing the words to sink in. A phrase might pop out of the text, and we might linger over or ponder that "word" in our hearts early in the morning and come back to it later. This is meditation.

Whether we simply turn a phrase over in our hearts or use our imagination, we should be open to the work of the Spirit praying within, stirring our affections, drawing our will closer to God. Sometimes nothing much will happen and that's fine, because prayer is not automatic. We must remember that we dispose ourselves as best we can, but we don't control God.

Sometimes when we've been faithful to prayer, we will experience a deeper prayer which stirs up our faith, hope, and love, and other times we'll simply rest in the Lord in a way that goes beyond words or concepts. Such is contemplation, a gift bestowed more often than many realize. When prayer is drawing to a close, then one *thanks* God for His presence (for He was present whether experienced or not), for any graces, or insights into one's life or the truths of the Faith.

Supplications follow as I intercede for others: family and friends; the world and its peace; the Church and the Pope; and finally, my own needs. I present them to my loving Father who always gives me what I need, though not always what I want.

Having a way of prayer (and one should use whatever works) is helpful even when I experience spiritual dryness because I know I have done what I could; I have disposed myself as well as I could and in this dry time God wanted me simply to wait in loving and humble faith.

Fidelity to prayer each day will yield a rich harvest this Lent. It will draw us closer to that contemplation we are all called to in this life, and prepare us for that heavenly contemplation that is our destiny.

5.   The Meaning of Holy Week

"During Holy Week, the Church celebrates the mysteries of salvation accomplished by Christ in the last days of His life, beginning with His messianic entrance into Jerusalem."

In reading these words from a circular letter of the Congregation of Divine Worship on Lent and Easter, we need to remember that we are that Church and we, like the disciples, must go to Jerusalem with Him.

The first Christians celebrated only Easter itself with a vigil and Eucharist.   But when the "Edict" of Milan (A.D. 313) made Christianity licit, pilgrims began to travel to the Holy Land.   They wanted to act out each aspect of the whole mystery in the very spots where the Lord suffered, died and rose.   So, they developed there the ceremonial of Palm Sunday, Holy Thursday and Good Friday, which they took back to their local churches and added to the Easter Vigil.

Holy Week begins on Palm Sunday and, as we march in the Procession of the Palms (or watch others do so) we need to see ourselves in the company of the victor King. Jesus is not some tragic hero being dragged along to meet His fate in suffering and death. He is marching forth clad in royal red vestments, joyfully accepting His suffering for all of us.   But the red of His garments becomes the color of blood, as we listen to readings from the Passion story and meditate on the price of our salvation.

Holy Thursday begins the Easter Triduum.   It recalls the Last Supper in which the Lord gave His Body and Blood as a sacrifice in the form of bread and wine.   He shared this humble meal with the Apostles so that they might continue His priesthood, and so that we all might participate in this communion of love.

In the early Church, Holy Thursday was a favorite time to reconcile sinners. Have we prepared ourselves for this special Mass by going to Confession earlier in the week?

As we hear St. Paul's account of the institution of the Eucharist, we ponder the Lord's love in giving us so great a gift. And as we listen to the story of His washing of the Apostles' feet, we are struck by His Humility – not only in performing so menial a task, but also by His coming to us sacramentally in so humble a way.

At the end of the Mass, when the Blessed Sacrament is carried in procession to the Altar of Repose, we should meditate on all these themes, especially the Lord's abiding presence with us as our food and drink.

Good Friday is so focused on the historical event of Christ's Passion and Death that the re-enactment of the mystery in the Mass is not allowed. There is only the stark reality of John's account of the Passion and the adoration of the cross itself.

After the homily, we have the Prayer of the Faithful in its most ancient Roman form. On this day when the world was reconciled to God through the Cross, the Church prays solemnly for all people to open their hearts to reconciliation, and we must do so, too.

The cross is lifted high for us to gaze upon: "Behold the wood of the cross on which hung the Savior of the World." Rejoicing that what was once the tree of death has now become the tree of life, we come forward to venerate the sign of our Savior's love.

The Triduum concludes and the Easter season commences with the Easter Vigil – in St. Augustine's phrase, "the mother of all vigils." The whole of creation is now sanctified by the Resurrection: water, earth and fire. From the new fire the paschal candle is lit and carried into the darkened church. This symbolizes the Risen Lord, the Light of the World, scattering the darkness of sin and death.

Readings follow from all of salvation history, and we should link them to the stories of God's grace and love in our own lives. The Easter Alleluia will then reverberate in our hearts with joy, and we will welcome the newly baptized wet with water from the font and commit ourselves once again to our own baptismal vows.

We conclude our paschal feast with the Eucharist of our Risen Lord, welcoming Him with thanks into our hearts and lives. Through prayer we have entered into the mystery of the Cross and tomb, and have discovered there Jesus, our Risen Savior.

6.   Lenten Forms Change; Human Nature Doesn't

"Lent isn't what it used to be." How often do contemporary Catholics hear that during this holy season?

Most of us who are 40 or older have bittersweet memories of Lent in the pre-conciliar Church, some feeling that the discipline was too harsh, others missing it deeply. We once observed Lent not just as an intellectual exercise, but in ways that affected our bodily senses: ashes, fasts, Stations of the Cross, purple vestments, no flowers. All of these signs created a Lenten environment that one experienced as a different and special time to do penance for one's sins, to atone for temporal punishment, to get ready for Easter.

In order to comprehend the Church's present understanding of Lent, it is necessary to go back to the beginnings of Lent in the early Church. This should not surprise us since the general thrust of Vatican II has been to uncover the richness and vibrancy of earlier ages to help the faith of the people of God today shine in traditional ways of worship.

A good guide for this historical investigation is my old liturgy professor at San Anselmo in Rome, Father Adrian Nocent, OSB. His four-volume work, *The Liturgical Year*, is excellent.

In examining the ancient tradition, we find that the first thrust of Lent was that of preparing catechumens for Baptism. In the very early Church, Lent was the time when those who were undergoing instruction in the faith completed their final instructions. They were prayed over by the bishop for strength and courage in their struggle with the Evil One. The whole Christian community fasted and prayed for them that their reception of Baptism, Confirmation, and the Eucharist at the Easter Vigil might really be fruitful in their lives.

At first there were three weeks of fasting, but eventually it became a favorite time to do penance to recapture one's baptismal innocence if one had lost it by serious sin. The penitents went before the bishop dressed in sackcloth and had ashes sprinkled on their head as a sign of penance after having done very severe penances (by modern standards). They were received back int the Church by the bishop on Holy Thursday. Favorite penances recommended by all the Fathers of the Church were the ancient triad of fasting, prayer, and almsgiving found in Jewish tradition. Fasting, prayer, and almsgiving were considered interrelated by the Fathers of the Church. One's fast heightened prayer and enabled one to share food with the hungry, while prayer kept this whole enterprise from being an exercise of pride or egoism.

When the catechumenate disappeared (about the sixth century) and public penance was no longer practiced, then all Christians began to see Lent as a penitential time. By the 11th century all wanted to receive the ashes that had originally been restricted to public penitents: thus, our custom of Ash Wednesday.

Penitential practice flourished in the Middle Ages, but some liturgists and theologians feel that it was not sufficiently oriented toward the Paschal Mystery or focused enough on Baptism and the community of the baptized. I wonder if this is not a too negative judgment on their part.

It is true that the medieval Lenten observances were less Resurrectional and more Passion oriented, but they still attempted to redress the imbalance caused by sin and were deeply incarnated in the Catholic culture of Europe. Among these practices we find the traditional Stations of the Cross, brought from the Holy Land by Crusaders and pilgrims; the Lenten cloth, hung across the sanctuary of the church to symbolize the separation of the penitent congregation from the altar; and the cessation of all amusements during this season, with many of the people wearing black, the color of mourning. Many of these customs filtered down to our own time and were part of the total penitential environment of Lent that shaped our consciousness as Catholics during this sacred season.

It is good that the Church is trying to lead us to a deeper awareness of the community dimension of keeping Lent and help us to maturely and freely choose our practices of penance. But we might ask now whether the people of God are fasting more on their own, whether they are more conscious of their need for penance, whether they are more aware than ever of their communal need of redemption. I suspect we've all fallen into the easy way, and it is only by reexamining the theology of penance, reparation and restoration that we will again become convinced of the importance of our Lent and be challenged for our own good.

Since we are sinners, we must do penance, not only in the sense of *metanoia*, conversion of life, but also in terms of penitential practice. As to the first, clearly Jesus preached the good news of the nearness of the Kingdom on the basis of repentance coming first: "Repent and believe the good news."[263] Christ's Kingdom is an entirely new way of reality, grace, and life in Him that demands that the followers of Christ slough off the old existence and turn around (*metanoia*) to embrace this new mode of existence.

Acts of penitence, self-denial of satisfaction, are important to insure that the conversion isn't simply a passing emotion, but that it becomes a way of life, a discipline of the unruly body and a

---

[263] Mark1:15

recognition of the superiority of the demands of the Gospel over the world, the flesh and the devil. Christ himself set the example for his followers when he went into the desert to fast and pray for forty days.[264]

On this level, penance is important in terms of Christian self-control and discipline. If we must cater to the body in all its demands, we will not be able to deny it when the demands are sinful. Further, the person who fasts is often aided in concentration on his prayer.

Another reason for doing acts of penance is to make satisfaction or reparation for our past sins. Some feel that this is no longer a valid emphasis. Jesus died to reconcile us to the Father, and that reconciliation is a more positive concept than satisfaction, which is seen as "medieval." It is true that the introduction to the new rite of Penance or Reconciliation stresses that, as we can see in this moving passage:

In the Sacrament of Penance, the Father receives the repentant son who comes back to him, Christ places the lost sheep on his shoulders and brings it back to the sheepfold, and the Holy Spirit sanctifies this temple of God again or lives more fully within it. This is finally expressed in a renewed and more fervent sharing of the Lord's table, and there is great joy at the banquet of God's Church over the son who has returned from afar.[265]

Yet Paul VI in *Doctrina Indulgentiarum* does not hesitate to remind us of the importance of expiation in terms of rooting out the remnants of sin in our lives, strengthening the holiness of the moral order, and restoring the glory of God.[266] This can only be understood if we see how the effects of sin harm the individual, society and the Church, upsetting the universal order of God. When this truth is perceived, then the need for reparation is easily seen. The Church has always understood this, recognizing that the imbalance of evil must be corrected here or hereafter.

Sin harms the individual believer, and, if left unchecked, will flourish in such ways as to lead to sin in other areas of one's life. The Christian is not only restored sacramentally but also the actual penance assigned (or any voluntary act of penance) can be remedial.

---

[264] Mark 1:13

[265] *Doctrina Indulgentiarum*, n. 6.

[266] *Ibid.*

Indeed, the new Rite of Penance (or Reconciliation) recommends that "the satisfaction should be suited to the personal condition of each penitent so that each one may restore the order which he disturbed and through the corresponding remedy be cured of the sickness from which he suffered."

Sin also affects the community of the Lord. As good acts edify or build up the Body of Christ,[267] evil acts tear it down or at least diminish the fervor of ecclesial charity. Thus, the remedy for sin comes through the Church of Christ in her minister, the priest. Because this ecclesial dimension of the Sacrament of Penance was not always so clearly seen, we now have the new communal rite for reconciliation in what is commonly called a penance service. This is in fact a sacred sign showing us Christ's forgiveness in the midst of the community.

I was very moved to read in Bernhard Poschmann's great book on the Sacrament of Penance that the early Christians who prayed for the penitents being reconciled to the Church felt that their prayers and good works (as well as the penitent's own) were necessary as part of the expiation of sin before the reconciliation could take place. This solidarity also existed with regards to Baptism in the early Church.

The possibility of reparation of sin, then, goes beyond the individual level: in and through Jesus Christ, the only mediator,[268] we can do penance, make satisfaction or offer reparation for one another in the Mystical Body, thus "making up what is lacking in Christ's sufferings for the sake of His Body, the Church."[269]

Though one does not equate private revelation with the Bible, the Catholic Christian must ponder the fact that there has been a constancy in the call for penance for oneself and others in the apparition of the Sacred Heart to St. Margaret Mary, and echoed by Our Lady at Lourdes and Fatima. The message is not only for personal conversion but also for penance for others to bring about *metanoia* for them, a tradition constant in the Church from St. Paul to Fatima. Now it is graphically carried out in the *palanca*, or penance, of the *Cursillo* movement when people pray for those on retreat so that they will experience new life as the fruit of conversion.

---

[267] cf. Eph. 4: 12-14
[268] cf. 1 Tim. 2:5
[269] Col. 1:24

It is clear that we cannot go back to the Lents of old that many may be nostalgic for. It is equally clear that we cannot ignore the deep need for penance in the post-conciliar Church. Our forms may change, but human nature doesn't, and our nature still needs the discipline, the uplifting, the change that appropriate penitential practice affords. If our Lents, our fasts and our penances were too harsh or too individualistic in the old Church, let us re-examine them now to see how they can be reclaimed. Let us not allow everyone but Catholics to fast and do penance for various non-religious reasons. Considering how respected the Church once was for its penitential life, that would be the greatest irony of all.

7. The Cross: Symbol of Suffering and Joy

Nothing so dramatically symbolizes the contrast between the Church before Vatican II and after than the way Catholics used to observe Lent. Lenten observance, with its self-imposed sacrifices, fasting, Stations of the Cross and daily attendance at Mass, showed that Catholics were serious about their religion, atoning for their sins, and that they identified with their Savior, Jesus Christ, and His Cross. Vatican II ushered in a paschal era, an Easter era with joyous banners and images of the Risen Lord decorating our sanctuaries, while we were exhorted to remember St. Augustine's statement that "we are Easter people, and Alleluia is our song." We found that the Cross of the Lord and His suffering were stressed less and less.

Some rejoiced in this swing from what they considered a too lugubrious spirituality of suffering and spiritual victimhood to a new, more adult spirituality of risen life in the Resurrection of Jesus.

My contention is that it is not a question of one or the other. Both Lent *and* Easter, the Cross *and* the Resurrection brings us into true, balanced, adult Catholic spirituality.

The Cross is a powerful symbol of the suffering of Christ, His sacrificial love for us and of our suffering and self-denial as well – "If any man would come after me, let him deny himself and take up his cross and follow me."[270] Suffering is a fact of life in our fallen state.

Pope John Paul II, in his masterful apostolic letter on the *Christian Meaning of Human Suffering* (*Salvifici Doloris*), does not spare us when it

---

[270] Mk 8:34

comes to dealing with it. He discusses the tragedy of collective suffering in this century: two world wars and the nuclear threat that hangs over our civilization, terming them "an incomparable accumulation of suffering." Dr. Peter Kreeft, in his excellent little book *Making Sense Out of Suffering,*[271] echoes the Pope and shows that the great problem of suffering is not to be solved with pat answers.

In Kreeft's work, he questions every aspect of human suffering and grapples with the in-depth solutions of Aristotle, Plato, the prophets, the saints and even Rabbi Kushner of *When Bad Things Happen to Good People* fame (although Kreeft points out that Kushner offers no solution and only compounds the problem).

Both Kreeft and the Pope show how the Book of Job deals with the suffering of the innocent in a way that sees Jesus as prefigured in Job's innocent suffering. For Pope John Paul II, Christ strikes at the root of suffering and death in His taking on both in the Cross. Our God does not stand distantly aloof from the work of evil, pain, suffering and death, but enters into this feared reality and conquers it. Our God psychologically endured abandonment and terrible physical agony in the human nature of His Son, and in that nature died, but rose again from the dead by the hand of the Father.

The Cross, which is the instrument of execution, then becomes the Tree of Victory on which the new Adam gives birth to the Church, while our Lady, the new Eve, stands below in intercession.[272] Here is the triumph of the Lord, the triumph of the Cross and our triumph if we will identify with the mystery and let it mold us.

The Cross does not take away all our sufferings but gives meaning and transcendence to them as Christ allows us to participate in His sufferings which continue in us, His Body, the Church, as both St. Paul[273] and Pope John Paul II remind us. Thus, the Cross is at the center of the universe in its message of our God entering our real and difficult world of suffering. Yet it is also the Cross of power of the Risen Jesus Christ. From this triumphant Cross, flows not only meaning, but also healing – sacramental and penitential. This last we receive through our acts of penance: fasting, almsgiving, praying, Mass-going, etc. These sacrifices – self-imposed suffering in some

---

[271] Kreeft, Peter, *Making Sense Out of Suffering,* (Ann Arbor, Mich., Servant Books, 1986).
[272] cf. Jn 19:25
[273] cf. Col 1:24

instances – help to restore the image of God in us, that image which had been hurt by sin.

Allowing ourselves to be crucified with Christ to the Cross sets free the power of the Cross to change our suffering into the glory of the Risen Jesus. Painful as suffering or penance may be, they are medicinal and unleash the grace that heals us at the root of our being.

The Catholic, then, needs both Lent *and* Easter, penance *and* rejoicing, fasting *and* feasting, for one goes before the other and prepares the way for it. At the center, in starkness and power alike, stands the Cross of Jesus – the sign of contradiction – representing both suffering and triumph. Perhaps this is the reason why the Extraordinary Synod of Bishops in 1985 reminded us that "God wishes to teach us more deeply the value, the importance and centrality of the Cross of Christ."

RENEWAL OF TRUTH, BEAUTY, AND GOODNESS

1. Fra Angelico: The Angelic Painter

Recently Pope John Paul II by means of a *motu proprio* confirmed the piety of the faithful by declaring the 14th century painter Fra Angelico officially beatified. Since Fra Angelico died on February 18, 1455, that day was set by the Pope as his feast day within the Dominican order.

Born Guido da Vicchio near Florence in 1386, as a youth he studied painting under several Florentine masters. At a young age, he and his brother entered the Dominican priory at Fiesole, a lovely little town overlooking the city of Florence.

Here, as Fra Giovanni degli Angeli, he was formed in Dominican life; his ideas were molded by the order's reform party of St. Antoninus, St. Catherine of Siena and her confessor, Blessed Raymond of Capua.

At first both he and his artistic brother illuminated manuscripts, choir books and the like. He later did altar pieces and his "Madonna of the Linen Guild" for the linen merchants of Florence won him renown in 1433. This triptych, like others that were to follow, was a delicate handling of Our Lady and the Christ Child framed by angels, all the figures richly clothed in the blues, reds and golds that Angelico loved.

His style has been variously described as late Gothic, early Renaissance or a transition from one style to the other. He painted many scenes from the Scriptures, set in gardens where the flowers of springtime suggest the freshness of grace, others against the medieval red gold of eternity, or the brilliant blue of the Tuscan sky, which we see in his "Coronation of the Virgin."

St. Antoninus said of him, "No one could paint like that without having first been to heaven." It was St. Antoninus who, as the prior of the newly constructed priory of San Marco, invited Angelico to Florence to decorate the religious house, cloister, chapter room, and even the cells of the individual friars with scenes from the life of Christ.

Here in San Marco, with its plain white walls and graceful early Renaissance arches upheld by slender columns, one appreciates the genius of our friar painter. As one quietly walks from cell to cell, from scene to scene depicting the Annunciation, Birth, Suffering, Passion, Death, Resurrection, Ascension of Christ and the Coronation of Mary, one senses that these delicate frescoes take one beyond each individual room into the event of the mystery itself.

Not only did Blessed Angelico portray the particular scene of the life of Christ, but he usually placed St. Dominic there as well. St. Dominic is usually a little distanced and in one of the nine postures in which he habitually prayed, contemplative in the presence of the very mystery of Christ's life. Time is telescoped: the historical event of Christ's life is made present to Dominic in his time, and both are rendered present to the friar occupant of the cell. Each arched cell becomes a little cosmos where time and eternity, heaven and the world meet. It is the genius of Angelico that he created such an atmosphere for his brethren.

So broad the scheme, so varied his landscapes and figure groupings, so fine his craftmanship, that many feel San Marco represents Angelico's major achievement in art.

At the apex of his career, Fra Angelico was summoned to Rome by Pope Eugenius IV to paint in the Vatican. Some of his paintings can still be seen there.

He lived in the Dominican Priory of Santa Maria Sopra Minerva, and there he died and was buried. The name Angelico was given to him after his death by the faithful, so convinced were they of his angelic purity. But his name also reflects the soaring and heavenly quality of his art. It emanates spirituality not by clever and dramatic conceits, but by the icon-like quality of his depiction of Christ, His

Mother and the Saints.

How much our bare, ruined churches and pale, imageless sanctuaries need such holy images today. Perhaps this is why John Paul has given us a heavenly patron of the arts in this humble but talented Dominican priest-artist.

2. St. Dominic: Contemplating a Saint

Imagine a society obsessed by sex but opposed to marriage, a culture against bringing new life into the world and not afraid of putting people out of their misery by helping them to end their lives, a civilization that hated family and the Church.

I think most of our readers would think I was describing our own secular society, but actually these are the conditions that existed in southern France when Dominic de Guzman, a canon of the Cathedral of Osma, was traveling through that territory with his bishop on a diplomatic mission. What Dominic saw was the fruits of the Albigensian or Catharist heresy: Eastern denial of goodness of material creation, the flesh, sex and marriage.

According to this heresy the perfect or holy ones were to abstain from food and sex as much as possible, but ordinary people didn't have to as long as they didn't marry or were able to avoid having children. Thus, this curiously modern sounding heresy attacked the very heart of the family and society, producing an atmosphere so pessimistic that death by starving or smothering was thought to be the *summum bonum* for the dedicated, releasing them from this world.

Dominic's first encounter with this heresy was not his last: He eventually returned to preach the truth of Christianity to the heretics. He was not the first. The pope had sent Cistercians to try to lead the people back to the Church, but with their beautiful mounts and vast retinues they seemed much more worldly than the abstemious holy ones of the heretics and so were unsuccessful. St. Dominic, whose earlier pious life had trained him well for such a challenge, lived simply, prayed, fasted and studied the Word of God. From this rich background he joyfully preached the Catholic faith in all its fullness.

He worked alone for several years without much to show by way of results, making his base of operations the picturesque little town of Fanjeaux. In desperate straits one night he prayed for help, pouring out his soul to his Lady, the Holy Virgin Mother of God.

Suddenly he saw a great flash of light over the place where he was later to found a convent for the first women converts from heresy.

It is at this time that tradition assigns the rosary as a gift from the Blessed Virgin. Paternoster beads as substitutes for the Psalter were known before, but this new form of prayer and preaching which had people fingering very real beads while meditating on the saving events of the Life, Death and Resurrection of the Word made Flesh proved an antidote to the super spiritual heresy of the time. Dominic, son of a Spanish knight, preached the great mysteries of faith with renewed fervor and joy and spread the use of the rosary.

Ultimately other apostolic men gathered around Dominic and joined in his preaching work. St. Dominic, a well-rounded man with a university education, lost no time in laying down simple legislation for this apostolic lifestyle and winning papal approval in 1216. His new band of preachers would be evangelical, live together simply and poorly, constantly study the Word of God, pray contemplatively and from this rich background preach the Gospel.

This structure grew from Dominic's own contemplative vocation as a Canon of the Cathedral of Osma. He chose to give his new community a monastic base, not like the large Benedictine abbeys in the countryside, but like the canonical urban monasticism with which he was familiar.

Blessed Humbert, fifth Master of the Order, tells us that Dominic took "whatever was difficult, beautiful and balanced" from the customs of the Cistercians and Norbertines. He did not jettison choir as St. Ignatius Loyola was later to do, for he loved the communal celebration of the Liturgy of the Hours, always attending it with the community while at home. On the road he celebrated Mass daily – a High Mass if he could – and if he heard the bells from a nearby monastery calling the monks to prayer, he would join that group in praying the Hours.

Thus St. Dominic gave his followers a mode of life that was a balance of elements normally in tension with one another – apostolic preaching and the monastic choir, intense study and contemplative meditation, the priory cloister and the highways of active evangelism. This balance reflected Dominic himself, whose own contraries complemented one another, rendering his rich personality responsive to the needs of the Church.

The life of study and liturgical prayer as a background for

forthrightly evangelical and ecclesial preaching begun by Dominic and lived by his followers has enriched the Church for almost 800 years. His feast day is August 8th.

3. St. Martin de Porres: The Web of Grace and Charity

A friend of mine once coined the phrase "web of grace" to refer to the way the Lord brings together like-minded souls to support one another in their common Christian vocation and help them to dare great things for the Kingdom. St. Martin de Porres was caught in such a web with his Dominican friends in Lima, when the "new world" was first open to Christian and Catholic influence.

Martin was a good friend of the Dominican brother, St. John Macias, from the neighboring priory of St. Mary Magdalene in the same city. They were Dominican brothers and spiritual friends, though Martin was black, and John was a Spaniard. They were both baptized by a saint, St. Turibius, Archbishop of Lima, and both were friends with the Dominican Tertiary, St. Rose. Both loved animals, did severe penances, and served the poor.

On Sundays, each Dominican brother would leave his prior to meet the other and they would take a walk to the country. Their destination was an old barn where they prayed and encouraged one another in holy conversation. They were true friends, caught in the divine web of charity, calling one another on to sanctity. They both died at sixty years of age and were both beautified in 1837, although Martin was canonized in 1962 by Pope John XXIII and John later in 1975 by Pope Paul VI.

Martin was born in 1579 to a Spanish father and a black mother from Panama. His father, Don Juan, a knight, never bothered to marry Martin's mother, Ana, and indeed left her to raise Martin and his sister, Juana, as well as she could by herself. Finally, his conscience getting the best of him, Don Juan acknowledged his children as his own when Martin was eight and took him and his sister to Santiago. Later, when he had to return to Panama, he dropped Martin off with Ana, and Juana he deposited with his brother in Santiago.

Ana had Martin trained as a barber, which in those days meant practicing primitive surgery and dentistry. As he worked in hospitals and private homes, he added to his knowledge the medicinal properties of herbs. In his work, God often graced his practice of *natural* healing with the divine *gift* of healing, for so open to the Lord was this intense young mulatto.

Martin was drawn to the Dominican Church of the Holy Rosary, where he often visited the Blessed Sacrament. His own prayer life was beginning to image the founder of the Dominicans, though whether this was conscious or not we don't know. We know from his landlady, who spied on him, that like St. Dominic, he spent whole nights in prayer weeping and sighing as the holy founder did before him. So drawn was he to the Dominican spirit that at the age of fifteen he asked to be a Tertiary at the Church of the Holy Rosary, and nine years later, he made solemn vows there as a co-operator brother of the Order.

The Dominican friars worked their young charge as barber, infirmarian, and keeper of the common wardrobe. Despite his many duties, St. Martin always had time for the ill, whom he would check on frequently at their bedsides. He cured many, his natural healing knowledge augmented by the gift of healing as can be seen in this example: he came upon a black man with festering sores, cleansed them, sprinkled them with powdered rosemary and made the Sign of the Cross over the man, and all was healed. He loved the novices of the Order and often cured them, especially one severe case from a neighboring priory who had cut his fingers and had a severe infection as a result.

Martin's charity didn't stop with his own Order or with the ill, but especially extended to the poor. He never set out on an errand with empty hands. His constant "companion" was his basket filled with medicine, bread, and fruit for the poor. He often knew their needs by divine inspiration as with the soldiers five miles away whom he visited every day with provisions.

Some of the conquistadores on their death beds gave him money for feeding the poor. He used $1,000.00 dollars a week to feed over 160 people. He organized others in a web of charity in caring for the ill and poor and burying the dead. With their money, he bought a tract of land and on it planted fruit trees so the poor could eat. He brought so many beggars to the priory that the priory bade him stop. His love of the poor even extended to God's creatures of the animal kingdom. He raised a dog from the dead, pacified a wild bull with a gesture, convinced cats and dogs to eat from the same dish, and even struck a charming bargain with the mice of the priory that he would feed them if they left the priory pantry alone.

Martin's love of the poor and his concern that justice and charity be done them flowed directly from his intense life of prayer and penance. How refreshing an example for us today when so frequently the people emphasizing prayer and liturgy are in one camp and those crying social justice in another. Martin's spirituality was thoroughly in line with the Gospel in that he didn't see any contradiction in prayer leading to concern for one's brothers and sisters; and love and concern for them leading one back to prayer. In fact, he spent nights in prayer for others, a custom begun as a young man, and to that he added severe penance. Three times a night he would scourge himself with the discipline before the crucifix for sinners, as did Dominic, and for the souls in purgatory. He fasted on bread and water during Lent, never ate meat, and on feasts would partake of vegetables. An extremely observant friar, nothing was found in St. Martin's room but a pallet and the crucifix, an image of Our Lady and St. Dominic. These few things the Constitutions of the Order allowed. His habit was old and tattered. If given new clothes, he gave them to the poor and took their rags for himself. A true Dominican, he loved Our Lady and her rosary, and loved to decorate her altars.

St. Martin's intense prayer life spun a web of charity for others, his brethren and friends, sinners, the poor, and all in any need. Wisdom was often given him in prayer and in giving advice to his brethren, especially the younger ones, he would often quote St. Thomas – though he was unable to read and his references to the *Summa* were always correct! His gifts of healing, prophecy and bilocation were used for the comfort or edification of others. He was seen on God's business in Mexico, Algeria, Africa, France, the Philippines and China! The same grace and charity poured out by God into Martin's heart, which caused him to respond to God in prayer, to his friends in spiritual friendship, to his poor in generosity and service was indeed a web binding him to God and his brothers and sisters. May we be caught in such a web!

4. Theology and Christian Humanism

In this discussion of Christian Humanism, I would like to look back beyond the fifteenth and sixteenth centuries, both eschewing the new learning that emerged at that time emphasizing the ancient pagan classics, and even their use, in the hands of their Christian champions, Erasmus, Colet, and St. Thomas More whom we associate with Christian Humanism. I would like us to journey back to the Carolingian Renaissance of the ninth century to see the role of liberal arts in early medieval education, in terms of *Trivium* and the *Quadrivium*. The former consisted of grammar, rhetoric, and logic and was the basis of a young scholar's beginning education before advancing to the *Quadrivium* in the study of music, arithmetic, geometry, and astronomy. These seven liberal arts had to be mastered before one could go on to higher university study.

Grammar was, of course, Latin grammar, but in practice it meant more than grammatical rules learned, but a knowledge of pre-Christian classics of Latin antiquity and this was more widespread than we have been led to believe. Indeed, the Catholic historian Carlton Hayes detects a Humanist spirit in the ninth century in his famous history text.[274] The young scholars being formed in the *Trivium* also were expected to express ideas clearly and in their classes in rhetoric, they imitated what models they had of ancient classical oratory.

To speak well, of course, one must think well, that is, clearly, and to reason correctly. And so, they were taught to do this by study of Aristotle's *Organon*, which had been translated into Latin by Boethius in the fifth century. Emphasis on philosophy would grow out of this interest in logic, and would be heightened by the translation of Aristotle's other works into Latin by 1275. This would give rise to scholasticism aided and abetted by saints Albertus Magnus and Thomas Aquinas, not to mention St. Bonaventure and the Blessed if subtle Duns Scotus. Before the rise of scholasticism, however, Carleton Hayes is of the opinion that if by Christian Humanism is meant a love of literature and life which gives emphasis to both the natural and supernatural, then in the twelfth century we have a full-blown Christian Humanism.

The *Quadrivium* of what we would call the sciences was not left out of this picture. As the universities arose from cathedral schools, each had its specialty and it was clear in the scientific and mathematical

---

[274] Hayes, Baldwin & Cole, *History of Europe*

studies at medieval Oxford, that Christian scholars there had learned much from the Moslems in math, geography, chemistry, and astronomy, although in the latter were often found traces of alchemy and astrology. Padua was noted for medicine and though its art was based on Galen and Hippocrates, it too showed openness to Arabic contributions, even to the dissections of human corpses. Bologna was famous for law and offered a doctorate in both civil and canon law; while Paris, of course, was the university specializing in theology. Here the first *studium generale* grew on the left bank, an overflow from the cathedral school of Notre Dame, and came to be called the Latin Quarter because all the students spoke the universal university language there. Before students could study theology, or major in other higher studies, they had to have this base of arts and sciences – the *Trivium* and the *Quadrivium*.

How did theology regard the sciences and humanities during this time? It will surprise no one if I propose that we look to the Angelic Doctor to find our cue. In the very first question of the *Summa*, St. Thomas treats the nature of sacred doctrine, as he calls theology: "Since sacred science is learned through revelation and therefore proceeds from principles of a higher science, i.e. the science of God and the Blessed, it is nobler than its handmaidens which derive their certitude from reason, and therefore can err, even philosophy. However, since the certitude of theology comes from God's knowledge which cannot err, and since its end is eternal bliss, while other sciences have lesser ends, good in themselves, theology is seen as the queen of the sciences. Finally, since wisdom sees all in ultimate causes, and theology sees all in God, as cause of all, it is the highest wisdom."[275]

If we were to apply this medieval understanding of the *Trivium* and *Quadrivium* and St. Thomas's understanding to modern Western education in a free and pluralistic society while pleading Christian Humanism, it might sound like we were building a seminary curriculum with tight niches for the arts and sciences with theology dominating and keeping each inferior branch of knowledge in tight control.

I do not believe that was the medieval spirit, for that of St. Thomas was architectonic, an ordering of truths in the light of truth,

---

[275] S.T., I, Q1

itself; nor do I see evidence of narrowness in Joh Paul II's *Ex Corde Ecclesiae* in which he promotes "a kind of universal humanism" in which "a Catholic university is completely dedicated to the research of all aspects of truth in connection with their essential connection with the Supreme Truth which is God."[276] Each science and art have its approach in which "scholars scrutinize reality with the methods proper to each academic discipline and so contribute to the treasury of human knowledge."[277] So we are not advocating, nor is the Pope, a kind of theological imperialism over the other arts and sciences, rather a working "towards a higher synthesis of knowledge, in which alone lies the possibility of satisfying that thirst for truth which is profoundly inscribed on the heart of the human person."[278]

In such a context "scholars will be engaged in a constant effort to determine the relative place and meaning of…the various disciplines within the context of the human person."[279] This we must strive to do as scholars, it seems to me, and so form our students that they have a unified vision of reality which respects the integrity of the wisdom offered by all the arts and sciences, and sees them as related to the highest wisdom and meaning, "Christ, the Logos, as the center of creation and of human history."[280]

The Pope sees the authentically Catholic university as promoting the "dialogue between faith and reason so that it can be seen more profoundly how faith and reason bear harmonious witness to the unity of all truth."[281] He sees theology, especially, as enabling both the synthesis of knowledge to take place and providing the wisdom which mediates between the human and the divine, both faith and reason, and I see this as one wholistic medieval vision endorsed by Aquinas and echoed by John Paul II. If we have such a vision of the utility of the sciences, the human wisdom of the arts and philosophy which so ennoble human thought and work; and if we have the openness to the Divine Mystery which divinizes the human heart, and allow it to permeate all other knowledge; and if we mirror this holistic vision of the human person, not so much as individuals, but

---

[276] *Ex Corde Ecclesiae,* n. 4.

[277] *Ibid.,* n. 15.

[278] *Ibid.,* n. 16.

[279] *Ibid.*

[280] *Ex Corde Ecclesiae,* n. 16.

[281] *Ibid.,* n. 17.

as an academic community, we will pass on to our students a vision that is truly humane, thoroughly Christian, and Catholic with both a small and a capital "C."

5.   Will the Real St. Thomas Please Stand Up?

I understand what Abbot David Geraets was trying to do in his recent response to Fr. Mitch Pacwa's article on the enneagram,[282] but I am not sure I agree with him. I understand his using the example of St. Thomas Aquinas and his life and teachings to show that facts may be slanted in such wise as to give the wrong impression, and so he overstated certain facts about Aquinas to make his point. I am afraid, however, that Abbot David's use of historical fact is misleading and not always accurate despite his good intentions.

He calls St. Thomas neurotic because he was afraid of lightning. It is true he was afraid of lightning and even developed an acrostic on the words, *Crux mihi Salus*, "The Cross is my Salvation," for protection against lightning. When I was a child, we lit a blessed candle for protection in a thunderstorm, a reasonable thing to do, it seems to me. Martin Luther sat under a tree in a lightning storm that struck near him and vowed to St. Anne he would enter religious life, which put him in a situation which did not help his scrupulous nature. Was he neurotic because he feared lightning? Am I?

St. Thomas was a big man physically, and Fr. James Weisheipl in his definitive biography says he was tall and somewhat corpulent. Does that mean he was "so lacking in self-control he was obese" as Abbot Geraets asserts? He seems to be influenced by the popular legend that Aquinas was so fat that they had to cut a hole in the refectory table at his place to allow him to sit at the meal, but that allegation is without historical evidence.

It is true that St. Thomas did reform Catholic theology by being open to the newly emerging "Pagan" Aristotle, as Augustine had used the "Pagan" Plato and the Neo Platonic School before him. Following the lead of St. Albert the Great, he purged it of its acquired Muslim errors and used its insights because they were metaphysically *true*, which was easy to do because of Aristotle's basic realism. One might remark that this made it easier to discern the truth than today

---

[282] cf. N.C., July/August 1991

with certain modern systems of thought such as Marxism, Jungian psychology, or secular humanism when similar attempts are made. The "Pagan" philosophy he adapted had more innate truth to mine for St. Thomas, who took truth wherever he found it.

It is true that some of St. Thomas's teachings were condemned along with many that the theologians of the University of Paris submitted to the Archbishop, who in turn submitted them to the Pope. They were few, mixed in with the many Muslim interpretations of Aristotle, and Aquinas was later exonerated, but we have no record of a book burning as Abbot David suggests.

Aquinas is charged by Abbot David as believing in astrology. In the *Summa*, his most famous theological work[283] St. Thomas asks whether our wills are moved by heavenly bodies (stars and planets), and he answers that they can have no direct influence on our wills since we are free. He admits they might have an influence on our bodies and emotions, as we notice at the time of the full moon which can stir our passions, but "the wise man governs the stars," that is, we need not be ruled by our emotions but rule them instead. It is difficult to call this balanced approach of Aquinas believing in astrology as Abbot Geraets does.

St. Thomas followed the Aristotelian biology of his day and thought that *materially* women were misbegotten males. However, it is not true as Abbot David asserts that he thought them inferior *as persons*. In his *Summa Contra Gentiles*,[284] he proves polygamy is immoral because it reduces women to slaves, which Aquinas says is wrong because a woman is equal to a man on the level of soul. His biology was wrong, not his theology!

Did St. Thomas have good things to say about prostitution as our Abbot suggests? Or does he simply tolerate it as did St. Augustine in his day to control it and restrict this vice to which fallen human nature is prone and thereby try to protect home and family in other areas of the city?

It is true that St. Thomas did not ascribe to the Immaculate Conception in his *Summa*[285] as our Benedictine Abbot points out. He saw such a privilege as putting Our Lady outside the human race redeemed by Christ. The subtle doctor, Duns Scotus, later saw her

---

[283] cf. I-II, Q9, Art.5
[284] Bk.4
[285] cf I-II, Q9

immaculately conceived through Christic grace received in anticipation of whom she was to bear and so by that grace which redeems us, protected her from the slightest taint of our fallen human nature while still receiving our human nature. Aquinas followed most of the theologians of his time who held for the sanctification of Our Lady in St. Anne's womb and that she was quite sinless. However, in his commentary on the Hail Mary, from Lenten sermons preached to the people of Naples, he seems to have held the Immaculate Conception, perhaps moved more by the devotion of the people than his own strict reasoning.

At the end of his life, St. Thomas did see everything he'd written as so much straw and would write no more despite the promptings of his friend and secretary, Reginald. It is commonly thought that because of a profound mystical experience that Aquinas had while celebrating Mass on the Feast of St. Nicholas, that what he had written seemed as straw in comparison to the Divine reality he'd experienced. Perhaps, but precious straw to us.

I do not really wish to enter the substance of the discussion between Abbot David and Father Mitch on the enneagram but only add this postscript. Suffice it to say that the state of the question is, can this tool be removed from its origins and background as Abbot Geraets asserts? Certainly St. Thomas took truth wherever he found it. He used the ancient understanding of the four humors of the body to discuss how we are influenced by our temperament and those insights are valid although the underlying biological theory is not. Is Fr. Mitch correct in saying that the enneagram is often taught even in Catholic circles with a lot of spiritualist and new age trappings which are dangerous to the faith? Can one become so dependent on the type given one's personality or others, that grace and the power of the Spirit are discounted? These weighty questions make me very cautious in endorsing the enneagram.

6. The Beauty of Holiness? (Liturgical Music Today)

As a religious priest, on Sunday mornings I am often sent out to help neighboring parishes by celebrating Mass for the over-worked pastor. Although the people and their pastor are usually kind and hospitable, the liturgy is frequently depressing. Often the church has been poorly remodeled for the current liturgy. The readings are badly proclaimed (sometimes by children who can barely read), but the overwhelming memory that one carries away is of the dreadful music, the listless singing and bad selection of hymns. Surely low Mass would be better than this – at least it would not aesthetically offend the ears. What's wrong? Why have we come to this impasse? Why isn't the present approach working? I tackle this question as one who is trained in liturgy, not in music, which I dearly love, recognizing that there are wonderful exceptions to the dreary picture I paint, but I fear they are few and far between in the United States.

For years I have been teaching liturgy, and having scanned the document *Musicam Sacram*, issued by Congregation of Rites in 1967, I had assumed rather blithely that *Music in Catholic Worship*, issued by American Bishop's Committee on the Liturgy in 1972, was substantially the same in its approach. Recently, having studied both documents, I realize how wrong I was. It is true that there are similarities, but the differences in the two documents far outweigh them.

In the Bishops' statement, there is really no theology of sacred music explicated and the term seems not to be used. "Sacred song" is referred to, but not "sacred music," which term carries the stamp of Pius X's insistence that it be characterized by universality, holiness and artistry. *Mucicam Sacram* actually defines the term as "that which (is) created for the celebration of divine worship and is endowed with certain holy sincerity of form."[286] The Bishops' document sees music as one of the sacred signs that should let their "full meaning and impact shine forth in clear and compelling fashion...must be humanly attractive... meaningful and appealing to the body of worshippers."[287] It does say that this music should assist the assembled believers to express and share the gift of faith that is within them and to nourish and strengthen their interior commitment of faith,[288] but nowhere do we find the sublime task of sacred music described as in the Roman document:

Liturgical worship is given a more noble form when it is celebrated in song...Indeed through this form, prayer is expressed in a more attractive way, the mystery of the liturgy, with its hierarchical and community nature, is more openly shown, the unity of hearts is

---

[286] *Mucicam Sacram*, n.4a.
[287] *Mucicam Sacram*, n. 7.
[288] *Ibid.*, n. 23.

more profoundly achieved by the union of voices, minds are more easily raised to heavenly things by the beauty of sacred rites and the whole celebration more clearly prefigures that heavenly liturgy which is enacted in the holy city of Jerusalem."[289]

It is this transcendent dimension which gives sacred music its exalted, though ministerial, role. Since we find it lacking in the American document, it does not surprise us that we find the same lack in practice on the parochial level.

It is not only the failure to provide a liturgical, theological underpinning that flaws the American document, but also its rigidity and lack of flexibility in pastoral application. Whereas *Musicam Sacram* upholds the possibility of low Mass (read) *Missa Cantata* (with many musical possibilities) and Solemn Mass, the American document sees these distinctions as outdated, which is less serious than its cavalier jettisoning of the distinction between the ordinary and proper of the Mass. Pastorally, the people can be taught to sing a simple ordinary, while the proper can be easily done by the choir. The disregard for this distinction has been disastrous in our recent history. *Music in Catholic Worship* also banishes to the concert hall the classical *Missa Romana* with its *Kyrie, Gloria, Credo, Santus-Benedictus,* and *Agnus Dei,* while admitting that *parts* of these composed Masses might be used. *Musicam Sacram* is gentler, stating that these Masses may yet be sung by the choir provided the people are not completely excluded from the singing. Indeed, in Germany and Austria, when the great Hayden and Mozart Masses are performed, the people chime in lustily during the vernacular hymns at other parts of the Mass. I don't wish to prolong this criticism any further but reiterate that the Roman document is truly far more pastoral and flexible in its approach.

From what has been said, could this document's teaching be of help in the parish settings described above? First, it is often said that people vote with their feet, and I think this is true of the followers of Archbishop Lefebvre with their little churches springing up all over and the large numbers who attend Tridentine Mass when it is celebrated with due authorization under the indult of *Ecclesia Dei.* I deplore, of course, Catholics going into schism although I think I understand what may have driven them to that point. I am delighted

---

[289] *Ibid.,* n. 5.

to see the Tridentine Mass offered more freely so that real pastoral needs might be addressed, but I do not feel that this is the final answer for the future. If the current liturgy outlined in the Missal of Paul VI were celebrated with the richness of the musical tradition of the Church, we might have quite a different story to tell. People also vote with their mouths. If, after almost twenty years, many American Catholics won't sing at Mass, including many of the young, are they telling us something?

The thrust of this article is not directed at those places where people are singing well. Sometimes, one could broaden and expand their repertoire and wean people away from the omnipresent St. Louis Jesuits. It was my good fortune to teach at the Franciscan University of Steubenville, where most of the students and staff are charismatics who love to sing. Since the chaplaincy asked my liturgical advice, we left well enough alone in general, but added to the lively charismatic standards, more traditional Catholic hymns that the students were actually requesting. We encouraged all to learn some simple Latin chants, the *schola* to do more complex and meditative chant and a little polyphony.

Choirs need to be encouraged in their task and re-founded where a misunderstanding of Vatican II brought about their untimely demise. The Council in its *Constitution on the Liturgy* sees an important role for choirs, whether large or small. They are not only to lead the people but preserve the great treasury of sacred music with great care.[290] *Musicam Sacram* especially speaks of large choirs doing this in cathedrals, basilicas, and monastic churches. It seems that while all sacred music should inspire the people, all need not be equally "pastoral" especially in larger city churches with mobile congregations. There it seems that classic Gregorian Masses or those of the great composers, can still be used with sufficient acclamations and hymns interspersed to insure popular participation. In fact, in our parish church in New Haven, Connecticut, it is precisely at those Masses where the choir sings a Gabrielli or Mozart Mass that the people nearly take off the roof in the singing of hymns at appropriate times.

However, there are places where hymn singing hasn't caught on at all. Is it because many of the hymns are Protestant? I rather like

---

[290] *Constitution on the Liturgy,* n. 114.

these hymns since I grew up singing them in public school, but are they the answer? First, it might be noted that whenever Catholic hymns like "Holy God, We Praise Thy Name" or "Immaculate Mary" are sung, the nave rings with sound. Further, the *Notre Dame Study of Catholic Life*[291] in its liturgical survey, found that the people respond in singing best with the organ to fill the church rather than a guitar.[292] They doubtless feel more confident of musical support.

Secondly, while recognizing the wonderful hymn tradition of Catholic Germany and of our Protestant brethren, one wonders how well in general that musical form accords with the Mass. Historically, hymns were sung at the Liturgy of the Hours and the entrance and communion processions had simple antiphonal responses for the people to sing in alternation with the *schola*. Ought we to use more of this tradition? Also, one might note that Protestant hymns were spread when the printing press newly invented made possible hymnals, as indeed newly printed Bibles made a *sola scriptura* approach to Christianity possible. The Protestant hymn (often based on a psalm) is a very wordy vehicle of praise. Is this what we need now, when our people are bombarded with cheap words in advertising, and an all vernacular liturgy with three Sunday readings and endless *ex tempore* homilizing nearly suffocates them? Is our medium too *hot*? Do we need more of the *cool* medium of Gregorian chant or chant-like music? Is that not more in our Catholic tradition?

The Notre Dame Study also found that the congregation does slightly better with repeated texts like the *Sanctus* than with hymns that are changed from week to week.[293] It seems to me that this is a good reason to teach the congregation one ordinary in English or Latin, a staple of its worship life. I have heard little altar boys unselfconsciously singing these unchangeable parts. In our parish at the five o'clock Sunday afternoon Mass, during which hardly anyone will sing the hymns which are played, there are many who join in the English ordinary. Aidan Kavanaugh used to say that priests and religious who were used to daily Mass needed much more variety than those who were Sunday Mass goers; for them one ordinary will do. If people won't sing hymns (e.g. the five o'clock Mass crowd – made up, I might add, of mostly young people), why not use

---

[291] *Notre Dame Study of Catholic Life*, (11. Of N.D. Press, 1984-88).

[292] *Ibid.*, p. 7.

[293] *Ibid.*

instrumental processionals and recessionals? *Musicam Sacram* has a whole section on sacred instrumental music and it recommends preludes, offertory and communion music as well as postludes. Might not such instrumental music give a more contemplative dimension to our often too verbose celebrations of the Mass?

I said at the beginning of this article that I wanted to tackle the question of what was wrong with liturgical music today, but in re-reading my article I find I have mostly asked questions. Still, that may not be a disservice if part of getting the right answer is asking the right questions. I hope my questions will stimulate discussion of this most important topic, even though there are many aspects of it I've left untouched. Yet, I suspect I've "stepped on enough toes" to elicit responses, both friendly and unsympathetic, but any reaction at all is welcome if it helps to get us out of our contemporary musical morass.

7. Will Beauty Look After Herself? (Church Art and Architecture)

The fine arts are rightly classed among the noblest activities of man's genius; this is especially true of religious art and of its highest manifestation, sacred art. Of their nature, the arts are directed toward expressing in some way the infinite beauty of God in works made by human hands. Their dedication to the increase of God's praise and of His glory is more complete, the more exclusively they are devoted to turning men's minds devoutly towards God.[294]

It may seem strange to those familiar with the "bare ruined choirs," which our churches have become in the aftermath of Vatican II, to see the council's words of praise for the fine arts placed within its treatment of sacred art and sacred furnishings, which the Church wants to "worthily and beautifully serve the dignity of worship."[295] This same section of the *Constitution on the Sacred Liturgy* makes it clear that while "the Church has not adopted any particular style of art as its own," she has inherited "a treasury of art which must be preserved with every care."[296] That this *magna carta* of the visual arts in the service of the liturgy has not caused a great flourishing of sacred

---

[294] *Sacrosanctum Concilium*, n. 122.
[295] *Ibid.*
[296] *Constitution on the Sacred Liturgy*, n. 123.

images, architecture, stained glass, murals, and the like, I think can be explained by certain principles embodied in the *Constitution* itself. Ordinaries are exhorted to encourage "noble beauty rather than sumptuous display,"[297] and while sacred images are encouraged, "their numbers should be moderate, and their relative positions should reflect right order."[298] While these two sensible *caveats* were welcomed by me as a young seminarian, when the *Constitution* was first promulgated in 1963, I have lived to see these ideas profoundly misinterpreted, perhaps even officially. Noble beauty or simplicity has simply become the Bauhaus look or LeCorbusier's poured concrete predicated on Louis Sullivan's dictum that form must follow function.

According to one theory, if this is done well, then "beauty will look after itself," as Eric Gill used to say. The splendor of the inner form will shine forth in honest making, the theory continues, but we can wonder if bare concrete walls simply do not manifest the cult of the crude rather than the inner splendor of the sacred. Such an approach is taken in the bishops' statement on art and environment and seems rather dated in our postmodern era. In this era when in painting, recognizable form is returning, and in architecture, Palladian arches are universal in current building design – just liberated from its Bauhaus prison by Philip Johnson's whimsical and courageous placement of a Chippendale top on the AT&T building in Manhattan.

Even though these principles seen in germ in *Sacrosanctum Concilium* have been carried to extremes in current church buildings, aided by "secular theology" and the fad of multi-purpose buildings replacing churches, I think a careful consideration of the whole of *Sacrosanctum Concilium* in tandem with the *General Instruction of the Roman Missal* [299] can help to correct the situation, especially if the problems in the document *Environment and Art*[300] be noted.

Let us state at the onset that building a new church for the current liturgy is quite a different challenge than remodeling an older edifice, but the same principles lie at the core. Frankly, I have seen so many wonderful old interiors of Irish Victorian and German neo-baroque

---

[297] *Ibid.*, n. 124.
[298] *Ibid.*, n. 125.
[299] Chapter V.
[300] NCCB, 1978.

churches gutted that I am more concerned with the latter than with the former, although I also think that the present situation, with the younger generation of clerics more open to the sacred, may help to balance the scales more on the side of the glory of God in the visual arts as well as in music.

Because the document *Environment and Art* focuses on hospitality, the human experience, the contemporaneity of art – all valid points – it tends to see the experience of the sacred (or of the mystery) in terms of a "simple and attractive beauty"[301] and the liturgy as demanding quality in artifacts, which comes when there is "love and care in the making of something, honesty and genuineness with any materials used, and the artist's special gifts in producing a harmonious whole, a well-crafted work."[302] The liturgy also demands that works of art bear "the weight of mystery, awe, reverence and wonder" and serve the liturgical action carried out in the assembly of worshippers.[303] While these guidelines are well intentioned, they clearly flow from the "form follows function" school of aesthetic and do not give us a clearly transcendent vision as the brief but pithy sentence in the opening paragraph of Chapter V of the *General Instruction of the Roman Missal* which states: "The buildings and requisites for worship as signs and symbols of heavenly things, should be truly worthy and beautiful."[304] I think it is the loss of the vision of the heavenly Jerusalem that has given us such lack-luster environments in which to pray and such dull service music to sing when we do so.

The *General Instruction of the Roman Missal* reminds us of the hierarchical nature of the liturgy and that the church building should reflect that nature in a unity of space with diversity of roles,[305] whereas the bishops' statement seems to be chiefly concerned with showing that different ministries do not imply "superiority" or "inferiority."[306] It is interesting to note the Roman document recommends some kind of emphasis on the sanctuary as special and different from the nave,[307] whereas the American document does not

---

[301] *Environment and Art,* n. 12.
[302] *Ibid.,* n. 20.
[303] *Ibid.,* n. 21.
[304] *General Instruction of the Roman Missal,* n. 253.
[305] *General Instruction of the Roman Missal,* n. 257.
[306] *Ibid.,* n. 37.

– an omission that reflects a less sacred view of the altar.

The altar itself is seen in the *General Instruction* as the table of the Lord and the place of sacrifice as well,[308] and ought to be free-standing so that "Mass can be said facing the people."[309] A fixed altar, made of stone, is recommended (especially the *mensa*), but moveable altars of other materials are permitted.[310] Relics may be enclosed in or under the base of the altar, though this tradition is no longer required, and the altar ought to be blessed.[311] From the care of this legislation one can see the dignity and specialness of the altar. The bishops' document calls the altar "the holy table," and sees it as the common table of the assembly, not making any sacrificial reference, though it does say it" should be the most beautifully designed and constructed table the community can provide."[312] It recommends a square or slightly rectangular shape since it is for the "community and the functioning of a single priest – not for concelebrants,"[313] but one can find no such bias against concelebration in the Roman document. It also presumes that candles and the cross will never be on the altar,[314] whereas the *General Instruction* allows this provided they do not block the view of the congregation.[315]

It is interesting to note that the altar is the first item treated in the Roman document, and the celebrant's chair is first in the American adaptation. Does this reversal hint at a different ecclesiology or liturgical theology? Both documents stress the chair as the symbol of presiding – presiding in charity would be the understanding of Saint Ignatius of Antioch of the role of the Bishop of Rome and so of all bishops and of all priests who act *in persona Christi* and show forth the ordered, hierarchical nature of the communal celebration of the liturgy. The Roman instruction warns against the appearance of a throne in the celebrant's chair,[316] and while this admonition is not

---

[307] *Ibid.,* n. 258.
[308] *Ibid.,* n. 259.
[309] *Ibid.,* n. 262.
[310] *Ibid.,* nn. 262, 263.
[311] *Ibid.,* nn. 265, 266.
[312] *Ibid.,* n. 71.
[313] *Ibid.,* n. 72.
[314] *Ibid.,* n. 71.
[315] *Ibid.,* n. 269.

mentioned in the American document, illustration #13 is a throne that would put Bernini's altar of the chair to shame! In a wonderful old German Victorian-gothic church in Minnesota the carved reredos has been preserved by Frank Kacmarcik, but rather than being a backdrop for the altar facing the people as one might expect, it has instead become an extension of the chair, towering to the heavens, while the altar is shunted to the side to share equal honors with the ambo or lectern. While it may be true, as *Environment and Art* alleges, that the altar need not be "spatially in the center or on a central axis,"[317] nonetheless, the Latin of the *General Instruction* says that the altar should be *revera centrum* (truly central), which seems not to permit this casual off-center treatment which gives the lectern and altar equal billing.

The lectern is described in the *General Instruction* as a suitable place for the proclamation of the Word of God and states that the dignity of its function demands that ordinarily it not be moveable,[318] whereas the American document describes it simply as "a standing desk for reading and preaching" though it wants it to be "beautifully designed, constructed of fine materials, and proportioned carefully and simply for its function...(it) represents the dignity and uniqueness of the Word of God and of reflection upon that Word."[319]

Of interest to our readers would be the contrast in the discussion of the placement of the choir, musicians and their instruments in both documents. The Roman document is concerned about the sign function of the choir and its special mission,[320] but that of the bishops is more pragmatic,[321] worrying simply about placement, although it does encourage good organs, while warning against their concert use.

Images for the veneration of the faithful (statues, icons, murals) are encouraged in the *General Instruction*, although as we have seen, there is a *caveat* against having too many or placing them in improper order.[322] The American document treats them along with seasonal

---

[316] *General Instruction of the Roman Missal,* n. 271.

[317] *Environment and Art,* n. 73.

[318] *General Instruction of the Roman Missal,* n. 272.

[319] *Ibid.,* n. 74.

[320] *Ibid.,* n. 274.

[321] *Ibid.,* n. 83.

[322] *Ibid.,* n. 278.

decoration, and warns against their competing with the assembly,[323] a negative treatment more suitable for a Quaker meeting house than a Catholic church, it would seem. This concern is echoed in the treatment of the Eucharistic chapel where "iconography or statuary…should not obscure the primary focus of reservation."[324] Both documents recommend a special chapel for the reservation of the Blessed Sacrament, a widespread European or at least Roman custom. The *General Instruction* sees this as helpful to "private adoration and prayer,"[325] whereas the American document seems most concerned that "no confusion can take place between the celebration of the Eucharist and the reserved species since active and static aspects of the same reality cannot claim the same human attention at the same time."[326] Not only do I think this preoccupation is overblown for ordinary Catholics who seem to know little about the Church's teaching on the real presence of Christ in the Eucharist, but it seems to me, that many of the unworthy solutions to the question of where to place the Blessed Sacrament have contributed to the breakdown in Eucharistic faith and the decline of devotion. The Roman document sagely notes that if no special chapel is possible, the Blessed Sacrament should be on an altar[327] or in some other place (wall safe, sacrament tower, a special niche) that is prominent and properly decorated *in parte ecclesiae pernobile et rite ornate.*[328] Finally, I might point out there is no treatment of the baptistry or confessionals in the Roman *Instruction,* whereas the bishop's document treats of fonts permitting immersion for infants[329] and reconciliation rooms.[330]

My comparing of the two treatments of the church edifice from an artistic and liturgical point of view is not to exalt one perspective over the other, but I do find it curious that the Roman perspective is more flexible. Is that because it is more truly universal, needing to enunciate the tradition for all climes and cultures? Finally, it seems to

---

[323] *Ibid.,* n. 98.

[324] *General Instruction of the Roman Missal,* n. 79.

[325] *Ibid.,* n. 276.

[326] *Ibid.,* n. 78.

[327] Forbidden by the bishops in n. 80.

[328] *General Instruction,* n. 276.

[329] *Ibid.,* n. 76.

[330] *Ibid.,* n. 81.

me that it is clear from the comparison that the American document despite its good intentions sells the sacred short and with that, no longer gives our artists, architects, and designers transcendent goals for which to strive, unfortunately impoverishing us all. The glory of God, the heavenly Jerusalem, needs to be incarnated in paint, stone, and glass to give us hope for the journey and a glimpse of the ultimate beauty for which we yearn.

8. Sacred Art: A Brief Reflection

The Constitution on the Sacred Liturgy of Vatican Council II speaks of the Liturgy as "the summit towards which the activity of the Church is directed...also the fount from which all her power flows,"[331] because it is "an exercise of the priestly office of Jesus Christ," head and members therefore are a sacred action surpassing all others.[332] Because this is true and this sacred action participates in eternity by means of the eternal priesthood of Jesus Christ, the Liturgy is also a foretaste of that heavenly Jerusalem towards which we travel as pilgrims.[333] It does not surprise us then that the *Constitution* sees the arts as "expressing in some way the infinite beauty of God in works made by human hands" and goes on to state that "all things set apart for us in divine worship should be worthy, becoming beautiful signs and symbols of things supernatural."[334]

We need beauty to arouse wonder and awe because as Jacques Maritain says, "the beautiful goes straight to the heart; it is a ray of intelligibility which reaches it directly and sometimes brings tears to the eyes." Pope John Paul II said in the *Letter to Artists* that we need artists and musicians to "give us a glimmer of the splendor which flared for a moment before the eyes of their spirit."[335] The *Catechism of the Catholic Church* states that sacred art expresses the surpassing beauty of truth and love visible in Christ, who reflects the glory of God and bears the very stamp of his nature."[336]

Both the *Catechism* and the *Constitution on the Liturgy* in speaking of

---

[331] *The Constitution on the Sacred Liturgy*, n. 10.

[332] *Ibid.*, n. 7.

[333] *Ibid.*, n. 8.

[334] *Ibid.*, n. 122.

[335] *Letter to Artists*, n. 6.

[336] Heb. 13

the church building discuss one altar, ambo font and other items of furnishings as being beautiful and well made. *The General Instruction of the Roman Missal* defends the use of sacred images as aids for prayer:

Venerating the memory of the Saints, the Church hopes for a small part and company with them…and so in keeping with the Church's very ancient tradition, the images of the Lord, the Virgin Mary and the Saints may be displayed for the veneration of the faithful.[337]

Now the documents we have quoted stress sacred art, but how is that different from religious art, or is there a difference? We have not seen religious art mentioned as a category in the plastic arts or architecture. However, in *Musicam Sacram's* definition of sacred music, it says that it is that "which is created for the celebration of divine worship" as we have noted above, but when it lists the types that come under that category, we find Gregorian Chant, polyphony, instrumental music, sacred popular music and that which is simply *religious*.[338]

Earlier this document quotes Pius X's *Tra le Solicitudine* to the effect that sacred music is "endowed a holy sincerity of form."[339] Pius X explicitly ruled out ballads, overly operatic music, that which took its inspiration from the secular. Much of what now passes for sacred music was not written for the Liturgy, or if it was, it has received its inspiration from the secular world. We could say the same for religious art, which might be appropriate for home, but not for the liturgical setting of the church building. It seems that the documentation restricts sacred art and music to that which is directly involved with the Liturgy, but we must recognize that a fine line exists between the sacred *per se* and the broader category of the religious.

9. So, You're on the Building Committee

Your parish priest has asked you to serve on the committee to help to plan your new parish church, or perhaps to remodel the old. You panic, for although you want to be of help, you know nothing about the task at hand. You know that since Vatican II, church

---

[337] *The General Instruction of the Roman Missal,* n. 318.
[338] *Musicam Sacram,* n. 4.
[339] *Ibid.*

architecture has taken a different turn and has produced buildings to worship in that "don't look like churches." You wonder if you're supposed to be involved in planning something for your parish along those lines. Your pastor gives you a copy of the *General Instruction of the Roman Missal*[340] and points out the section "The arrangement and ornamentation of churches for the celebration of the Eucharist" for your reading. He also hands you *Built of Living Stones,*[341] the guidelines of our own American bishops. You glance through the two documents; what to make of it all?

A very handy guide is Denis McNamara's *Catholic Church Architecture and the Spirit of the Liturgy.*[342] He takes seriously the contention that many of our churches today no longer "look like churches," and explains this phenomenon in the light of the historical situation. He also provides a rich theology of the church edifice based on the tradition of the Church, Sacred Scripture, and texts of the Liturgy itself. Above all, the sacramental symbolism of the church structure is stressed – that it is more than simply a functional covering for God's people at prayer, but also a "symbol of the Father's house towards which the people of God are journeying."[343] The church, itself, and all the "requisites for divine worship should be truly worthy and beautiful and be signs and symbols of heavenly realities."[344]

It has been my good fortune to know several young and talented traditional architects with whom I have worked – James McCrery, Duncan Stroik, Thomas Gordon Smith, Steven Schloeder – who do excellent work in recovering the Church's architectural tradition. Dr. McNamara is quick to point out that the Church has never "canonized" any one style as the Church's style. The illustrations in his profusely illustrated book are from all periods, even the contemporary, showing that a monumentality, symbolism, and serious materials all help to make a church "look like a church." It should stand out in our neighborhood as a sign of the Body of Christ, the Temple of the Lord, a symbol of the Heavenly City, and a

---

[340] *General Instruction of the Roman Missal* (USCCB, 2011).
[341] *Built of Living Stones* (USCCB, 2000).
[342] *Catholic Church Architecture and the Spirit of the Liturgy* (Hillenbrand Books, 2009).
[343] *CCC,* n. 1130.
[344] *GIRM,* n. 288.

sign of God dwelling with his people here and now. To help the parish building or remodeling committee and its members, I'd like to walk through the church and its components in that article with these sources in mind.

The *General Instruction of the Roman Missal* (*GIRM*) has the church building reflecting the people of God at prayer with its hierarchical orderly structure.[345] Thus, the sanctuary for the altar and ministers is to be marked off from the body of the church, by elevation or some other means. Traditionally, it was often a rail which some are using again. The people have their place affording active participation and the choir has its place as well.

The heart and center of the church is the altar, a multivalent symbol. Of late, all the emphasis has been on the table aspect, but the *GIRM* stresses the sacrificial aspect as well. The altar is primarily a symbol of Christ. He is the altar, for in his humanity dying on the Cross, he was the sacrifice, victim, priest, and altar, and as such is made present to us at Mass. Since Christ is one, normally there should be one altar. The altar should, if possible, be made of stone or marble, evoking the sacrificial rock. As a table, it symbolizes the heavenly banquet and the Last Supper, at which the Eucharist was instituted. Tomb aspects can also remind us of the Lord's saving Death and Resurrection. It should be free of the back wall so Mass may be celebrated facing the people and yet have adequate room on either side, so Mass may be celebrated *ad orientem* (facing liturgical East), as Pope Benedict has taught. No matter which way we face, he reminds us, we face God, and a reminder of that is the cross suspended over the altar, on the altar, or the processional cross (of a size to be easily seen), so we offer our sacrifice with that of his Son to the Father in the power of the Holy Spirit. Candlesticks may be on the altar, or on either side of it.

The *Catechism* places the tabernacle after the altar, and I think that is fitting because, in a way it is an extension of the altar. Pope Pius XIII, at the Assisi Liturgical Conference in 1956, warned against disassociating the two. My own opinion is that more harm has been done after the Council by removing the Blessed Sacrament from the main body of the church than any other change. Before, people were quiet in prayer waiting for Mass to begin, and now our assembly is a

---

[345] *Ibid.*, n. 294.

noisy one of socializing rather than prayer. Liturgists tended to think that if the tabernacle were in a separate chapel like in cathedrals, people at Mass would not be distracted by the Blessed Sacrament and would pay more attention to the unfolding modes of Christ's presence at Mass. I think this fear was unfounded, an academic preoccupation, rather than a pastoral problem. The *GIRM* states that the Blessed Sacrament must be reserved in a tabernacle in a part of the church that "is truly noble, prominent, conspicuous, worthily decorated and suitable for prayer."[346]   In many churches the back wall behind the altar and on the central axis is the favored spot. This seems to be a good solution if there is a suitable distance between altar and tabernacle. The bishop may opt for a special chapel for the reservation of the Eucharist, especially if the church is historic with many tourists visiting or if the church has the practice of continuous adoration of the Eucharist. In remodeling an old church, it is possible to use the old high altar as a place of reservation, and many fine old altars would serve this function well. In the words of Max Thurian, once a monk of Taizé, before becoming a Catholic priest:

"The church by its beautiful layout, its tabernacle radiating Christ's real presence, should be the beautiful house of the Lord, where the faithful love to recollect themselves in the silence of adoration and contemplation."

The ambo is the place for the reading of the Word of God. It should have an inherent dignity but should not be equal to the altar. Some think that the Council said the altar and ambo should be similar because the Liturgy of the Word and of the Eucharist are equal as two modes of the presence of Christ. Christ is present in the proclamation of the Word in a real but transitory way and not in the enduring sacramental way he is present in the Eucharist, so such a theory is quite erroneous. The ambo should have a big enough top for the Lectionary (or Gospel Book) and sermon notes. The microphones and acoustics should be adequate.

The celebrant's chair is not to be a throne (unless in the cathedral), but a dignified chair showing the function of the priest who presides over the Mass in *persona Christi capitis* (in the person of Christ, Head of the Mystical body). He presides in charity and makes the sacrifice of the Mass possible and his chair symbolizes that

---

[346] *GIRM*, n. 314.

authority. The *GIRM* expresses a preference for the basilican position of the chair at the head of the apse, but admits other possibilities, especially if the tabernacle is placed there. The deacon's seat should be near and there should be places for concelebrating clergy.

The *GIRM* waxes eloquently about sacred imagery as a foretaste of the heavenly liturgy and encourages images of the Lord, the Blessed Virgin Mary and the saints.[347] Dr. McNamara distinguishes between liturgical art, which draws the connection between the earthly liturgy of the Mass being celebrated and the heavenly liturgy of which it is a foretaste and an eternal memorial. The apse may well have a mural of all the saints gathered around the throne of the Lamb, or a Crucifixion scene with the Father, the Spirit, and angels in attendance. Such would draw one into the Liturgy, whereas devotional images, statues, paintings, icons of particular saints, patron saints, and shrines need their own niches or side chapels that are a part of the whole, but not the major feature. A misunderstanding of "noble simplicity" has banished all such from white-washed churches and made them very antiseptic, not filled with heavenly light and color that murals, mosaics, paintings, and stained-glass windows would provide, all helping our churches to "look more like a church."

The *GIRM* does not treat baptisteries, although in many places they are placed near the entrance of the church to symbolize it is through Baptism we enter the Church, and the font is often placed on the same axis as the altar to show Baptism as leading to the Eucharist. Sometimes the sacrament can be administered by immersion, so that possibility should be foreseen. Confessionals and/or reconciliation rooms may be situated nearby to draw out the connection of Penance as a quasi-extension of Baptism.

I hope this little walk through the church building and its furnishings, its purpose, its layout and symbolism will encourage the faint of heart to take their place in working with pastors and architects that are trying to build beautiful churches for the Church, the Body of Christ, to worship in until they reach the Heavenly Liturgy in the Jerusalem, which is above.

---

[347] *GIRM*, n. 318.

10. Religious Art in the Service of the Eucharist

The Catechism of the Catholic Church (CCC) sees sacred art as expressing the "transcendent mystery of God, the surpassing Invisible beauty of truth and love visible in Christ who reflects the glory of God and bears the very stamp of his nature,"[348] and reminds us that genuine sacred art draws us to adoration, prayer and the love of God. Vatican II's *Constitution on the Liturgy*[349] mandates that "all things set apart for us in divine worship be worthy, becoming and beautiful signs and symbols of the supernatural." First and foremost, this must apply to the Church itself. The Rite for the Dedication of a Church states:

Because a church is a visible building it stands as a special sign of the pilgrim church on earth and reflects the church dwelling in Heaven…it should be dignified, evincing…a noble beauty and should stand as a sign and symbol of heavenly things.[350]

My elder brother, St. Thomas Aquinas, says the same thing more laconically when he points out that:

*The house in which this sacrament is celebrated denotes the Church and is termed a church and so is fittingly consecrated **both** to represent the holiness which the church acquired by the Passion… and the holiness of those (receiving).*[351]

Clearly, if we are dealing with signs and symbols of holiness, of heavenly realities, of the Paschal Mystery, then these signs must communicate to the faithful of today. While it is true that the Church has not adopted any historic architectural style as her own,[352] and this means that we need not confine ourselves to building in past styles, one could ask whether our modern concrete bunkers symbolize the transcendence of the All Holy God. It is also true that the same *Constitution* encourages "noble simplicity rather … than ostentation."[353] One wonders whether that *Constitution* envisaged all the "bare, ruined choirs" that would spring up as a result of the encouragement.

---

[348] cf. Heb. 1:3

[349] *Constitution on the Liturgy,* n. 122.

[350] n. 2.

[351] ST. III, Q 83, art. 3, ad. 2.

[352] *SC,* n. 123.

[353] *Constitution on the Liturgy,* n. 127.

Fortunately, there is a new breath of the Holy Spirit abroad in the Church. People are asking why our churches can't be more like churches." Our own bishops are refurbishing the *Domus Dei* or House of God in their document *From Living Stones*. The wonderful *participatio actuosa* of Vatican II is being balanced by the silent adoration in Eucharistic exposition, which renders active participation deep and actual. The Church is like the good steward who brings out of her treasury things old and new, and I believe this is a time in the new millennium when it will not be a question of liberal or conservative, old church or new church, conciliar or pre-conciliar, but the *Church*, and all things Catholic in the richness, diversity, tradition, and Spirit-led innovation that is our inheritance and which will guide us in the new millennium.

Max Thurian, monk of the ecumenical monastery of Taizé who later was quietly received into the Catholic Church and later was ordained a priest, signaled this new movement towards beauty and transcendence in an article on church art that appeared in *L'Osservatore Romano* shortly before he died. Of the church building, he said:

The whole church should be arranged so as to invite adoration and contemplation even when there are no celebrations. One must long to frequent it in order to meet the Lord there...The church, by its beautiful liturgical layout, its tabernacle radiating Christ's real presence, should be the beautiful house of the Lord and of his Church, where the faithful love to recollect themselves in the silence of adoration and contemplation. Every church must be praying even when no liturgical celebration is taking place; it must be a place where in a restless world one can meet the Lord in peace.

Thus, the church building is more than just a functional covering for the assembly. The assembly is not the primary symbol, for though they are the People of God, they are not the whole of God's People and the Church in Heaven, our goal and destiny, must be symbolized too. The great cloud of witnesses[354] the saints, our brothers and sisters who have gone before us as well as the choir of angels surround us as the timeless eternal heavenly liturgy is brought to our altars in time so we can participate in this saving sacrifice and heavenly banquet. And even where the liturgy is not being celebrated, the sacred atmosphere should enable us to lay aside

---

[354] Heb. 12:1

earthly cares and enter into the contemplation that refreshes us and gives us strength for our work on the journey. Thurian says of the altar that it should be:

> ...*the center of liturgical celebration. It must be built and adorned so as to attract one's gaze and to cause admiration ... it will sometimes be covered with beautiful fabrics in our liturgical colors (frontals, antependia) ... The altar and the objects used for the Eucharistic celebration should rouse wonder in the presence of the beauty that leads one's whole being to adore the glory of the Lord. The altar is actually the sign of the sacrifice of the Mass as memorial, the table of the Eucharistic meal, the symbol of the tomb left empty of the Risen One.*

The newly reworked and reissued *GIRM* has some interesting points to make about the altar which are not amiss to note here. After reminding us while it is the table of the Lord,[355] it is not just that but also symbolizes elements of sacrifice (of the Cross) and thanksgiving. It stresses a fixed stone altar representing Jesus Christ the Living Stone,[356] although moveable altars are permitted.[357] While the *GIRM* emphasizes the centrality of the one altar,[358] it admits that in churches already built an old altar can be retained if artistic and another new one "artfully made" and used,[359] hopefully the new blending in with the old which can serve as a backdrop for it. More is said about the adornment of the altar.[360]

A subtle and interesting change has taken place in the *GIRM*'s discussion of the reservation of the Eucharist. The 1970 edition stressed a separate chapel for the Blessed Sacrament and admitted other possibilities, if necessary, because of the structure of the church or local custom.[361] The new legislation seems to reverse that order. The first consideration is that the Eucharist be reserved "in a part of the church which is noble, worthy, conspicuous, well decorated and suitable for prayer,"[362] and that it is either in the Sanctuary apart from the altar of celebration (upon which Mass *versus populum* is celebrated whenever possible),[363] and the old high altar is not excluded. The

---

[355] *GIRM*, n. 296.
[356] 1 Pet. 2:4
[357] *GIRM*, nn. 298 – 301.
[358] *Ibid.*, n. 303.
[359] *Ibid.*
[360] *Ibid.*, nn. 304 – 308.
[361] former *GIRM* n. 276.
[362] *GIRM*, n. 314.

separate chapel suitable for adoration and prayer is still an option if it is conspicuous to the faithful and integrally connected with the church.[364] In discussing the chair *GIRM* sees the head of the apse as the best place but recognizes that if a Tabernacle is directly behind the altar, another place is possible.[365]

I'm delighted with these subtle changes. It seems to me that a separate chapel makes sense in Roman basilicas, historic cathedrals and pilgrimage shrines or tourist sights. I'm less convinced that it is the solution for all parish churches. I watched the first consultation on Domus Dei (as it was then called), and bishop after bishop stood up and said the faithful want to be able to see the Blessed Sacrament in our churches! I'd call this an exercise of the *sensus fidelium*. In old churches the old high altar is a marvelous place for reservation, and a new center of liturgical gravity can be created for the central altar closer to the people. Even in a new church a central position is not ruled out, nor is it required! As we find more worthy and beautiful solutions for reservation of the Eucharist, our churches will benefit in becoming more prayerful.

Finally, there is a richer treatment of sacred images. The former was rather negative and restrictive, and while there still are caveats about the number of images and their reduplication, the images of our Lord, the Blessed Virgin, and the Saints are seen as part of the heavenly liturgy of which ours on earth is a reflection: and so we begin where we started, with the church building as a sign of the Heavenly Jerusalem toward which we journey as pilgrims.

11. The Placement of the Tabernacle

Everywhere I go, I hear people speaking of churches, the churches of today, the churches of their youth, or the great churches of Europe. They often express the desire to see "churches that look like churches." They mourn the loss of statues, murals, stained glass, marble altars, etc., but most of all, they ask why the tabernacle was moved. They remember it in the most important place in the middle of the high altar in their parish churches and do not understand why the tabernacle with the Real Presence had to be moved. And frankly,

---

[363] *Ibid.,* n. 299.
[364] *Ibid.,* n. 315.
[365] *Ibid.,* n. 310.

looking over our collective experience since Vatican II, nor do I. Our churches now are perceived as barren, without color or symbolism, without the living presence of Christ in the tabernacle, and are treated by our people as assembly halls, where they chatter before and after Mass, rather than pray. There used to be a hushed silence in the church, all waiting for the unfolding of the holy mysteries.

I tend to think that "Ressourcement," the movement which had the laudable desire to rediscover the biblical and patristic roots of theology is unintentionally responsible. Suddenly after the Council, the patristic model rather than the medieval, became the norm. We started using the vernacular at Mass, received under both species and eventually in the hand. Deacons were restored as were consecrated virgins and the minor orders were abolished. Architecturally the basilican arrangement seemed to be given preference for the building and decoration of churches, the chair at the head of the apse, the altar facing the people, the placement of the choir all seem to suggest the basilican plan. The old *GIRM*[366] with its preference for a separate Eucharistic chapel seems in line with this emphasis.

Even though Eucharistic reservation was allowed in the sanctuary, the notion that the tabernacle had to be moved to the side became standard with the result that often the old altar with its reredos, dorsal, or baldachino was torn down and the back wall was left bare except for the celebrant's chair which was not to look like a throne. Old churches were left without a visual center and yet all their lines converged on the nearly empty sanctuary, because fine old marble altars were often destroyed. Noble simplicity was interpreted to mean no decoration, no images, no statues. The latter were often moved to an alcove in the back of the church for "peasants" who needed them, but mainly so they'd not "distract" those participating in the liturgy. Where is the "great cloud of witnesses"[367] who joins us when the heavenly liturgy comes to earth on our altars? The present *GIRM* treats the whole question of sacred images in a richer way than did the old, as does the *Catechism of the Catholic Church*.

One begins to see new trends, a possible reversal of the present situation. In my opinion, the new *GIRM* is an improvement over the former one. In terms of the placement of the tabernacle, it no longer

---

[366] Issued 1970.
[367] Heb. 12:1

sees a separate chapel as the first option, but the second, giving pride of place to the sanctuary, but leaving all up to the local bishop. It is interesting to note that the *Catechism* treats the tabernacle, immediately after its treatment of the altar, whereas the new *GIRM* treats it after discussing the altar, the ambo, the chair, places for the faithful, the choir, and the organ. I think the *Catechism* is more correct theologically because, as Msgr. Elliott points out in his book on the present Roman Rite, Pius XII warned against disassociating the Real Presence from the altar. It is true that the present directives state the Eucharist should not be reserved on an altar where Mass will be celebrated to make a clear distinction between the signs of the Mass being celebrated and that of the reserved Sacrament. Still, where an old altar is no longer used for Mass, it is allowed in an old church to reserve the Sacrament there. It would seem that an existing high altar of artistic merit would be a perfect solution for reservation. A new altar could be built further out and receive the attention during the Mass (perhaps by lighting), but after Mass the focus is on the tabernacle for quiet prayer and contemplation.

It should be clear by now to the reader, that I favor reservation of the Eucharist in the sanctuary. The *GIRM* says the "most Blessed Sacrament should be reserved in a tabernacle in a part of the Church that is truly noble, prominent, visible, beautifully decorated and suitable for prayer." Why couldn't the chair in such a case balance the ambo of the other side? While the basilican plan of the apse seems to be recommended, it is not mandated.

One could argue that the custom of most of the English-speaking world was to have the tabernacle "in medio" and altars to Our Lady and St. Joseph on either side. One today would not want to fashion non-functioning altars merely to be the bases for shrines to the saints, nor would we want to obscure the symbolism of the one altar in a new church. Still shrines without altars can still be erected. Is our custom part of American enculturation? I'm not arguing for a return to yesteryear, but I do think that the restoration of the tabernacle to a prominent place in the sanctuary (and I would argue for a central focus) would help to restore the atmosphere of reverence and silence that was once so characteristic of our churches.

Proper catechesis would be necessary, but Catholic teaching on the Real Presence of Christ in the Eucharist would be "incarnationally realized" in the sanctuary setting. People would know in what direction to genuflect and faith expressed in the bent knee would symbolize and undergird faith held in the mind and heart. The concern of some liturgists that reserving the Blessed Sacrament in the sanctuary where the altar for Mass is, sets up a "conflict of mysteries" is in my opinion overdrawn and is not a real problem for our people. True, the altar ought not to be "smack dab" in front of the tabernacle and a suitable distance should be observed. The tabernacle might be on a higher plane as it is in the monastic church of Solesmes or in a wall niche as is skillfully done in Stroik's Church of All Saints in Walton, Kentucky. A beautiful reredos or dorsal could be the backdrop for the tabernacle when Mass is not being celebrated and serve as the glorious background when it is.

A separate Eucharistic chapel is an option but in my opinion this ought to be reserved for cathedrals, historic, or pilgrimage churches where the number of visitors, pilgrims or tourists so overwhelm the edifice, that a separate quiet place to pray is necessary. One immediately thinks of St. Peter's in Rome. If this became the rule in ordinary parish churches, Sunday Mass Catholics might think that prayer before the Blessed Sacrament is an esoteric rite for devout souls and not for ordinary Catholics. This is Msgr. Elliott's fear. If there is a separate chapel, the *GIRM* directs that it be "organically connected to the church and readily visible to the Christian faithful." There should be easy access from the altar.

The tabernacle, itself, must be solid, unbreakable, immoveable, and not transparent. There should be one tabernacle and it may be on a pedestal, in a sacrament tower or a wall aumbry. Veils are not forbidden, and the lamp (candle or oil lamp) may hang in front of the tabernacle, be on a wall bracket or on a stand. The former rubric was that there could be one, three, five, or seven lamps. Clear or white glass is preferable for the Blessed Sacrament, but red has become traditional in the English-speaking world.

Our churches are not "simply gathering places but signify and make visible the Church living in this place, the dwelling place of God with men reconciled and united in Christ." God dwells with His people in the Eucharist celebrated and reserved and outside of the Mass, it is the tabernacle that is the "living heart of our churches" according to Paul VI. We'll give the last word to Msgr. Elliott who thought:

Devotion to Our Lord in the Eucharist is embedded in the religious psyche of our people. It is not an optional extra for devout souls. This devotion remains essential for the continuity of the living tradition, not only of our rite, but of the faith itself.

Let us then design churches that embody this principle and let us return the *tabernaculum*, the dwelling tent of God with his people, to a place of glory.

12. Where Have You Gone, Michelangelo?

On sabbatical last summer, I visited many parts of the United States and Mexico to observe the changing fashion in the Church's liturgy and architecture.

Many of us, in the 1950s, used to decry ugly pseudo-Gothic churches cluttered with sentimental plaster statues, but now many of us would be glad to return to them to escape the bare concrete bunkers that have replaced them. While the *Constitution on the Sacred Liturgy* (*Sacrosanctum Concilium*) of the Second Vatican Council encourages "noble simplicity," the wholesale rejection of images, crucifixes, statues and paintings is a complete misunderstanding of the Council.

My first engagement on sabbatical was to preach at the first Mass of a former student, now ordained, at a historic old church in the nation's capital that is slated for renovation. As we entered, we could see the plans to remove an interesting '50s reredos, which gave focus to the altar facing the people, and to replace it with a plain Celtic cross against a bare sanctuary wall. The décor will clearly be Presbyterian – scant consolation to the Irish who built the church.

The highlight of my sabbatical was a pilgrimage to Guadalupe. Recently built at this Mexican shrine was a new church to house the miraculous *tilma* with Our Lady's image because the lovely Spanish baroque structure previously used is sinking into the earth. This very contemporary basilica has none of the starkness of its cousins to the north. It is full of shadows and light, marble and rich use of wood, as well as sacred images. Of course, the sacred *tilma's* luminosity sheds Mary's radiance on this delightful modern church, fully consonant with Vatican II's call for participation, and yet it is not cold, sterile or bland.

The last leg of my journey took me to a four-week sabbatical in South Orange, New Jersey, to Seton Hall University. Our Lady of Sorrows Church, nearby, shows how a magnificent pre-Vatican II Gothic church can be tastefully and sensitively remodeled for current liturgical participation without sacrificing aesthetics.

Unfortunately, some designers of contemporary churches do not bother reading the documentation of Vatican II, come up with instant answers based on the opinions of "experts," and do not grapple with trying to incarnate our faith in wood, stone, glass and concrete.

Why is it that the post-Vatican II Church seems to have given up on decorating churches to make them beautiful places that invite contemplation of God and the things of the Spirit through images, icons, statues, murals?

Thomas Day, in his thought-provoking and, at times, amusing book *Where have You Gone, Michelangelo?* (a kind of sequel to his uproarious, *Why Catholics Can't Sing*) puts his finger on the problem. He examines the provisions of the *Constitution on the Sacred Liturgy*, with its suggestion that sacred works of art turn our thoughts to "God and to the cause of His honor and glory."[368] The *Constitution* glories in the "treasury of art," which has developed in the Church through the ages and exhorts that new churches strive after "noble beauty rather than sumptuous display."[369]

Day then carefully considers the 1977 document *Environment and Art in Catholic Worship,* put out by the U. S. Bishop's Committee on Liturgy. He charges that while this document states that the "liturgy's climate is one of awe, mystery, wonder, reverence, thanksgiving and praise,"[370] it also subtly suggests that the primary purpose of a church building is to promote hospitality, a feeling of togetherness. Churches should help us to be "comfortable with one another, either knowing or being introduced to one another."[371] Day suggests that this sounds like the bylaws of a country club.

Day humorously exaggerates, perhaps, but his critique of the modern carpeted church as a "comfy" living room where we encounter God in one another and sing songs that celebrate

---

[368] *Constitution on the Sacred Liturgy,* n. 122.

[369] *Ibid.,* n. 123.

[370] *Environment and Art in Catholic Worship,* n. 34.

[371] *Environment and Art in Catholic Worship,* n. 11.

ourselves is very much to the point.

The Fathers at Vatican II wished to have us all more involved in the liturgy. They envisioned churches built for participation in the Mass. The problem is that many "experts" see art as a distraction rather than an aid. Statues are often banished to a back alcove. Why must it always be either participation or devotion, liturgy or folk piety, modern music or Gregorian chant?

We need to get back to the broader, more universal, more historical perspective of the Church of Rome, and this, I believe, will enable us to reclaim our rich tradition of Church art and God's beauty afresh for our time as the medieval cathedrals did for theirs.

13. A.W. Pugin: Prophet or Dreamer?

This fall in London a comprehensive exhibit of the art of Augustus Welby Pugin (1812-1852) was held at the Victoria and Albert Museum and the catalogue was replete with the most breathtaking photographs of his work: cathedrals and churches he designed, their architectural plans, altars and their reredoses, rood screens and carvings, decorative floor tiles, Mass candlesticks and reliquaries, golden chalices and ecclesiastical vessels and vestments of all styles. There was no aspect of ecclesiastical design that was not tackled by this gothic enthusiast and convert to Catholicism whose quest for beauty had brought him from the cathedrals of his native England to the great churches and abbeys on the continent where he found the faith. His crusade was to restore to the Catholic Church in England (then small and beleaguered) medieval splendor in the gothic style "for the revival of Catholic art and ecclesiastical dignity." The photographs of the Pugin catalogue suggest that he accomplished this mission nobly, but a recent renovation of his Irish cathedral in Killarney and the booklet describing its metamorphosis according to the ideas of the renovating architect, Ray Carroll, seem to disagree.

Thomas O'Caoimh's booklet, while replete with many excellent photos of the renovated church, shows nothing of the old cathedral. When I was a teenager, my parents gave me Msgr. Cartwright's book, *The Catholic Shrines of Europe*. I well remember its views of the noble gothic revival pile that its exterior made as well as the spacious cruciform interior. The inside with its white plaster walls and medieval stenciling contrasting with the stone trim of the great arches, the deep cathedral choir with rows of choir stalls before the gothic high altar needed the decorated floor tiles to create a unity of the space connecting the nave with the many jewel-like chapels that fanned out from the main design. The architect, Mr. Carroll, had a difficult task adapting this building for the liturgy of Vatican II. He recognized the genius of Pugin:

Who can view for the first time, the heart-stopping solemnity of the succession of perfectly continued spaces and not recognize with a degree of awe and delight the exact fulfillment of a powerful vision, the hallmark of genius? Those things are Pugin.[372]

Mr. Carroll's redesigning stripped away all the plaster, so the stone rubble underneath is now featured, making the church seem much older than gothic, vaguely reminiscent of Irish round towers and early Irish Romanesque. The high altar, most side altars, altar screens, choir stalls, and floor tiles have all been removed. The crossing of the cruciform cathedral under its central lantern has been built up to be the main sanctuary *in medio* with its altar *versus populum*.

Dominating the old sanctuary is a huge modern white marble sacrament tower for the reservation of the Blessed Sacrament which is truly prominent and beautiful. The baptismal font balances the lectern on either side of the sanctuary. It reminds one of medieval cathedrals in Germany with good modern fixtures, noble and simple and the effect is not bad. I liked what I saw of the old cathedral in Cartwright's book and when I visited Killarney, I liked the new. I do wonder whether such radical changes were necessary, however. Mr. Carroll is quoted several times in the booklet on what he sees as the "errors" in Pugin's thought. In describing his cathedral, St. Chad's in Birmingham, he says its design is:

...powerful and beautiful and medieval which, so effective was its artistry, (that it) drew them back each Sunday to a nostalgic fairyland of a distant past, a land of false promise. One might ask whether he drew them too much out of their real world and away from their duty to change it.[373]

Carroll sees this as the nineteenth century Church's "world of

---

[372] *Killarney Cathedral Booklet*, Dublin: Eason & Son, 1990, p. 17.
[373] *Ibid.*

false otherworldliness" which Pugin fostered, and which was a restraining force on the liturgy, "divorcing the activity of the altar from the people kept at a distance."[374] Though Carroll kept many Puginesque features of the north transept and Kenmare chapels, the tracery in the baptistry, the stations of the cross, he felt it would be wrong to leave the building as a "museum of Victoriana." He spelled out his principle of discernment as follows:

> Where the inevitable conflict arose between Pugin's medieval philosophy of liturgy and the... modern one, we deferred to Pugin (namely his sense of the sacred, and his sense of mystery), took into account the internal built-in commands of his building, and simultaneously followed as faithfully as we know the new guidelines set down by Rome.[375]

Clearly the above was the architect's intent, but one might ask whether his reaction to Pugin's "philosophy of liturgy" isn't overdone. Doesn't even the *Constitution on the Liturgy* remind us of the heavenly dimension of the liturgy?

In the earthly liturgy we take part in a foretaste of that heavenly liturgy which is celebrated in the Holy City of Jerusalem towards which we journey as pilgrims, where Christ is sitting at the right hand of God, minister of the holies and of the true tabernacle.[376]

And this is echoed in the *Catechism of the Catholic Church* (1994) using this same quote in n. 1180. The *Catechism* also moreover emphasizes the eschatological sign value of the church building as the sign of "our Father's house, the goal of our journeying" in n. 1186. Could it be that English Catholics, despised and discriminated against in 19th century Birmingham, were lifted momentarily from their distress at St. Chad's to focus on "the things above" and perhaps similarly disenfranchised Irish peasants might have been grateful for the glimpses of otherworldliness that the great cathedral of Killarney afforded them? Those of us today who are used to worshipping in "bare ruined choirs" and sterile concrete bunkers would welcome just such a glimpse. Perhaps that's why the Pugin exhibition in London drew so many visitors.

---

[374] *Ibid.*
[375] *Killarney Cathedral Booklet*, Dublin: Eason & Son, 1990, p. 18.
[376] S.C. in *Documents of Vatican II*, ed. Flannery, OP, n. 8.

RENEWAL OF THE CHURCH'S MISSION

1. Tale of Two Marches and The Journey Between

January 22nd found me in Washington, D.C. for the March for Life. Washington had been experiencing bitterly cold weather, but that afternoon, as 70,000 of us marched up Constitution Avenue, the sun warmed us a bit on our way to the Supreme Court. The atmosphere was hopeful (having heard the President speak to us by phone), even festive.

I was among the Dominicans who marched from our House of Studies; the Knights of Columbus from Providence College were also there. There were bearded Jewish rabbis from New York, Evangelical Protestants from Liberty College in Lynchburg, Virginia, Catholic Traditionalists from the Tridentine Church of Saint Pius V and Episcopalians for Life (with the parade's most tasteful banner!).

Surrounding us was a great multitude of ordinary Catholics of all ages and from parishes all over the country. The overwhelming impression, however, was that the majority of marchers were young, and this augurs well for the future.

As I marched along the parade route with my brothers, I found myself remembering another march of almost two decades ago. I had participated in a protest against Catholic University because it was threatening to dismiss the dissenter, Father Charles Curran, the school's controversial moral theologian.

It seemed to me then, as I marched in my Dominican habit, that I was upholding academic freedom for the right of all professors to teach what their consciences dictated. Naturally, I was against the narrowness of *Humanae Vitae*, and wondered how the "open" Paul VI could issue such a document.

Gradually, however, I came to see the harm that came from separating sex from procreation in marriage: once that separation which contraception afforded was effected, there was no logical way to say "no" to premarital sex or to homosexuality except through Scripture – which was increasingly portrayed as only teaching the vaguest moral principles – or the authority of the Church, which was seriously questioned.

While studying in Rome, I began to rethink these issues. I found myself more and more convinced by the inner logic of the papal teaching, while I was more and more drawn personally by the warmth and genuineness of Pope Paul VI, whom I saw at Vatican Masses and Papal audiences.

It all came together for me later when I read an article by Father Curran, a retrospective on *Humanae Vitae*, in which he articulated how his moral theology had "grown" since then. Now he was more "open" to pre-marital sex, homosexual relations and abortion in certain instances.

It is perhaps true, as a Dominican professor of moral theology maintained, that in morals, the domino theory works! Once one no longer respects the nature of things as given by a wise Creator, one is on the slippery slope sliding from contraception to abortion.

These are the thoughts that were in my mind as I marched with my Dominican Brothers last January 22nd. I only hope that my marching and this column are accepted as reparation for the other march at Catholic University.

2.   Freedom Behind Bars

On the Feast of Corpus Christi this year, Father Ed Wade and I travelled across the state of Pennsylvania from the Franciscan University of Steubenville in Ohio to visit the pro-life prisoners, Father John Osterhout (a Franciscan, now in rescue work and formerly on the University staff), Joseph McCormick, Joe O'Hara and Mark Nelson, a young man recently married.

It was arranged for us to celebrate Mass in the prison in

Bethlehem for the prisoners. A Catholic prison chaplain joined us to make sure there would be no problems. We were escorted to the cafeteria where we arranged the Mass vessels and vestments on the cafeteria table. At the other end of the room newly admitted prisoners, all shackled, were watching videos to acclimate themselves to prison life. The chaplain kindly offered Father John vestments as we all vested. We asked Father John to be the principal concelebrant. Father John led us in music and presided at the Mass, explaining the ceremonies to the many Protestants who attended along with the Catholic prisoners. Father Ed and I preached; the Mass went as usual.

Following Mass, I gave Father John a rosary from Germany. We were then concerned that we would be asked to leave because our request for a visit with the pro-life prisoners had not been made in the required amount of time. However, the guards were helpful, and we were allowed to visit with our friends. They all expressed their joy in being permitted to attend the Mass, a privilege they had not enjoyed for a month. Father Ed and I on leaving felt ashamed at not appreciating the Eucharist more. Our friends were so hungry for the Lord's Body and Blood. When we left their shining faces, Father asked me, "who is most free, we or they?"

Shortly after we left, prison officials charged Father John with all sorts of infractions of the rules of the prison – disguising himself as a priest, preaching illegally (which he did not do) to an illegal gathering (which had permission to be there) and receiving contraband goods (a rosary!). He pleaded innocent to the first two charges. The chaplain didn't know prisoner priests couldn't vest in prison, yet the guards stood by and said nothing about his vesting or presiding! Father pleaded guilty to receiving the rosary. One bystander asked if the prison officials thought Father John would use the rosary to escape. (Perhaps, in a sense, it might cut through the walls!)

Father John was penalized to eight hours labor for his offense of receiving a rosary, but that never had a chance to take effect because he and Joe McCormick were assigned an outside work detail which they refused in accordance with rescue principles. Rescuers will not take work assignments because they think work assignments are an admission of guilt. Nor will they cooperate with any penalty which helps the judicial system as it continues to support the holocaust of the innocents. Because of their refusal to work, Father John and Joe

McCormick were sent to neighboring Allentown prison where they were placed in solitary confinement. They were confined in their cells 23 hours a day. During their one free hour they were placed in handcuffs. After several days in solitary confinement, they received a hearing for their "mutinous" refusal to work, and they each received a penalty of 25 days in 23-hour "lock-up." One week later, Joe O'Hara and Mark Nelson were also placed in solitary confinement for refusing a work assignment.

What had these people done to be imprisoned in the first place? On July 17th of last year, Father John Osterhout, Joe O'Hara, Joe McCormick, Mark Nelson, Gretchen Schmiedicke, Kathleen Doherty, Nancy McNulty, Debbie and Beth Bond and their mother, Virginia, trespassed on the property of an abortion mill in order to close the place for the day, thus preventing the killing of unborn children. They broke a law of trespass to uphold a higher law that innocent life should be protected and not slaughtered in the womb.

At the May 19th hearing this year, the judge would hear no discussion of a higher law, and then sentenced each rescuer according to prior convictions. Joe O'Hara and Mark Nelson received a sentence of 3 months to a year; Gretchen Nelson (recently married to Mark) and Debbie Bond were sentenced to 2 months to a year; Father John, Kathleen Doherty, Beth Bond, and Joe McCormick received 1 month to a year. Virginia Bond was placed on a year's probation. Nancy McNulty, who was in prison in Pittsburgh was sentenced to 6 months to a year. She had recently been brought to Allentown for the sentencing procedure. At the time of this writing the Bond girls have been released on parole. The other seven remain in jail.

The prisoners are all in good spirits. On July 12th, I visited them all and gave them communion. The young women, Kathleen and Gretchen, are in maximum security. Father John, Joe O'Hara, Joe McCormick, and Mark Nelson have been moved from disciplinary lock-up to administrative segregation. Now they are allowed out of their cells two hours each day. They are permitted one phone call a day, and they receive mail and limited visitors. They may not attend Mass at the prison if offered by the chaplain. The only religious ministrations they may receive are those planned explicitly for them. Bishop Welsh of Allentown has visited the girls in prison, and Bishop Timlin of Scranton flew himself down to visit imprisoned members of his flock. He was able to see Debbie Bond in Allentown but was kept waiting one-and-a-half hours in Bethlehem, a relatively small prison, and had to return to Scranton without seeing Joe O'Hara, who incidentally had some devotional literature confiscated while there.

These brave prisoners of conscience are fasting and praying for all of us, for our nation, for the prison officials and the judge. They pray that this nation will be saved, and that the scourge of abortion might be lifted from our land.

3.   Reclaiming Catholic Colleges: How One School Did it

One of the saddest commentaries on the difficulties of Catholic education in our own time was related to me by a priest-friend who had studied at what was once a prestigious Catholic college. This school (which shall be nameless), in order to receive state funds, had removed crucifixes from all the classrooms of the institution; my friend related the eerie feeling he experienced gazing on the shadowy imprints left on the walls where the crucifixes had once been.

This incident is a kind of negative image of what secularization had done to our Catholic colleges, not only in the realm of curriculum, but especially in the area of the total learning experience which may, in the long run, be even more important than the subjects taught. Many of us who attended Catholic colleges remember taking a prodigious number of courses in theology and philosophy, probably at least a course in either discipline each semester for four years.

In most Catholic universities before Vatican II, students studied logic, metaphysics, ethics, some history of philosophy as well as apologetics, moral and dogmatic theology treating God, Christ, the Church and sacraments as well as the Ten Commandments, and virtues and gifts of the Spirit. At least such was the curriculum I was subject to at Providence College in which the Dominican faculty, using texts that popularized the *Summa* of St. Thomas, brought us through the essential points of the Faith as well as the philosophical underpinnings that were useful in its explanation and defense.

Some schools at that time (the late '50s) were moving away from such a scholastic approach to emphasize more the Bible and Church history, but the basics of the Faith were nonetheless reviewed and elaborated on in greater depth.

Educators find today that most Catholic students haven't the foggiest notion of Catholic doctrine. While it may be true that an awareness of the Christian life needed to be emphasized to balance the intellectual and dogmatic stress of the *Baltimore Catechism*, the end result now is that neither the truth of the Faith nor the experience of its mysteries is familiar to young Catholics entering our Catholic colleges.

However, hand-in-hand with the question of the curriculum of Catholic education, and in my opinion equally important, is the question of the total environment of the Catholic campus. Many Catholic schools – if not hostile to the practice of the Faith – are at least lethargic in creating an atmosphere of virtue, where young people are encouraged not only in Christian belief, but also in keeping the Commandments. No one would openly advocate immorality in itself, but do not coed dorms, unenforceable visiting hours in single-sex dormitories, courses in morality endlessly emphasizing exceptions and presenting dissenting opinions in place of the clear teaching of the Church; do not all of these factors not create an atmosphere that practically invites our young people to experiment with drugs, alcohol, and sex?

It was into such an atmosphere as this that Father Michael Scanlan stepped as president of the College of Steubenville in 1974. He describes it in his recently published autobiography, *Let the Fire Fall,* as a school that was following the general trend, abandoning or soft-pedalling the Christian and specifically Catholic character of our institutions of higher learning. He characterized student life there (as at other schools) as "increasingly permissive, individualistic, hedonistic and riddled with drugs, alcohol and sex." Nominated by the search committee and the board of trustees precisely because of the strong Catholic and Franciscan identity he said he would stress, not only in the classroom but in all aspects of campus life, Father Scanlan was faced with the challenge of enfleshing those ideals in a practical way.

Wanting to build a faith environment but not sure exactly how to go about it, Father Michael spent three months mingling with the students, getting to know them and their problems, and found them angry, lonely, and depressed. Promiscuity, achieving numbness by drugs and alcohol, vandalism, and even attempts at suicide were all escapes from the isolation of student life as then lived.

As he prayed and consulted, the new president began to formulate a plan which he unfolded at the end of the first semester. He had been asked to cancel Sunday morning Mass in favor of a couple of afternoon Masses for the few who attended. Before a meeting of the whole school he announced that he would be the celebrant of the Sunday morning liturgy, which would be celebrated more fulsomely with solid preaching and would probably take twice as long.

He also announced that he was refusing the petition to start coed dorms and end curfews, but he was going to change dormitory life so that it wouldn't be so impersonal. He proposed that students live in "households" – small groups inhabiting a wing of a dorm where one could share one's life, pray with one's brothers and sisters, and find encouragement and support.

Though they have changed and developed, this aspect is still very much a part of the student life of the university now. As his presidency went on, Father Scanlan invited people of faith to help provide an atmosphere of Christian belief, not only to serve on the faculty, but also to run other programs serving the Church and the charismatic renewal. Little by little, the college that was going to close and be sold to the highest bidder to pay off its debts changed so that it is now debt-free and prospering. But far more important from a Catholic perspective, the school has turned around so that it reflects the ideal of Catholic education in every aspect of its being.

Father Michael likes to describe the function of the Catholic college in terms of "the Way, the Truth and the Life," reflecting its Lord who is indeed these very realities.

The *Way* is the pattern of life that Jesus, the Way, left us to live in true freedom and joy, and that pattern is taught at the University of Steubenville so that young people learn how to handle their relationships, emotions and temptations in a Christian way – experiencing the support of their peers in so doing.

The Truth is that of the Gospel of the Lord as understood by the Church. At the university, theology is not a welter of opinions of dissenters from the magisterium, but the teaching of the Church in all its theological richness and variety. Our one hundred and fifty theology majors and graduate students again see theology as "Queen," as the highest of the sciences harmonizing all human wisdom with Divine Wisdom.

Finally, the Life of the Christian is that of the Holy Spirit within him, and the power to live the Christian life that only the Spirit can give. The university has a rich life of prayer open to all the gifts of the Spirit which, of course, draws many charismatics to study there.

However, it is not only charismatics who benefit from the rich and joyful liturgies that use Latin chants as well as upbeat contemporary music, or the deeply reverent Holy Hours before the Blessed Sacrament exposed, or the little groups praying Our Lady's Rosary, all of this enlivened by the same Spirit whose power is felt dramatically in larger gatherings for prayer and praise.

This article is not meant to be partisan praise for the University of Steubenville as some Catholic academic utopia, but one must admit that the totally academic environment found there can be an object lesson for so many Catholic colleges which are searching to affirm their Catholic identity in positive, joyful, and contemporary fashions. Steubenville has led the way – will others follow?

4. Spirituality and the Needs of Youth

My experience of teaching young people in colleges and seminaries for almost twenty years has put me in touch with all sorts of young people, with their hopes and dreams, their fears and problems, their sins and their desire for authenticity or holiness. In my experience, too many educators and youth ministers tend to talk down to our youth, tend not to expect much of them, tend to water down the gospel message for them so that it loses its punch as the salt loses its savor.

I think John Paul II in his many talks to young people around the world gives us a model of the approach we ought to take. On one hand the Chief Shepherd of the Church is approachable – enjoying contact with the young, talking to them, listening to them, and singing with them. We might apply to him the words he addressed to the youth of Turin in 1980, speaking of St. John Bosco, who was able to understand the young: "But it must be added at once that the reason for this particular depth in 'understanding' the young was that he 'loved' them just as deeply." Yet this love of Pope John Paul for the young never keeps him from challenging them with the hard sayings of the Gospel – a challenge that youth with its desire for heroism accepts in papal youth rallies in country after country.

Young people surrounded by rock music, the drug culture, and sexual promiscuity are so often presented such a deterministic gospel of despair that they want someone to evangelize them – to raise their consciousness to the fact that there is a truly human way, a way of holiness and wholeness which can answer the needs of the human heart. The Pope is not afraid to do just that. He said to the young: "Be on the lookout for real values, which are important you; look for ideals which will enrich your life and for which you are ready to fight. I exhort you: do not let yourselves be hindered in your search, do not be satisfied with easy answers, and examine with clear vision what you have chosen to serve as your real happiness in life." And in his letter to youth he stated: "To be truly free does not at all mean doing everything that pleases me or doing what I want to do. Freedom contains…the discipline of truth. To be truly free means to use one's own freedom for what is truly good."

At the Franciscan University of Steubenville where I, a Dominican, teach, the thrust is the same as that of the Holy Father – loving and yet challenging. The opening conferences for enrolling students deal squarely with sin and the need for conversion in frank terms that the young can relate to, and yet against a background of God's love and mercy offered to those who turn to him. They are encouraged to go to confession to knowledgeable and sympathetic confessors who are kind and yet call them on to a more virtuous life and who, when absolving, often pray for whatever inner healing these young penitents may need.

The young people I have met are searching for God, and they are looking for the people who can help them set their sights on attaining him. At Steubenville's orientation program, young people are encouraged to work out their priorities in terms of prayer, study, social life, and Christian support so that they have a plan for daily living and do not simply drift along. The keystone of this life plan is of course prayer, and pains are taken to give a rudimentary instruction in the art of prayer, which, if followed becomes meditation, and which under the breath of the Spirit often blossoms into contemplation even among the young.

I would like to outline this method of prayer taught at the University, adding a few comments of my own, because I think this is so often where we fail the young who ask us to teach them to pray. Instead of bread we hand them a stone, for frequently we have nothing to say. The method – praise and thanksgiving, receiving the

Word of God, repenting, and interceding – is simply a framework of the essentials of prayer which furnishes the raw materials for the Holy Spirit to use, the Spirit who hovers over us, enabling us to cry, "Abba, Father," as that same Spirit prays in us.[377]

Before we can begin to pray, we need to find a quiet place where we can pray undisturbed – a corner of our room, before our favorite crucifix or icon. At Steubenville, the young people love to pray, to "take their prayer time" as they say, before the Blessed Sacrament either in the main chapel or in one of the four dormitory chapels, or in the recently built replica of St. Francis' Portiuncula, which is reserved exclusively for adoration and exposition of the Blessed Sacrament. Once we have found the right environment and have our Bible in hand (beginners find it usually better to start with the New Testament) we are ready to begin.

Praise and thanksgiving are the first steps, because as the President of Steubenville, Fr. Michael Scanlan, TOR says, it is necessary to put oneself in the proper stance before God – we are creatures, he is Creator. The Lord told St. Catherine of Siena, "I am he who is, you are she who is not." As we realize that we would not even be here without God's creative word, that we would not even continue to exist without his sustaining word, we find praise welling up in our hearts and expressed on our lips. As we thank him using various titles and names of God, Father, Son and Holy Spirit, from the Old and New Testament, other motives for thanks often come forth – especially for family, friends, and special events in our own particular story of salvation. Very often in such a context we experience the presence of God – the kingdom of God is within!

We are now open to experience God's Word. It may well happen that we will experience the Holy Spirit speaking within our depths the Word of God for us now. If not, we open to the Scriptures and read a passage – perhaps that of the day's liturgy – and allow the words to sink in. A phrase might pop out of the text, and we might linger over or ponder that "word" in our hearts as did our Lady. In fact, at Medugorje, Mary recommends that we ponder the Word early in the morning and keep coming back to it from time to time during the day.

Whether we simply turn a phrase over in our hearts (this

---

[377] cf. Rom. 8:15-26

ruminating or pondering is what the ancients call meditation) or whether we use our imagination to put ourselves in the gospel scene, as recommended by St. Ignatius of Loyola, we should be open to the work of the Spirit praying within, stirring our affections, and drawing our wills closer to God. Often, we will experience a deeper prayer, a quickening of faith, hope, and love, or we may rest simply in the Spirit in a way that goes beyond words or concepts. Such is contemplation which is the perfection of love to which all Christians are called as Vatican II's *Lumen Gentium* reminds us. Other times the Spirit will reveal to us those areas of sin in our lives for which we need to repent. This is not so much a "feeling" of sorrow as the resolve to change, to ask God's grace so that one might be changed and thus experience a growing conversion. Sometimes nothing much will seem to happen, and this is fine because prayer is never automatic. We must remember that we can dispose ourselves as best we can, but we do not control God; rather we humbly wait for him. When we know that prayer is drawing to a close, we thank God for his presence (for we know by faith he was present whether experienced or not) and for any graces or insights into our lives or the truths of the faith.

Petitions follow as we intercede for others – family and friends, the world and its peace, the Church and the Pope, and finally our own needs. We present them to God, our loving Father who always gives us what we need, though not always what we want. Giving the young a method of prayer (and this is not the only model) is helpful even when they experience spiritual dryness (as indeed they will) because they know then that they have done what they could – disposing themselves as best they could – but that God at times wants faith and trust in him alone rather than experience, rich as that is. In general, this is the method of prayer taught to our youth at the University with some of my own observations added.

Of course, individual prayer is not the whole of the prayer life of the Christian, and our students know that. The center of life at the university is the Mass. Many of the young complain that the liturgies they attend are dull and lifeless. This is certainly not true at Steubenville where the Eucharist is celebrated in a vibrant fashion with the chapel ringing with the young people's songs, and with popular preaching being directed at students' needs, with no watering down.

Just as preaching for the young should be in their language and yet not sell them short by descending to a childish or incomplete Gospel, so young people should be exposed to that rich heritage of Church music that is their birthright as Catholics. And so, at university Masses on great feasts, the *schola* sings Latin Gregorian, polyphony and leads the young in Taizé chants. The report on the Extraordinary Synod on Vatican II pointed out that today people, especially the young, are searching for the Sacred. If they do not find it in the rich mystical and liturgical heritage of the Church, they search for it in the non-Christian East. Our celebrations need to be lively and yet sacred.

Two devotions that draw out that transcendent quality in a mystical atmosphere are Exposition of the Blessed Sacrament and the Rosary of our Lady. In the former, one Host is placed in a monstrance and becomes a holy mandala for all to focus on in their prayer. Of course, we have not only a sign aiding contemplation (which is so necessary for prayer, especially in the beginning) but the sign (bread) has become in this case the very reality toward which it points – the Lord in his sacramental presence. The young, I find, are very drawn to this experience, so sacred and mystical. They are fed by this silent prayer before the face of the Lord as indeed they are by meditating on the mystery of his Incarnation, Death, and Resurrection in the Rosary of his Mother. Here too, we have incarnational signs or aids to help prayer – the mantra of the Hail Mary and Our Father, the beads running through the fingers while the mind ponders the gospel events by which we were saved. Paul VI in *Marialis Cultus* compares this prayer to the Mass, pointing out that the mystery of the Death and Resurrection of Christ, which is made present in the Mass, is the very same one on which we meditate in the rosary so that its recitation is an excellent preparation for the liturgy and the extension thereof.

Today young people are keenly aware of their need for others and are seeking personal relationships, sometimes wrongly. They need to be brought into vibrant community situations with other young people who share their values, will support them in prayer, and have fun with them as well. At the university this is done through households or gatherings of the men who live side by side on their floors, and the same for women on their floors. These groups of twelve to twenty that live in the wing of the building provide prayer support of various types, social occasions, and a matrix from which friendships are formed. The students even encourage one another to study and to do their academic best so that the priority that study should have is maintained.

The young need to have the Gospel preached to them so that they can respond in their moral life and in their prayer. They need to be taught how to grow in prayer, to center their lives on the Lord especially in the celebration of the Eucharist, and to let their social lives flow from that experience. Young people formed in this way want to share their experience with others, and thus evangelists are born. What I have described as the needs of the young are not theoretical, rather they are the needs I have observed over the years and at my present teaching assignment. At the University of Steubenville these needs are being met.

5.   Italy's Lay Movements: A Renewal Ever Ancient, Ever New

Many are apt to think of Rome only in terms of the Vatican and its curial offices, its color and ceremony, the Pope and his teaching. Obviously when the throne of Peter is filled by as dynamic and spiritual a man as John Paul II, the temptation to focus on him and his curia is understandable. But I would like to highlight other signs of hope and spiritual renewal here in Rome, a city that too many dismiss as living off past glory.

The hundreds of thousands of teenagers and young people who came to the eternal city Palm Sunday to meet one another and the Pope obviously do not share this view. There were gatherings for them sponsored by Taizé, Opus Dei, the Emmanuel charismatic community of Paris; there were all night vigils before the exposed Blessed Sacrament for them in St. Mary Major and San Clemente, the Irish Dominican church; as well as an opportunity to sing folk songs with and for John Paul II in a great open air audience in front of the Basilica of St. John Lateran.

This youth congress culminated in the celebration of the Palm Sunday Liturgy with the Pope in St. Peter's Square with many young people present from England, France, Italy, Spain, Yugoslavia, and the United States. The Basilica of St. Mary Major was jammed with young French students listening to a French bishop while all around the edge of the crowd young priests were hearing their individual confessions. The assembly knelt on the marble floor, prayed together for the coming of the Holy Spirit, and went forth into the city with youth banners and icons of Our Lady to witness to their faith.

The signs of hope, however, are not confined to visitors from outside Rome. The community of Sant' Egidio (St. Giles), for example, originated in the part of Rome which is across the Tiber (Trastevere) at the time of the student revolutions and spread throughout the city. The communities are made up of young people both married and single, many of whom are social workers who work with the poor and those caught in drug addiction.

They also live an intense life of prayer, praying Vespers together when they can, and in the little baroque Church of Sant' Egidio they gather for Mass on Saturday evenings. In the semi-darkened, white-washed church, lit only by candles flickering in front of the numerous icons, young people sat on every inch of available floor space, while those of us who were older sat on the benches. The Mass commenced with the lively singing of Byzantine-like chants. As we approached the Liturgy of the Word, the Paschal Candle was brought in procession from the back of the church to the sanctuary and, as more lights were turned on, we knew that Sunday, the day of the Lord's Resurrection, had begun. After the homily, there was a long spontaneous prayer of the faithful. The gifts were brought up, the Canon sung by all the concelebrants, Communion received with great reverence, and the Mass concluded an hour and a half after its inception with the same spirited hymn with which it had begun.

Another Mass that attracts many young people in Rome is that of Rome's *Comunione e Liberazione* (CL) community. Every Sunday morning at 11:45 at the Basilica of Santa Maria di Trastevere (a block away from Sant' Egidio), the community gathers for Mass.

Here again the church is jam-packed with students and young married couples singing joyful melodic hymns to the accompaniment of guitar, as well as some Latin Gregorian, e.g., the *Sanctus* and the *Regina Coeli*.

I attended the Sunday before Italy's recent regional elections. The sermon touched on the vote by emphasizing the need to preserve the Christian values of Italy. After the post-communion prayer, a layman spoke for those candidates favored by *Movimento Popolare*, a political movement related to CL. (While it was good to see Catholics organizing to make their influence felt in a political system growing increasingly secularist, to an American it seemed strange to hear political policy outlined directly from the pulpit.)

Later that day I attended a charismatic prayer meeting at which an international group of youth leaders, half of whom are Maltese, performed an extraordinary dramatization in dance and song of the story of salvation. It was a mystery play in modern dress done wherever young people might gather. Afterward the performers talk to young people about Christ and His Church.

Lumen Christi, the charismatic prayer group hosting this presentation, was founded by Dominicans (including myself), seminarians and lay people in 1970. It still meets every Sunday afternoon at the Gregorian University under the able direction of Father Frank Sullivan, SJ. Prayer groups all over the world have sprung from this group, many of them flourishing in Italy. At a recent meeting I attended, an African bishop informally spoke to us about the Lord, the Spirit, and the devil in a delightfully amusing way.

Besides these, there are other youth groups, such as the *Focolare* and the *Neo-Catechumenali*, which also testify to the fact that the Holy Spirit is at work enlivening the Church, ever ancient, ever new.

Quite aside from these various movements, one also finds many ordinary people praying in Roman churches, especially in Eucharistic chapels where the Blessed Sacrament is exposed.

In the major basilicas now, by order of the Pope, Eucharistic adoration is a daily occurrence. Men and women, young and old, religious and lay, pray before that sign which is the very reality toward which it points – the Body of Christ.

Personally, I do not feel that any deep renewal of the Church can take place until we rediscover the deepest value of the Mass. One way of plumbing the various aspects of this central and holy mystery is to pray in the presence of the Lord as He graces our altars. Humble people have always known this, and to see the growing numbers of people silently so engaged may be the central sign of spiritual renewal in the eternal city.

ABOUT THE AUTHOR

Fr. Giles Dimock, O.P. grew up in Stonington, CT. He attended public schools and is a graduate of Providence College. He entered the Order of Preachers, and upon being ordained, taught at Providence College. He studied Liturgy at Notre Dame and at Sant'Anselmo in Rome, earning an STL in Liturgy and an STD in Theology from the Angelicum, i.e. the Pontifical University of Saint Thomas Aquinas in Rome. A priest for over 50 years, he has taught for 46 of them at Providence College, the Angelicum in Rome, Franciscan University of Steubenville, the Dominican House of Studies in Washington, D.C., and Dominican novices in Cincinnati, OH with summer terms at St. Charles Borromeo Seminary for the Archdiocese of Philadelphia.

www.ingramcontent.com/pod-product-compliance
Lightning Source LLC
Chambersburg PA
CBHW051725040426
42447CB00008B/975

9780988627055